WANTON
WEST

WANTON
WEST

MADAMS, MONEY, MURDER, AND THE WILD WOMEN OF

MONTANA'S FRONTIER

LAEL MORGAN

CHICAGO
REVIEW
PRESS

Library of Congress Cataloging-in-Publication Data
Morgan, Lael.
 Wanton West : madams, money, murder, and the wild women of Montana's fron-
tier / Lael Morgan.
  p. cm.
 Includes bibliographical references and index.
 ISBN 978-1-56976-338-4 (hardcover)
 1. Frontier and pioneer life—Montana. 2. Women pioneers—Montana—His-
tory. 3. Women—Montana—History. 4. Prostitution—Montana—History. 5.
Women pioneers—Montana—Biography. 6. Prostitutes—Montana—Biography.
7. Montana—History—19th century. 8. Montana—History—20th century. 9.
Montana—Social conditions. 10. Montana—Biography. I. Title.

 F731.M77 2011
 978.6'02—dc22

                                                              2010053911

Interior design: Jonathan Hahn

© 2011 by Lael Morgan
Published by Chicago Review Press, Incorporated
814 North Franklin Street
Chicago, Illinois 60610
ISBN 978-1-56976-338-4
Printed in the United States of America
5 4 3 2 1

To Madeleine, our sisters in sin, and good women everywhere who pushed the envelope.

And to the men, good and bad, who made way for us.

". . . there is not a respectable woman in the territory!" Charles Otis, superintendent of the Overland Stage Line, New York City, exclaimed on hearing that Methodist preacher A. M. Hough planned to move with his wife, Anna, to Montana Territory in the summer of 1864.

"If there is not a respectable woman in the territory of 15,000 or 20,000 inhabitants, it is time there was one," Mrs. Hough responded. And off they went.

CONTENTS

ACKNOWLEDGMENTS

Jacq Siracusa, an off-duty anthropologist, and I drove into Butte, Montana, in 1998 pretty much as a lark. She planned to visit a friend. My only agenda was to tour America's longest-operating whorehouse, long since closed. Yet the trip spawned a book that was fascinating to research, and I thank Siracusa for suggesting it.

My appreciation also extends to Norma Jean Almodovar, founder and president of the International Sex Worker Foundation for Art, Culture and Education, and Rudy Giecek, still the owner of the old Dumas brothel. I am indebted to writers Paula Petrik of George Washington University and the late Michael Malone, a prolific historian who also served as president of Montana State University in Bozeman, whose careful research provided the foundation of this work. Author Ellen Baumler, coordinator of Montana's National Register of Historic Places; Amorette Allison, historic preservation officer of Miles City; Ellen Crain of the Butte–Silver Bow Public Archives; and author Mary Murphy, a down-to-earth historian who teaches at Montana State University in Bozeman, helped keep me grounded.

I am indebted to James L. Lopach and Jean Luckowski, University of Montana at Missoula; Diane Sands, a gifted researcher from Missoula; Joan Hoff, Montana State University of Bozeman; and author/journalist Kevin Giles for their insights on Jeannette Rankin. Roy Millegan, founder and curator of the Jefferson Valley Museum in Whitehall, also helped fill an important gap in Rankin's history. Professors Pat Gordon and the late George Proctor, my teaching colleagues at University of Texas at Arlington, encouraged me when long-distance research seemed most foreboding.

The efforts of researcher Cindy Shaw and Father Robert Maloney, who documented Celestine Healy Bottego and her family, were vital. Nancy Silliman of the Kohrs Memorial in Deer Lodge unearthed new material on Anna Eugenia LaChapelle. Robin Gerber, history instructor at Miles Community College; Bob Barthelmess of the Range Riders Museum; Mark Browning of the Custer County Art Center; and Jean Nielsen, Miles City Public Library, contributed excellent material. Jay Moynahan, retired from Eastern Washington University, whose field is criminal justice with a focus on prostitution, proved an excellent sounding board.

For new thinking on Madeleine Blair I thank Canadians Bill Hillen of the Galt Historic Railway Park; Lindsey McMaster, Department of English Studies, Nipissing University; and book dealer David Ewens of Ontario.

Peggy Pascoe, History Department, University of Oregon, generously shared notes from her research on *Relations of Rescue: The Search for Female Moral Authority in the American West, 1874–1939*, after I discovered the archives from which she took them had closed.

My gratitude to the staff of the Montana Historical Society Research Center in Helena, most especially Brian Shovers and former director Charlene Porsild, whose suggestions were invaluable. Rosalie L'Ecuyer of Fairbanks, Alaska, and Marilyn Talmage, originally from Havre, not only traveled many Montana miles with me but helped rehabilitate a very rough, rough draft. Sally Pomeroy Backus, a special education teacher from Burnhan, Maine, deserves congratulations for her editing insights.

Last, but certainly not least, my thanks to Mable Deane of Three Forks, Montana, whose determination to locate the origins of babies sold by Gertrude Pitkanen inspired this book as surely as did the Dumas brothel.

INTRODUCTION

SINFUL CITIES, 1863–1919

Having researched and written about sin in America for several decades, I assumed I fully understood the economic and emotional cost of being female in the long, bleak era before governments began to grant women rights. During this period, prostitution was generally a woman's most lucrative job option and sometimes her only viable strategy for survival. Raised with a stout set of New England values, I understood the dangerous downside of that career choice early on. In the first book I read on the subject, the English classic *Moll Flanders*, the heroine finds herself on a bumpy road that is mostly downhill, and other classics tell a similar story. So I was later startled to learn that a good number of women had apparently prospered at the trade—especially in the American West.

It wasn't until a visit to Montana in 1998, however, that I witnessed a compact example of how good and how bad that career option would have been. Norma Jean Almodovar, a strikingly beautiful Los Angeles policewoman who quit to become a call girl, had just founded the International Sex Worker Foundation for Art, Culture and Education. A friend of a friend, she suggested that I tour the historic Dumas brothel she was hoping to purchase in Butte to serve as a museum for her trade. Rudy Giecek, then (and still) owner of the establishment, who had been running it as an antiques mall, welcomed me.

Considering the Dumas was built in 1890 and is the last of Butte's famous "parlor houses" still standing, it was in remarkable shape. We started on the second floor, where the dark wainscoting gleamed in the morning sunshine that poured down through the skylights. Large, airy bedrooms ringed a spacious open balcony around an elegant staircase leading to the first floor with its many parlors, fancy dining room, and grand ballroom.

The three or four women who worked here would have been among the most beautiful in Montana—elegant, well spoken, with class and style. When things went well, a Dumas girl could earn more in a single night than the average schoolteacher did in a month. Her chance of landing a rich husband was excellent, and, if prudent, she wouldn't have to stay in the trade too long to tuck away a good retirement.

But an evil alternative lay just below, waiting for the unwary. Beyond the doors of the Dumas's restaurant-sized basement kitchen lay a dank, dark tunnel, part of Butte's subterranean street system by which customers could access the red-light district from respectable addresses away from the eyes of the staring public. There, cut into the tunnel's earthen walls, were shallow caves just big enough to hold a small metal bed, where down-and-out prostitutes too ill, old, or ugly to ply their trade aboveground sold themselves to low bidders.

———◇———

Norma Jean Almodovar's attempt to turn this unusual establishment into a museum was not welcomed by the town of Butte. Ultimately her purchase of the Dumas fell through, and Rudy Giecek no longer opens it for tours, which may be just as well, for I found myself haunted by my exposure to the Dumas. The unexpected shock of walking from the sunlit second floor to those awful caves just two flights down jolted me into taking a second look at this era, most particularly in Butte but also in Montana in general, which in some ways remains a world unto itself.

America's Western frontier was launched from hundreds of boomtowns, most of which featured instant millionaires, laissez-faire law enforcement, and women of beguilingly ill repute. But rare was the boomtown—no matter how wild—that couldn't be tamed in a decade. Butte, Montana, "the Richest

Hill on Earth," beat the odds for nearly a century, running red hot and wide open in the face of half a dozen regional and national purity crusades, not to mention Prohibition. To some extent Helena, Butte's neighbor and genesis, also qualified for some time as a renegade, embracing convention only after it became the seat of state government in 1898. And dozens of small, isolated Montana towns enjoyed similar traditions.

The Montana story is fascinating because nowhere else in America was open prostitution a given for so long. Because of the extraordinary independence of its women, not only those from the demimonde but those who escaped it, and because open cities apparently worked for the majority of Montana citizens without leaving visible scars, the legacy of Madeleine Blair, Chicago Joe Airey, Lizzie Hall, and their sisters is worthy of attention.

LAEL MORGAN
Saco, Maine

WANTON
WEST

MADELEINE: A SELF-MADE WOMAN

1894

Bertie Simpson spotted her as soon as she walked into the grand lobby of the staid Butte Hotel, and he chuckled to himself. Though young—just over twenty, he guessed—Madeleine Blair carried herself like a duchess. Her simple but smartly tailored blue traveling suit complemented her elegantly arranged auburn curls, which were topped by a pert little hat. She wore no makeup and she was no beauty, but it was subtly obvious that, beneath her demure dress and the encumbrance of a fashionable hourglass corset, she possessed a stunning figure.

Her clean-cut features brightened with her dimpled smile when she spotted him, and Bertie Simpson knew that luck had gone his way. Few, if any, would guess Madeleine was a whore, but Bertie, who had recently purchased her services in Chicago, had not only enjoyed her erotic talents; he found her charming. How she had come by her cultured East Coast accent she would not say. But she was well read, intellectually curious, and a delightful companion.

Simpson, although a confirmed bachelor with solid banking credentials, had made less of an impression on Madeleine. A stray tomcat, she thought. But since she knew no one else in the town where she had arrived that morning, she greeted him like a long-lost friend.

"What in the world are you doing in Butte?" he asked. "But pardon me, are you here with someone?"

"I came out to see the wild and wooly West, and I am alone," she said.

"Good!" he answered. "I have to go to Missoula tomorrow, but I can show you the elephant tonight."

"I think I have seen him this afternoon," she murmured with a grimace.

———◦———

Depressed after the death of her young son and a subsequent miscarriage, which had been carefully engineered, Madeleine had traveled from Chicago to Butte on a whim, hoping to find her longtime lover, Paul Martin, with whom she had recently quarreled. Anxious because she had failed to warn Martin that she was coming, as she checked into the busy hotel she paid little attention to the town perched precariously almost a mile above sea level on the side of a monstrous barren hill. She was further distracted to learn her lover was working in a remote section of the state and would not return for several weeks.

Overcome with gloom and finding herself unable to breathe in the thin atmosphere, she rushed to open the window of her hotel room, only to close it hastily when smothered by the sulfur-laden air.

"As I stood looking through the window at the hurrying throng in the street, I wondered if I had not lost a day somewhere," she later told Simpson. "I had thought it was Sunday, but surely I was mistaken, for men who wore the garb of labor hurried through the streets, carrying dinner-pails in their hands, and Chinamen with laundry baskets on their heads mingled with the crowd of alert-looking business men, debonair gamblers, pasty-faced pimps, overdressed shop-girls, and painted, gaudily garbed harlots."

As she stood at the hotel window, she recalled having overheard a well-dressed man in her Pullman car describe Butte to a party of women from the East as "the greatest mining camp on earth." She wasn't sure what that involved beyond ore in the ground and perhaps savage Indians, but, rattled from her self-absorption, she put on her hat and went into the street for a better view.

It *was* Sunday! The street was named Broadway. But beyond that, nothing looked familiar. Unlike those in Chicago on a Sunday, most of Butte's 212 licensed drinking establishments were open, and some never closed as demonstrated by the fact that they had no locks on their doors. Scantily dressed women strolled the sidewalks in broad daylight, explaining graphically the sexual services they were prepared to render. Men in working clothes mobbed the city's sixteen licensed gambling halls. Private games for higher stakes were equally busy, but with a better-dressed crowd. The red-light district also ran three shifts.

The *Denver Sun* had just admitted on page one that Butte was the liveliest town in the United States, and the local paper boasted Butte had produced $300 million in mineral wealth since 1864. Montana led the nation in the percentage of men employed, and Butte, of course, led Montana.

The most notorious joint for trouble was Clipper Shades, a bar, dance hall, and brothel where clients were likely to be rolled if drunk or welcomed with mail if they were old customers and used the place as a forwarding address. The Atlantic claimed to have the longest bar in the world, employing fifteen bartenders at a time. The Casino, a dance hall, saloon, prizefight arena, theater, and brothel where gunfights were no surprise, hired a couple hundred girls around the clock. The Comique featured nationally known vaudeville stars and local talent in the form of "pretty waiter girls" and supplied boxes from which wealthy patrons could view the show with their mistresses discreetly hidden behind a screen. Clothing, dry goods, and grocery stores were also open.

Outraged at the blasphemy, even though she never kept the Sabbath herself, Madeleine walked the neighborhood feeling no temptation to enter the gaudy establishments.

Commentary on horse races bellowed from the bookie joints. "They're off at Hawthorne!" someone yelled, relaying the news from a telegraph. "Wildfire in the lead! Rubicon against the field! It's a hundred-to-one shot you can't win. You're crazy with the heat. They're off at Oakland."

The noise, with the foul air, made her head swim, and soon Madeleine retired to a side street to get her bearings. But there, from an open window, she overhead a clear voice announcing, "She is seventeen, gentlemen, and a black one."

Certain she'd heard the auction of a black woman, she hurried back toward her hotel, encountering Bertie Simpson on the way, and she soon unburdened her fears to him. Much amused, he assured her there was no

cause for alarm. "Seventeen and a black one" was simply the number that had
won on a roulette wheel, he said.

———◈———

Later that evening with her Chicago patron, Madeleine toured a couple of
fancy parlor houses and got her first look at Butte's filth-ridden back alleys
full of cribs—tiny rooms fronting the walkways where her sisters in sin casually displayed themselves in open windows and doorways. Hundreds of flimsy
little buildings stood so crowded together that stairways led to precariously
built second tiers. Who owned them was a mystery, she learned. And, miserable as they were, the girls paid a stiff rate to work there.

"The sight fascinated even while it repelled me," she later wrote, resorting
to the purple prose of her Victorian era. "It gripped me by the throat and
forced me to examine it, even though I was sickened and faint at the horror
of it. I drew my skirts back from contact with the poor creatures who represented this seamy side of prostitution; I could not help it. I wanted to take
them by the hand and tell them that I was one of them, but I could not touch
them. I could barely touch my lips to the glasses of beer they served."

She felt particular pity for a forty-year-old prostitute from whom she
bought many drinks when Simpson refused, simply so the old girl could
show a good profit at the end of the night. And when the woman cursed her
on leaving, calling her a "stuck-up parlor-house tart," Madeleine told Bertie
that she didn't blame her.

A few doors down, she was surprised to see a girl dressed in little more
than a wrapper beckoning from a flimsy crib, and she recognized Norma,
with whom she'd worked two years earlier at Lizzie Allen's palatial brothel
in Chicago. Once Allen's star boarder and one of the most beautiful women
in Chicago, the girl seemed to have aged ten years. Sobbing, she clutched
Madeleine's hand, pathetically eager to talk with someone who had known
her in better days.

Norma had moved to Denver after leaving Allen's and had fallen for a
gambler who took her out of the business and lavished money on her for
several months, she explained. They'd come to Butte a year ago for its famous
horse-racing season, where her lover planned on making a killing. Although

Butte and the track at neighboring Anaconda were regularly listed nationwide in the racing news, and some considered them the best in the West, he figured the odds would be easier to beat than those of long-established East Coast establishments. So when he lost, Norma pawned her furs and jewels to give him a new start, which also failed. Then she had gone into one of two first-class houses in town.

"But no girl can meet the expenses in a big parlor-house and keep a man at the same time, even if the landladies would stand for a *macque* [pimp] in the house, which they won't," Norma insisted. "The girls in the big houses are all hundreds of dollars in debt, with no chance to get out. Board is not high, because they pay twenty-five dollars a week straight. All the rest they make is theirs, which would be fine if they cleared anything over their board. But they don't, and the cost of clothes, and laundry, and cleaners' bills, and toilet articles—in fact, everything we use—is double the price it would be in Chicago."

"I do not see why business is not good, if there are only two big houses," Madeleine countered. "I never saw so many people on the streets and in the places of amusement; and at the hotel I saw so many well-dressed, prosperous-looking men that I concluded that any girl who was in business in Butte would have a gold-mine of her own."

"Forget it," Norma said with an air of disgust. "If you stay in Butte a while you will discover that Montana liberality runs by buying booze and playing the races and 'stacking them up' on the high card, never giving women a good price for their services."

Norma went on to explain she now made her profit mostly in selling drinks and occasionally rolling a drunk or two if she thought she could get away with it. This disgusted Madeleine's escort, who insisted they move on.

As an afterthought, Madeleine ran back to make an appointment to see Norma later, only to find her friend eagerly talking to a big, dirty laborer so drunk that he swayed from side to side, although he tried to steady himself on the window casement. Norma appeared embarrassed, and Bertie had to rescue Madeleine when the would-be customer lurched to grab her.

Later, over supper before they bedded, Simpson questioned Madeleine closely. "It struck me in Chicago that night that you were a haughty dame and a darned poor mixer. Or, as one of the other girls in the party said, you were not a good fellow," he recalled. "Yet here you pick up a low crib woman who by her own voluntary confession is a thief, and you invite her to break bread with you. I'm wondering why you did it?"

"I thought I knew all the horrors of prostitution, but I have learned tonight that I know very little about them." She considered. "I have learned that there is a sheltered class, and that I belong to it, yet I would have laughed yesterday had any one spoken of 'sheltered prostitutes.'"

"But you can't do anything for this girl. Why do you harrow your own soul by association with her?"

"It may be a premonition of what is coming to me that makes me want to be kind," she replied. "It is something I have never felt before."

"Madeleine, it is a premonitory birth-pang of the social consciousness," he said.

"What is the social consciousness?" she asked. "I never heard of it."

"It's summed up in the question you are now asking yourself. 'Am I my sister's keeper?'"

———◇———

In Butte, Norma had worked for Lou Harpell, who had been Lizzie Allen's rival in Chicago before retrenching in Montana under the patronage of one of the state's most influential mining magnates. Madeleine did not know Harpell's background, but she was impressed by the opulence of her Butte bordello and by the straight-talking madam herself. Who better to help rescue Norma? And Madeleine had picked the right time to enlist Harpell's help.

It was the morning after a busy night that had been hard to manage. Bertha, one of Lou's girls, had sprained her ankle while horseback riding with a patron that afternoon. The sprain wasn't bad, but weekends were busy, and at the last minute Lou had been forced to find a stand-in for her.

"Stand-in" was a ridiculous term for the replacement of a whorehouse inmate, Lou realized, and it was high time she recruited to fill Bertha's position. The girl had come there with the express goal of finding a rich husband. Her solicitous riding companion—who had spent the evening at her bedside (not in it), paying well for the privilege—was the perfect candidate. And Lou's customers would welcome a new face.

Another potential problem was a minor war. Lola and Suzette were lovers who usually worked in tandem, but last night they'd had a monstrous fight. Lou had temporarily kept things under control by refereeing them into separate parlors, where they vied to outdo each other for high-tipping customers. For one night, at least, it had worked: in competition, they sold twenty-eight bottles of champagne, which Lou had priced with an intoxicating markup. Not bad for the nightly receipts, she realized as she reconciled her account books. If business kept improving, she'd soon be able to leave this forsaken hole for a new life as a rich widow in her native Germany.

Sam Jung, the butler, interrupted to present a silver tray bearing a rectangle of heavy bond finely engraved with the name MADELEINE BLAIR. Although startled at receiving a formal visiting card, the madam managed to place her. A day earlier, Lou had noticed Bertie Simpson, a frequent visitor from Chicago, entering her parlor with a young woman she assumed was a young society matron, which was not unusual. Tours of the red-light district's high end were considered daring, and Bertie, with his impeccable manners, was an ideal escort. Lou's orchestra was the best in town, and Bertie had taken to the dance floor with his charge, displaying his usual dash and skill.

It wasn't until about two hours later, when the crowd had thinned, that Lou had a chance to meet the newcomer. Unhesitatingly, Bertie introduced her as a working girl from Lizzie Allen's house in Chicago, and Lou, who was seldom wrong in judging appearances, was surprised. Assuming that the girl had come today to seek work, she pushed aside her books, more than willing to hire away an employee of her former rival.

She was disappointed to learn Blair was on a rescue mission for Norma, now for sale with the lowest of the low in Lou's back alley. The madam snorted. She had four girls of her own to look after, and they all had problems. Besides, she'd fired Norma because the girl had became addicted to drugs, and the madam was reluctant to break that news to her friend. Madeleine appeared sincerely appalled at what she described as the general squalor of the district. She spoke harshly against unscrupulous landlords and the gruesome fate of Butte's crib girls.

"You've got to help her," she pleaded. "No working girl can survive in Butte for long. The town is brutal."

"Perhaps you're just not used to the frontier," Lou suggested tactfully. But Madeleine, who readily conceded that most of her five years in the trade had been spent in high-rent districts, had recently worked six months in the raw boomtown of Winnipeg, Canada. She'd enjoyed it and returned with bundles of money.

"You're doing well here," she said accusingly. "Perhaps you don't see how different Butte is."

Having worked Chicago for a decade, few were more aware than Lou Harpell of Butte's abnormities, but she held her tongue, if for no other reason than her fondness for Bertie Simpson and not wanting to offend his young friend, even one with the misplaced zeal of a Salvation Army worker.

"I'm to meet Norma at two o'clock at the Chaquamegon," Madeleine said. "What do you think? Can we get her out of that awful place?"

Lou sighed. "We can try, I guess," she said reluctantly. "But many women do make good money in this town, even if it's not as rarefied as some you are used to. I had to let your friend go because she had other problems beyond the usual expenses."

The private meeting with Norma did not prove successful. It became obvious her drug habit was serious. The fallen beauty had no intention of leaving her gambling man, who apparently had no intention of supporting himself. And Madeleine soon had so many problems of her own that she gave up the rescue attempt.

"Poor little fool that I was," she would later write. "I could not even heal myself."

———◈———

Madeleine Blair had been born with a silver spoon in her mouth, only to have it taken from her. Her well-educated father had turned to drink, losing his fortune and leaving his wife and children destined for the poorhouse. When their fine home was repossessed by the bank, he dismissed their servants and moved the family to a slum occupied by prostitutes working under such respectable guises as laundresses and seamstresses. The old man disappeared for months at a time, leaving his wife, pregnant with their sixth child, to cope alone, with no source of income. Pulled from school for want of money, Madeleine had spent much time with her notorious neighbors despite her mother's forbidding it. At sixteen she had experimented with sex out of curiosity and had gotten pregnant by a family friend from whom she sought no help.

Madeleine did not claim rape, and she showed no self-pity. Leaving home unaware she was pregnant, she had worked briefly as a factory girl and had done well as a department store clerk. But when she learned she was pregnant and her mother was without resources, prostitution seemed an obvious option.

Her entry into that profession was anything but smooth. She acquired a venereal disease from her second customer because she had no idea diseases could be transmitted through intercourse. The cure, which kept her in the hospital for some time, was brutal but effective. The man, ten years her senior, had not only been supportive but was, in fact, her current lover, Paul Martin. Despite his consideration, she entered a house in Kansas City's red-light district at age seventeen and then moved up to one of the most famous and fashionable bordellos in Chicago.

Her first pregnancy resulted in the death of that unwanted child shortly after she became a prostitute, and her doctor, who told her she could never get pregnant again because of her earlier infection, was wrong. The death of her second child, a five-year-old son whom she'd raised against considerable odds, left her devastated. On the verge of a nervous breakdown, she'd treated her lover harshly and then abruptly dismissed him.

To compound the problem, Madeleine had recently been disowned by her father, who had finally sobered up enough to discover how she had been supporting her mother and siblings. Hurt, too distracted to return to Allen's, and rudderless, she had fled to her lover in Butte only to learn that Paul Martin was away on business. She was overjoyed, however, when he finally learned she was in Montana and invited her to the pretty little town of Bannack, about sixty miles southwest of Butte, where he was overseeing a gold-mining operation for the summer. He proved delighted to resume their relationship, which had always been passionate, and he installed her in a room at his hotel and appeared quite openly with her.

"I was an object of much curiosity to the natives, both as to my social status and my occupation," she later wrote. "They were not long in discovering that I was Paul Martin's girl, and they soon concluded that I must be an Eastern school-teacher, for no one else could possibly be so eager for information."

As the site of Montana's first major gold discovery, Bannack had a rich history of highwaymen and the vigilantes who hung them, and while Paul attended to his mining business, Madeleine pestered longtime residents for stories of the early days. Worst of the outlaws, they told her, was a handsome man named Henry Plummer, who led a double life as sheriff while murdering anyone who got in his way, including women and children. It took the vigilantes some time to discover his duplicity, for he appeared to be a good lawman and was charming to boot. Before they finally hung him, he had begged for his life.

"Oh, God! I'm too wicked to die," he had cried.

Why, if he believed in hell, had Plummer been so wicked? Madeleine pondered this, considering her own double life. Although she'd long since put religion behind her, at certain moments she felt the hand of God in Montana's wild panoramas. She reveled in Bannack's mountains and woods, exploring on horseback from Road-agents' Rock to Hangman's Gulch and the still-wild outback. Delighted to be free from the pawing of endless clients, she dared hope that, unlike the highwayman, she could still escape her past and a grim fate like that of Norma.

Of course, her reasons for staying with her profession remained sound. When things went well, prostitution was an easy way to make money—more than any other trade a woman could enter—and Madeleine enjoyed the power over men that it gave her. Taking their money. Making them jump through hoops, even when they thought they were in charge. This was not the case in marriage, where women lost the rights to their earnings, their children, and their very lives. No! Madeleine Blair had no regrets about the life she'd chosen because, for the most part, it had gone far better than what had originally been handed to her. But in Butte, particularly, she'd been forced to see a dark side, which horrified her.

Paul had offered to send her back to school, but she had declined, unwilling to let him know how little formal education she had, believing she would never get into college for want of it. Still, she possessed a photographic memory, and education might lead to an interesting life. She'd recently noticed a pretty young woman lawyer named Ella Knowles making a good run for the job of Montana's attorney general, the first woman in the nation to do so. There was a female doctor in Bannack and another in Helena who had a remarkable practice. Or perhaps marriage to Paul would turn things around for her . . . if he gave her enough freedom.

Madeleine would later view her two-month idyll in Bannack as one of the happiest times in her life, but to her frustration Paul never proposed as he had done in the past. He did invite her to return to Butte with him that fall but insisted that they live apart to avoid scandal. Although he supported her handsomely, he became deeply absorbed in his business affairs and even more so with the Butte social set to which he could not introduce her as he had to friends in Bannack.

Feeling neglected once back in Butte, Madeleine began accepting invitations from other men. Then one evening during supper with Bertie at the town's best hotel, she listened half distracted as he held forth about a wild poker game he'd been in on the night before, where "the sky was the limit."

"Would you like to see one?" he asked. "Women are barred from the cardroom, but everything goes in Butte if you know the ropes."

Madeleine knew nothing of poker, but she liked the idea of being admitted where women weren't allowed. After a brief parley at the door, they were in, and her escort politely began to explain the game. Fifteen minutes later Bertie removed his coat and became intent on his cards. Madeleine pouted. Not used to being ignored, she was thinking about slipping out unnoticed when one of the players—a recent winner—handed her a stack of chips saying, "Try your luck, kid!"

She won, and then won again, mostly because her fellow players were being generous. They found her a novelty. They bought champagne. At 4:00 A.M. she emerged with $250.

Back at the hotel she found Martin pacing her room, white with jealousy and rage.

"Madeleine, where in the world have you been, and is there anything you want to tell me?" he asked in a steely voice.

Visibly relieved to discover her new love was cards once she explained, he began to lecture her on the evils of gambling. Madeleine promised her lover she would never play again, but the casinos of Butte were enticing, and many men were anxious to escort her. A few days later she won $100 at roulette, and her life changed course.

Soon she discovered the racetrack. Copper king Marcus Daly, a mine owner who had built the neighboring town of Anaconda around a smelter, raised thoroughbred racehorses, some of which were internationally famous. When one tired of Butte's casinos, Daly's fine racetrack was the place to mingle with high society, to see and be seen placing enormous bets. Norma and her gambler were long gone, but Madeleine was so busy with her wagers that she scarcely noticed. In fact, she barely had time to acknowledge Lou Harpell, who usually turned out with her girls garbed in Daly's racing colors.

"I played poker, roulette, faro, the races, or anything else on which money could be staked," Blair later confessed. "I had escaped the usual vices of my class, liquor and drugs, only to fall victim to as great an evil. There were times when I would have sold Paul for a stack of red chips."

Many of the men who frequented Butte's high-class casinos were cosmopolitan—titled Europeans and America's highest rollers, all in Butte to make a fast buck. They could do so in the mining business, which was virtually unregulated, but high-stakes gambling also had appeal.

Completely caught up with this fast crowd, Madeleine found Paul Martin's earnest lectures on the evils of gambling tedious, and she tried to keep her addiction from him. When he discovered she had broken her promise and tried roulette, he was furious. Again she promised with great sincerity to stop, but she couldn't. Soon she lost everything on what had seemed a splendid plan to "beat the wheel" employing her remarkable memory.

"It was the first time I had ever been completely broke since I had been in the 'business' and I could hardly realize that I did not have a penny in the world," she recalled. "I dared not confess to Paul that I had broken my word to him again."

Lou Harpell generously offered the girl a position in her parlor house to provide a new stake, but Madeleine declined. She couldn't work in the town where Paul lived, she said. And besides, working in Butte would ruin any chance she had of returning to Chicago. Eastern madams would not send a railway ticket or pay a bill for a girl who had sullied herself on the Montana frontier.

"They seem to think that the girls in the West, especially in Montana, become tough after they've been here for a short time," she explained, recalling an early conversation with Norma.

"Good thing I'm not longing to return to Chicago," Lou snapped. "Perhaps I should provide you with a train ticket back there before your reputation as a whore is truly ruined."

Instead, Madeleine pawned her expensive solitaire diamond, and when Martin noticed it was gone, she was forced to confess. To her surprise, instead of getting angry, he quietly paid for her to redeem the ring, gave her additional money to get her back on her feet, and disappeared for three days.

It was off again, on again with him after that, and Madeleine was ambivalent about her feelings for him, which were compromised by her new lust for excitement. Paul had grown stodgy. The precious Butte society that he valued so highly was just a laughable collection of pretenders and nouveau riche. Old Joe Nadeau and his ridiculous wife, Delia, were among them, for heaven's sake, when everyone in town knew their wealth came from the red-light district despite the fact they were sending their brat to Harvard.

Still uncertain, Madeleine lingered in Butte for a couple of months, hitting the casinos with increasing frequency before she disappeared. Lou Harpell— who had recently started drinking gin in her morning orange juice—feared for the girl's future and for her own. There were just too many addicting pleasures associated with their trade. She hated to be reminded of them. So it was a relief to see the last of Madeleine Blair and forget her dire predictions for whores who hoped to get ahead in Butte.

Later that year—1895—Bertie dropped by with the news that Madeleine was touring the casinos of Europe with a moneyed earl.

"She certainly gambled away a good marriage here," Lou observed. "Paul Martin is a fine man."

"Eventually he would have bored her silly," Bertie pointed out.

"Well, she's in on the fast life now," Lou observed. "You were right when you said she had problems. I wonder if she will survive."

"I think she will, and maybe come out ahead," he said thoughtfully. "Do you want to make a small wager?"

———◦———

Madeleine Blair was unique in that she wrote an unblushing and unapologetic account of her life as a prostitute at the turn of the twentieth century; no similar accounts exist. In contrast, most historians dish up grim portrayals of the fate of women lured into a life of sin. Yet Madeleine's success in her trade and her satisfaction with it were by no means an anomaly, and there are good reasons why.

Prostitution was the only avenue to wealth open to poor women of her day unless they managed to captivate a rich husband. Some colleges were beginning to open their doors to the fair sex, but few women had the resources or the brass required to compete in a man's world. Marriage was, of course, the only respectable option, but that respect came at the cost of freedom: married women had few rights, lacking even the power to deter a philandering wife beater. Madeleine, who viewed marriage for money as simply another form of whoring, enjoyed crafting her own destiny. And so did a surprising number of her Montana sisters.

1

THE SUMMER WOMEN OF HELENA

⚜ 1867 ⚜

The first boom began in a crude camp they called Bannack, in the foothills of the Rocky Mountains of Idaho Territory. A small party of Colorado prospectors was looking for a way over the Continental Divide but instead found gold at Grasshopper Creek near Badger Pass. By 1863 the town had about one thousand inhabitants, who, realizing the area's mineral potential, wrested it from Idaho to incorporate as Montana Territory with Bannack as its capital. In very short order they mined out about $5 million worth of precious metals, but John White, the original discoverer, was not among the happy survivors. He was murdered eighteen months after his arrival while prospecting the area for another strike.

White's widow and child were living in Illinois at the time, and word traveled fast. Prostitute Molly Welch, also known as Mary Welch, also known as Josephine Airey, also known as Chicago Joe, heard about Bannack from her friend Al Hankins, a Chicago gambler who took a professional interest. Hankins's older brother, Jeff, had been dealing cards at a casino in San Francisco when he learned about the strike and suggested Al and their younger brother, George, join him there in mining the miners. Too late to get in on the initial rush, Jeff had established headquarters at a low-class saloon and gambling den with the high-flying name of the California Exchange in a rough little mining camp near another gold deposit on the Stinking Water River.

By the time Al and George had navigated the rutted wagon trail south
from the Missouri River port of Fort Benton to join him, the place had been
rechristened Alder Gulch and its settlers—mostly rebel sympathizers, draft
dodgers, and deserters from the War Between the States—had officially organized as the town of Varina, honoring the wife of Jefferson Davis, the Confed-
erate president. It was the Yankee judge in charge of paperwork who changed
the name to Virginia City, causing never-ending trouble for U.S. postal clerks
who confused it with Virginia City, Nevada. But by that time the new settlers, whose ranks had swelled to about ten thousand, had made Virginia City
Montana's capital and were too busy getting rich to care. The Hankins boys
did so well at their game that within two years they found it prudent to move
on. The newest gold discovery was a place called Blackfoot City in Ophir
Gulch, about a hundred miles to the northwest, where the brothers enjoyed
even greater success running a clip joint called the Headquarters.

Meanwhile, Josephine Airey, who had been saving her money, grew impa-
tient with the economics of working on her back in Chicago's tenderloin and
decided to do some pioneering of her own. Clients flush from the Montana
diggings informed her that the remote territory had a serious shortage of
professional women. Mostly there was Lizzie "Nigger Liz" Hall, a strong and
enterprising black woman, and Carmen, described as a "full blossomed Spanish rose who would just as soon stick a stiletto into your gizzard as stand at
the bar and have a drink with you."

Prostitutes did so well there that sometimes respectable women also
turned to the trade, especially when starvation faced families whose claims
did not pay and those who had no savings to tide them through the fearsome
Montana winters that made mining impossible. One of Josephine's clients
produced a wrinkled clipping from a Virginia City newspaper dated New
Year's Eve 1864 and read it to her, knowing she had no formal schooling.

"Three little girls, who state their name to be Canary, appeared at the door
of Mr. Furgis, on Idaho street, soliciting charity," it began. "The ages of the
two elder ones were about ten and twelve respectively. The eldest carried in
her arms her infant sister, a baby of about 12 months of age."

Actually Martha Jane Cannary, who later become famous as Calamity
Jane, a prostitute, teamster, and pioneer scout, would have been younger

than the twelve years for which the Virginia paper gave her credit, but 1864 had been a desperate winter for her family, and selling herself might well have been their only out, as the miner who read her the clipping had suggested.

Josephine was moved by the story. She had escaped to America out of similar poverty in Ireland at age fourteen, reluctantly leaving two younger sisters behind. She'd gotten her start in the miserable sweatshops of New York but could not tolerate the brutal overseers she watched work some of her fellow wage slaves to death. Her strictly Catholic family would never condone the choices she'd made when she embraced a much easier lifestyle in Chicago, but she had good reason to have chosen her profession. There had been little help for exploited girls like her when she'd landed in New York.

Towns like Virginia City were too wild to organize any kind of relief. Nor was there any law enforcement to help the miners victimized by vicious prostitutes and their pimps, the Montana man reported. What the territory needed were honest whores.

Airey was no beauty, but a fresh-faced Irish lass of twenty-two with a delightful brogue and a stunning figure. She dressed her dark, curly hair in an exotic fall and sported an expensive wardrobe accessorized with frills, laces, and jewels. The fact that she was illiterate was countered by her extraordinary aptitude for math. Her social skills matched her sharp wit. She was, as reputed, a woman of her word, and she was physically as tough as a professional wrestler.

By the time Josephine got organized to leave Chicago, the stampede had moved to Last Chance Gulch, about eighty miles to the north of Virginia City, where a party had struck pay dirt on Prickly Pear Creek. Carmen and Lizzie Hall soon moved into the new camp, joined by a second black woman named Fanny Bird, who on June 14, 1865, became the first whore to put her name on land records there. That was just after General Lee surrendered to Grant, ending the Civil War, but despite heavy Southern sympathies, Montanans were apparently too busy chasing riches to draw color lines. In fact, most of the prostitutes servicing white men in some of the outlying gold camps were black or Chinese, although Last Chance soon enjoyed a white majority.

By 1867, when Josephine Airey arrived via stagecoach from Fort Benton, there were already forty ladies of the evening in residence, but as the county seat and port of entry with a virtually all-male population of more than a thousand, Last Chance Gulch welcomed her as Chicago Joe. It was a rude settlement of hastily built log houses, bars, stores, and hotels; its muddy streets were filled with splattered pedestrians and screaming teamsters and their wagons, oxen, and horses. Airey liked the action. On April 5, just after the settlement was renamed Helena, she purchased a crude, one-story log cabin on Bridge Street in the red-light district with a down payment of $375, with $675 due in three months. Then, investing her remaining capital in some minor carpentry and hiring three musicians and several pretty inmates from the district, she went into competition with Fred White, who had been running the town's only dance hall.

Airey was pleased to call herself a manager, but she worked regular shifts as staff, too, and found it rough duty. A hurdy-gurdy house, as Josephine's dance hall was disdainfully labeled, usually charged men a dollar a dance and strongly recommended the purchase of drinks at highly inflated prices for the customer and his lady at the end of each set. There was more money to be made by arrangement in the hall's back rooms and in smaller houses Airey would eventually purchase with the profits. But placer mining—panning gold out of surface gravel—which was Helena's main employment, was hard, dirty, mind-dulling work. Although wages were high, the mining season was as short as the work hours were long. Many unwashed customers arrived armed with pistols, drank to excess, and were hard, if not downright dangerous, to deal with. Since women were scarce, especially those who were single and respectable, Josephine and her girls were alternately fought over and manhandled. The town's police station was conveniently located in the middle of the red-light district, but since officers generally ignored "proprietor prostitutes," the girls ensured their own safety by hiring burly bartenders and bouncers to keep peace.

Luckily, veteran operators like Big Lou Courselle, who'd come north from a lively California district, and Carrie Whitney, a survivor of rough-and-tumble Kansas cattle towns, joined forces in dealing with the town's disruptive elements. Then there was Eleanor Alphonsine Dumont, also known as

Madame Mustache because of the dark hair that shadowed her upper lip, who had gambled her way through most of the West's famous boomtowns. A well-brought-up French Creole from the Mississippi Delta, Dumont dabbled in prostitution as a sideline but forbade swearing and rough behavior in her house, establishing a precedent for the district.

As in Virginia City, times were tough for many who found themselves in Helena without resources, and more than a few turned to Josephine, who could be as generous as she was obsessed with making money. Too often the loans she made were not repaid, but, mindful of her own harsh beginnings, she continued to make them because there were few community agencies to meet the needs of those in trouble.

Airey could definitely afford her philanthropy, of course, because she and the rest of Helena's thirty-seven independent, property-owning prostitutes were doing extremely well. According to public records, they made 119 separate property transactions totaling more than $50,000 in a five-year period as the district expanded, accounting for 44 percent of the town's real estate transfers. Respectable merchants dealt with them openly, buying and selling property, occasionally loaning capital for their ventures or borrowing from them. One-third of the town's white demimonde population (twelve proprietor prostitutes) reported an average of $2,500 in personal wealth in the bank. Even street whores without capital could expect to earn $223 a month.

By comparison, stonemasons and carpenters commanded no more than $100 a month and bank clerks earned $125, while the highest legitimate wage a female could make was $65 as a sales clerk. However, Helena's good money was guaranteed only from June through September during the mining season. Business slowed to a crawl during the frozen Montana winters, motivating so many prostitutes to leave town that they became known as the summer women.

It was during this hiatus, perhaps, that Josephine Airey reconnected with gambler Albert Hankins, her old friend from Chicago who had first alerted her to Montana's potential. He had become a rich man since she had last seen him, wisely moving out of Blackfoot City just before that stampede ended to invest his winnings in a fine club in Salt Lake City. There he'd fallen in with a group of Mormons who apparently found gambling no more sinful than polygamy. He had won their trust by joining their church, he explained.

In truth, Hankins had actually gone on trial in Blackfoot City for absconding with the savings of four prostitutes he and his brothers had imported from San Francisco to staff their dance hall. The girls, nicknamed "the herders," had been so popular with the town's mob of womanless miners that would-be customers had to be limited to just one dance an evening. Living together, pooling their resources, the herders had amassed a sum of $4,000 from their shares of the proceeds, which Al managed to convince the court he had not stolen. The local vigilantes proved more skeptical, however, and soon thereafter decided to hang all three Hankins brothers, whom they believed to be harboring murdering highwaymen and thieves in their crooked gambling saloon. Jeff broke his leg in a mad dash to escape. Al and George managed to rescue him and make it to safety, but Jeff would limp for the rest of his life, and they all agreed it had been a close call. The vigilantes were actually nothing but a pack of thieves themselves, the Hankins brothers would always explain when some version of the story surfaced. The vigilantes, in Blackfoot at least, simply used their guise as protectors of respectable folk to rob, maim, and kill successful miners and gamblers.

While Josephine Airey was established in Helena long enough to be aware that Al Hankins's reputation in the territory was dubious, she may not have heard the details of his adventures in Blackfoot. She may also have missed the news that criminal charges had been filed against him by a Deer Lodge County prostitute who accused Hankins of fleecing her of $2,000. Or perhaps Josephine just didn't care, for the handsome twenty-seven-year-old gambler, whose real name was Prince Albert Hankins, must have appeared a prince indeed in contrast to the unpolished mining men with whom she'd danced away the past two summers. A fine physical specimen, Hankins was famous in the region as a champion sprinter who won almost every footrace he entered, even against Indians. Although born on a farm in Indiana and trained as a saddler and horse trader, he had ornate taste, as did she. He loved horses and had plans for owning a stock farm as well as another gambling house. His ambitious business schemes matched or topped her own, and so Josephine Airey allowed herself to fall in love as she had never done before.

Elegantly garbed in the latest fashion, which favored her hourglass figure with a tight bodice, deep velvet hoop skirts, overskirts, and a provocative little bustle and ornamented by extravagant ruffles, flounces, and expensive jewelry, she wed the frock-coated dandy in Helena on Valentine's Day 1869. Marking the auspicious occasion was a fire that leveled much of Helena's legitimate business district. Built in a narrow valley, Helena was like a wind tunnel in a blaze. Two more conflagrations that followed set back the economy even further, but Josephine—whose property escaped all three of the disasters—took advantage of the lull. On June 15, 1869, she purchased a lot two blocks closer to the center of town for four dollars, then resold it that afternoon for $150 to Catherine Harrison, who thought even better of the new location. The reason for the quick turnover was undoubtedly word of a gold rush to White Pine, Nevada, which caused Josephine to put the rest of her property under the management of an associate and pack her portmanteau.

Albert Hankins had always found it hard to resist a good stampede, and the White Pine strike, billed as the "biggest and brightest of them all," attracted thirty thousand to the slopes of Mount Hamilton in the fledging state during the summer of 1869. British who had missed out on the California rush led the way, and there were also a surprising number of blacks encouraged by the ending of the Civil War and passage of the 13th, 14th, and 15th amendments to the Constitution guaranteeing them citizenship. The problem was that new gold deposits were discovered daily and all over the place, which made it risky to pick a site on which to establish a whorehouse or gambling hall. Al didn't like the look of it. The gold was quick to give out and so was Hankins's marriage to Josephine. Albert headed back to Chicago almost immediately to build a grand gambling casino in partnership with brothers Jeff and George.

Josephine's reaction to his leaving, and to his marriage to the fifteen-year-old daughter of a well-heeled Indiana farmer on Christmas Day the next year, is not known. Nor is there any solid proof that Hankins left Josephine pregnant, although it is believed that she had a son by him or someone else she met during this unsettled period. According to rumor, she placed the baby with a family outside the territory, paying his way but never seeing him after his adoption.

Having no close friends of record, Josephine appears to have kept her own council, although we do know she quickly dropped her married name. Then, a year after her wedding to Hankins (which is public record), Josephine Airey rejoined the summer women of Helena to take up where she had left off. Her story was simply that she and Hankins had gotten a divorce, although no record of it has ever been found.

—◦—

In the summer of 1870 James T. "Black Hawk" Hensley was disgusted with himself and with life in general. He hadn't come all the way from Missouri working as a teamster and surviving Chief Black Hawk's Indian War in Utah to live a life of abstinence on declining wages, holed up in a ten-mile gulch on the upper Blackfoot River. Although several million in gold had been taken from the long, narrow valley since Welshman Richard Evans had discovered it with a Yankee in 1865, Lincoln City remained isolated near Montana's Great Divide. It offered virtually no amenities except a piss-poor saloon selling rotgut liquor at outlandish prices. There were only nine grown women in a population of 187, and all of those were married except for seventeen-year-old Julia Galter. Unfortunately, Julia was the daughter of the richest man in town, who happened to be a rancher with nine other kids but who guarded her as if she were his prize cow. Most gold camps had a string of whores, but with the exception of some ranch hands, two doctors, and a couple of Chinese laundrymen, the rest of Lincoln's citizens were all miners, and business wasn't good.

When Hensley first arrived, the gulch's primitive little drift mines averaged $375 a set, but now it looked like the pay dirt was playing out. Even if it wasn't, Black Hawk had had enough. Stranded there during the long dull winter, he had discovered he was a pretty fair poker player. In fact, having accumulated $300 in dust and nuggets, he figured with a bit of luck he might earn a living by gambling or something similar. Just twenty, he had the makings of a ladies' man and was well aware of his dark good looks. After the fall cleanup, Evans, the gold-discovering Welshman, was moving to Helena, fifty miles to the south. Black Hawk knew that town had a lot of action, and he liked the idea of trying it out. He could always get a job as a bartender until he got really good at mining the gambling joints. With Richard Evans in residence, at least he'd have one friend there.

Josephine had just lost the services of dashingly handsome James "The Duke" Hamilton, who had given up his career as a butcher in the county jail to become her bartender and muscle man, only to leave for reasons unexplained. She doubted Black Hawk had much bar experience, except perhaps as a customer, but James Hensley didn't lie about it. He simply said he could handle the job, and she liked his looks. She actually needed a bouncer as much as she needed someone to peddle drinks, and there were no doubts about James Hensley's qualifications in that department. He was a big man. Driving mule trains and swinging a miner's pick had endowed him with a rock-solid physique. Of course, his weathered tan wouldn't last long, but he was nice to look at and surprisingly easygoing.

Black Hawk was up front with her, too, about hoping to become a professional gambler. However, until he was a bit surer of himself at the tables, he promised to work for her like a dog, which is just what he did. Even after he hit a winning streak that earned the respect of local cardsharps, he stayed on. She'd be losing him soon, she thought, angry at herself for growing to depend on him. Yet she was delighted with Black Hawk's success and the way he handled it. Unlike the departed Al Hankins and most of the local demimonde, he actually seemed to like Helena. He never voiced a desire to move on to a more sophisticated city and he doted on her. Yet, discovering he was five years her junior, and weary of entanglements, Josephine tactfully evaded his suggestions that they become romantically involved. Instead, with attendance at her dance hall slowing as gold deposits dwindled, she focused on business.

Helena still remained better off than most towns, however. Butte, which once rivaled it as a gold camp, was fast becoming a ghost town with a population of just 261, one-third of whom were Chinese. Bannack had already faded, and Virginia City, though still the territorial capital, was in decline. Meanwhile, Samuel T. Hauser, a Helena resident who was a civil engineer and one of the territory's most powerful capitalists, had early recognized the potential of silver mining, attracting outside capital in 1866 to build Montana's first silver smelter at Argenta, not far from Bannack. The operation was soon expanded successfully to the town of Philipsburg, and Hauser was known to be considering other developments closer to home.

Centrally located, with a steady population of more than three thousand and lusting to become the capital site, Helena had a future worth gambling on. At least that's the way Josephine sized it up after every building on its main street burned in October 1, 1871. One week later, the Great Chicago Fire wiped out the insurance companies many were depending on for recovery. Josephine, who once again had been spared, moved to get in on the distress sale that followed. She began by buying out veteran prostitute Henrietta Bischoff for $2,000, half of which she had on hand. The rest she borrowed, promising 2 percent interest a month to Harriet Truett, mother of the local judge and daughter of a U.S. congressman, who was waiting for an inheritance from the sizeable estate of her late husband.

The purchase reestablished Chicago Joe's presence in the red-light district although she didn't resort to personally turning tricks. Instead she rented to women who did, which proved so lucrative she paid back her loan to Mrs. Truitt in less than a year and went looking for similar opportunities. In April 1873 Airey paid $200 to buy back the downtown lot she'd sold to Catherine Harrison for $150 just before heading off to the White Pine stampede, and it became clear that Airey was determined to grow her business. By today's standards, of course, $200 may not sound like much, but in early Helena it equaled four to five months' wages made by legitimate working women and was a risky expenditure. Nor was that the only risk Josephine took. In July of that year the Helena police, who usually looked the other way, arrested Airey after she chased down Annie Glessner on Wood Street and beat her severely. The judge fined her ten dollars. While court records make no mention of what provoked the incident, Josephine demanded complete loyalty from the women she employed and was known to be merciless in dealing with her competition.

Later that summer, Airey mortgaged just about everything she had for a loan of $3,000 at 2 percent interest per month from Selig Lavenberg, a dry goods merchant in partnership with his brother on Bridge Street, a major part of the red-light district. Josephine's collateral included one gold watch and chain, five diamond rings, one fur cloak, a muff and cuffs, plus three dozen pairs of underclothes. What exactly the loan was to finance is uncertain, but the Panic of 1873—caused when the ambitious North Pacific Railroad went into bankruptcy—may have compromised Airey's finances.

National rail lines had been built only as far as Salt Lake City and Bismarck, North Dakota, and Montanans had hoped the North Pacific would soon connect their remote territory to a major rail center, reducing the price of ore transport and general shipping. The company's failure sharply curtailed mining. Outside capital dried up, and then, on January 9, 1874, a fire that started in a Chinese gambling den near Bridge and Main and spread rapidly in high winds destroyed some of Helena's most valued assets—the library and archives of its ten-year-old historical society and the red-light district. Property damage, estimated at more than a million dollars, included Chicago Joe's dance hall.

One year earlier, the territorial legislature had passed a law making "dancing saloons or hurdy-gurdy houses" illegal, and it later added a statute allowing women to own and operate a business in their own right. Since Airey had long been in business without territorial sanction and had enjoyed uninterrupted profits from her dance hall until the fire, she ignored the government action, determined to rebuild. Selig Lavenberg and his brother, however, who had also suffered major fire losses, were pressing Airey to repay their loan, which is when James Hensley found a way in. By that time, Black Hawk had more than proved himself as a professional gambler and was on a solid winning streak. With his backing, Airey managed to bankroll construction of a fireproof hall fronting on Wood Street and still pay off the Lavenbergs' loan six months early. Then, comfortable with the partnership, which didn't include Hensley's name on the building title, Airey again teamed with him to construct a business building across the street with ample second-floor living quarters, which she shared with the gambler and several female employees.

Josephine named the new dance hall the Red Light. In an attempt to make it legal under the new law and as a come-on, she allowed customers to dance for free while making drink purchase mandatory. Then, taking advantage of the rail link to Salt Lake City and scheduled stagecoach runs from there to Helena, she began to import dance hall girls from Chicago—fresh new faces much appreciated by her clientele—and the business boomed.

While Airey and Hensley were busy with urban renewal in the fire's wake, many prostitutes who had pioneered back when the town was called Last Chance Gulch could not muster the resources to rebuild. Lillie McGraw, a twenty-seven-year-old who had been working a crib in Portland, Oregon, arrived looking for bargains and picked up a good parcel of land that had earlier belonged to a Helena veteran, while Josephine bought out Big Lou Courselle, paying $150 for property that had been valued at $2,000 before the district's fire. Then, teaming with James Hensley and Delores Jarra, who already owned two district lots, Airey and McGraw petitioned the court to incarcerate Mary Kelly, a sister land-owning inmate of the line, on grounds of insanity. What exactly they had on Kelly is unclear, but the doctor who evaluated the girl for the court declared her the victim of designing demimonde leadership that sought to defraud her of her property, and the scheming foursome backed down. Airey, who would purchase no additional property for four years, focused on growing the business she had.

The next year Helena wrested the territorial capital from Virginia City and business picked up for the summer women. Of course many of the legislators were as uncouth and hard to deal with as the miners, but they kept the town operating in the winter, and there were also rumors that another gold rush was in the offing. Josephine heard it first from Lizzie Hall, who was still working the black district on Clore Street. Everyone knew the Black Hills of South Dakota were teeming with prospectors. They were there illegally because the country had been given to the Sioux by treaty, but neither the pugnacious lieutenant colonel George Custer nor soldiers from the expedition that followed him there in 1875 could discourage them. As far as most people knew there had been no big discoveries, but Liz and the other black girls working in Helena had an unexpected good run during the spring of 1875 when a group of black miners arrived loaded with gold and reluctant to discuss where they'd gotten it. It turned out they had stumbled on the find after white prospectors directed them to an area about twenty miles northwest of Deadwood, believing it was hopeless. Working quietly with remarkable speed and luck, the black miners panned out enough to make them rich but left early without filing to avoid the legal hassles and losses in the saloons and gambling dens they realized would follow.

By fall, about $10,000 per day was being mined out of Whitewood Creek in the Northern Hills, and the following March, Helena citizens organized a wagon train to get in on the action. The party of two hundred hit the Bozeman trail with a hundred pack mules for a nightmare trip. There were narrow escapes from the Indians, who killed one scout, and the wagons had to be lowered by ropes down the steep canyon walls. Nevertheless, most of the survivors decided to settle in Deadwood, sending back glowing reports. Word that Lieutenant Colonel Custer and more than two hundred of his men had been massacred by Indians out at Little Bighorn in June of that summer deterred very few. Nor was there much concern when Montana governor Thomas Francis Meagher disappeared after boarding a riverboat at Fort Benson about the same time. A second Helena expedition made the trip to Deadwood with sixty wagons that fall, with the majority reporting success at merchandizing if not in actual mining.

Chicago Joe Airey and James "Black Hawk" Hensley were not among them, however; they'd both had their fill of stampedes, and Helena had gotten into silver mining in a big way. In fact, silver production had doubled throughout the territory, and there were other options to consider. The discovery of a big silver lode at Leadville, west of Denver, lured many from Helena, but it was a sudden copper-producing boom in Butte that got the most attention—so much, in fact, that Helena's Board of Trade backed the building of a road to Butte over a rough trail that was getting heavy use.

Helena merchant John How opened a mill there. Sam Hauser had quietly gotten involved. Butte's red-light district was rapidly expanding because there were plenty of jobs and single men to fill them. Anton Holter, a member of the Board of Trade and respected pillar of Helena society, was building some cribs there and might back local girls who wanted to relocate. Even Lizzie Hall was planning to make the move!

Dolores Jarra, who intended to beat Lizzie on the scene, ran the idea by Josephine. Dolores was hoping to make the move with Helena bartender Charlie Stanchfield, who predicted that Butte would soon be the biggest city in the territory. This was a chance to get in on the ground floor. Had Joe ever been to Butte? she wondered.

Josephine said she had, and she didn't much like it. It was growing, but too fast—three thousand people already and more streaming in every day. Being on the ground floor wouldn't do you much good if you didn't know the major players, she pointed out. And there was little chance for a working girl in Butte to purchase property. Of course, after all the fires in Helena, renting didn't sound like a bad idea. But Dolores was only twenty-four while Josephine was thirty-two. Airey had a good foothold in Helena, and she decided to stick with it.

Black Hawk Hensley, still tending bar for Josephine, was of like mind and enthusiastic about Airey's plans for Helena expansion. He knew from past experience that she'd seldom include his name with hers on land titles, but she trusted him with management and they made a formidable team. On December 17, 1878, he was highly relieved to make it official by marrying her for the record.

2

BUTTE, THE BLACK HEART OF MONTANA

ℰ 1877 ℰ

Dolores Jarra's first impression of Butte was that of most newcomers: she had made an enormous mistake! The buckboard trip over the steep Rocky Mountain passes from Helena to Butte had been a rough, but a wonderful, adventure. Her two young daughters—Louisa, eight, and Minnie, just seven—had loved the deep woods, splashing streams, and early wild roses that bordered the trail. But Butte . . . the shock of seeing it for the first time frightened them all. It appeared suddenly as their team of horses strained over the Great Divide. Perched on the bleak hillside of a dark volcanic cone, it was a randomly organized mining camp of more than three thousand, almost as big as Helena, with a dozen or so gallows-like headframes that hauled workmen to and from the underground mines fringing the downtown.

Settled after a placer discovery in 1864, the site had early attracted a couple of thousand prospectors despite its reputation for wild lawlessness. When the surface gold played out, the population had dropped below one hundred. Recently, however, hard-rock miners adept at dynamiting their way to underground ore veins had discovered silver, and Butte was making a noisy comeback. The sounds of blasting continually topped the din of heavy equipment. Huge granite boulders and tailing dumps littered the barren landscape not yet altered by an enthusiastic building boom, and black smoke from various refining operations clouded blue skies. There were no birds. There seemed to be no grass anywhere. No wonder Butte had been nicknamed the Black Heart of Montana.

Park and Main streets, the heart of the camp, sported an odd combination of crumbling shacks, more substantial start-ups with second stories being added, and fine new buildings of sophisticated design. Livery stables and the shops of tradesmen selling food, clothing, and building supplies were crowded in among casinos, beer halls, and—of all things—a roller-skating rink. Young Minnie and Louisa were pleased about the rink, and Butte Public School in the next block looked substantial, but the apartment Charlie Stanchfield had rented for them provided another rude shock.

Situated at 182 East Park Street, it cornered China Town on lower Main Street, which featured gambling and opium dens and tiny cribs occupied by indentured prostitutes, along with noodle parlors, laundries, and tailor shops. Nor was Park much of an improvement with its saloons and a growing population of white prostitutes from many nations. Fortunately Dolores's daughters, who had been carefully raised in the rural isolation of the family's Prickly Pear Homestead, were taken by the color and excitement of their new world, which their mother explained to them as discreetly as she could. She worried about them, of course, but Park Street and its attractions were exactly what had drawn her to Butte. Despite the recent influx of newcomers like herself, the majority of prostitutes there were still Chinese, and there were no well-run dance halls.

———◆———

Dolores, whose roots were in Czechoslovakia via American-born parents, had come to Helena from Illinois in her early teens as an experienced working girl. Hired as a dancer at Fred White's saloon, she displayed real talent and a fine figure along with considerable flirtatious charm. When Chicago Joe Airey offered her better money she took it, forming a fast friendship with the ambitious dance hall owner and following her business advice. Saving her earnings, Jarra purchased two lots in the red-light district. By 1869 she had enough capital to make loans to other businesswomen and acquire the ill-reputed "Twin Cottages," which she leased out to prostitutes. It soon became obvious, however, that the Chicago madam would stop at nothing to gain a monopoly in the Helena red-light district, and Dolores, who hoped to strike out on her own, did not dare go up against her.

Dolores was living with Lewis Washburn, who had developed a fine homestead in the Prickly Pear Valley and had a good job as clerk for a local transfer firm. It was Washburn who had fathered her two daughters, but marriage was not an option. A priest had noted Jarra's relationship with Washburn as "concubina" on her daughters' baptismal certificates. So when Washburn decided to leave the territory in 1874, Jarra purchased his homestead but made no other claims on him.

Shortly thereafter, the twenty-two-year-old mother formed an alliance with a bartender from her home state, Charlie Stanchfield, twenty-four. He had learned his trade from a German saloon owner with whom he found lodging during the Virginia City gold rush before opening a bar of his own in Helena. When that venture failed, Stanchfield turned to his friend Fred Loeber, a Helena miner turned cowboy, who was headed to Butte in search of a job. Stanchfield's mother had recently moved to Butte with his older brother and his family. They were urging Charlie to join them, and Dolores, who wanted to start her own dance hall, jumped at the idea of moving with him.

Fred Loeber worked for wages just two months before asking to lease fixtures from the bar Stanchfield had just closed for one he was planning in Butte under the lofty name of Loeber's Opera House. Dolores was so enthusiastic about the idea, she extended a mortgage to Charlie on the bar fixtures to help her lover finance his own move.

Nor were they alone in wanting to relocate. Lottie Ables, who worked under the name of a popular race horse, Sorrel Mike, had recently made a couple of unsuccessful suicide attempts and hoped for a new start. Prostitutes Liz Hall and Carmen, who had pioneered early mining camps, were going to Butte. Sam Hauser, Helena's leading banker and an operator of successful silver mines to the west, was enthusiastically promoting similar operations in Butte while quietly laying the groundwork to expand the town's red-light operations. Even Anton Holter, a pillar of society who'd made a fortune in Helena as a builder and promoter, was said to be investing surreptitiously in sin there.

It was rumored that, in addition to silver, an amazing discovery of copper had been made in the area; that thousands of men, most of them single, would soon be hired to extract it. With the recent invention of the telephone, millions of miles of copper wire would be needed and the price of that commodity was rising. No business could fail if that rumor were true, and investments in vice would be golden. All that was needed was capital and a front man.

Still, Dolores's initial Butte venture proved every bit as discouraging as her introduction to the camp. Charlie had no sooner leased a hall on East Park, just a block from Venus Alley, which was certain to become one of the most famous red-light districts in the West, than authorities moved to close down dancing saloons and arrested him. Bail was $500, and he was stuck with court costs of $105. They reopened as the Variety Theater, but business was so slow that Charlie suggested Dolores take a more active role as an entertainer.

She had hoped that the move to Butte would provide a respectable cover for her daughters. While some of their near neighbors on East Park were gamblers and lowlifes, the majority had turned out to be families of miners and tradesmen. Encouraged, Dolores had accepted Charlie's offer of marriage just before Christmas in 1878 and taken back her given name of Laura, which she'd dropped when she became a working girl. Selling herself, scantily clad in a public dance hall, was hardly in keeping with the new image she hoped to foster, but Charlie had a point. She was very good at erotic dancing, and giving birth to two children had done nothing to mar her dark good looks. The opening of their second variety theater two doors farther east, with Dolores as the major attraction, proved a resounding success.

Unfortunately, Dolores found the assignment far rougher than it had been in Helena. Butte was fast developing a sophisticated criminal underworld that shocked her. Unlike Helena, where most of the property in the red-light district was owned by proprietor prostitutes, only a few sisters in Butte could afford to own the houses in which they worked, and even fewer could discover the true identity of their landlords. Butte's boom attracted many transients, whereas Helena's red-light customers were usually better known. And while Helena's tenderloin was consolidated in such a way that a sales force was not needed to draw in newcomers, Butte's was citywide, so prostitutes usually had pimps to promote them. Coyly, the working girls referred to these middlemen as their secretaries, but many were brutal and controlling.

As for the miners, who made up the bulk of the blue-collar trade, they worked under terrible conditions, sweating hundreds of feet below ground with very few safety precautions, emerging in winter to some of the coldest weather on the planet. Wages were good because Butte was a union town, but it was no secret that the life of a miner was apt to be cut short by accident or some terrible lung disease. Most drank hard, played hard, and were tough on sporting women, while law enforcement usually looked the other way.

Even more lethal was a pimp who married his charge, for Montana had yet to pass a law against wife beating. So Mollie Forrest Scott, a beautiful little dancer known as the Highkicker, would have had no recourse if she was worried when her husband arranged her hire at Butte's Union Dancing Saloon late one Friday evening in July 1880, with full understanding she might also utilize a private room reserved for prostitution should customers tire of tripping the light fantastic. Mollie had met and married Joe Scott during the Black Hills gold rush five years prior while still in her early teens. She was well aware of his mean temper, even before he had stabbed a Helena hotel clerk in a scuffle earlier that month. Yet she mustered the spunk to defy her husband when he interrupted her shift at the Union to insist she accompany him to another dancing saloon, probably Stanchfield's, a few doors distant.

Scott argued with Mollie at the back of the hall and then took her to the bedroom he had earlier reserved. No one at the Union paid much attention until five minutes after the couple's departure when a gunshot startled revelers to silence. The noise was so loud, in fact, that it caused Officer Micklejohn of the Butte Police Department to leave his sidewalk beat and head for Mollie's bedroom, from which Joe Scott was making a swift departure. The girl had been shot through the cheekbone with the bullet ranging backward and upward, taking out six of her teeth and the back of her head. She never regained consciousness. Fellow workers saw to it she was buried in a fine white dress with kid gloves when her husband showed no inclination to plan her funeral. Scott cursed Mollie as her coffin was carried to the hearse and later escaped the law by swearing she had committed suicide.

The grisly death was followed by what appeared to be a rash of suicide attempts, beginning with Anna Parker, who was charged with taking $300 out of the pants pocket of a patron of Allen's Saloon on East Park. Escorted to her room to collect her belongings following her arrest, Anna managed to swallow a large dose of laudanum (a tincture of opium), declaring she would rather die than go to jail. But that was not to be. A physician was summoned by the sheriff to save her, and an unsympathetic judge set her bail at $700, which she somehow managed to muster before disappearing.

Inez Mayberton, an inmate of what the local paper described as "a well-known house on Park Street," was more successful, ingesting about an ounce of morphine after being abandoned by her lover.

"As she lay yesterday afternoon in an almost dying condition she called continually on the name of the man about town who at one time was her friend, but who, it is said, had maltreated her of late," the paper reported. "Word was sent to him but he is said to have answered with an angry oath."

Her suicide note instructed a coworker to bury her all in black. "Tell _____ [the man who spurned her] he may thank himself for this," she concluded. "If there is any such thing as haunting, I will haunt him to his death bed."

Less clear was the supposed suicide of Lottie Ables, who had abandoned her nickname of Sorrel Mike when she left Helena in an attempt to start a new life. Following her move to Butte, she wed bartender James C. Pickett, only to be rescued from a half-hearted suicide try with laudanum ten days later. By October she was back at her trade when a man known as Bronco Bill was fined twenty-five dollars after pleading guilty to insulting her with foul language and striking her. The following June a census taker reported her as Lottie Picket, married but living alone in a small house at 78 East Park in the center of the red-light district. Things apparently went well with her during this period, or at least she didn't make the news again, until she died mysteriously at the same address fourteen months later.

According to a newspaper account that appeared under the headline "Who Did It?" Lottie's younger sister Dollie claimed to be visiting a neighbor but had rushed to the small house she shared with Lottie after hearing a cry of murder. There she found Lottie shot in the stomach. Dollie called a doctor who had treated Lottie earlier, but this time he could not save her.

In an unusual deathbed scene, Lottie declared she had been shot by a man with a gun she had used for self-protection, while Dollie insisted her sister had pulled the trigger herself.

"Lottie, you know that is not so; you did it yourself," Dollie was quoted as chiding the dying girl. "Some innocent may suffer from your talk; you know you did it yourself."

The coroner's jury found for Lottie.

"It seems to be the general impression among those best informed in regard to the facts of the case, and among several of the jurors, that the shot was not fired intentionally, if at all, by Miss Pickett herself," it was reported. "The position of the wound is such that the pistol must have been held in the left hand on the hypothesis of suicide, which would seem to negate any such supposition. The friends of the deceased, knowing of her previous attempts at self-destruction—by poison, think that if Miss Pickett shot herself her intention was to inflict simply a slight flesh wound."

No explanation of Dollie's suicide verdict was forthcoming, nor was the name of the murderer, who might well have been a valued customer of both sisters, if indeed they were sisters at all.

Because there had never been a successful suicide in the Helena red-light district, the Stanchfields found the deaths of their Butte neighbors unnerving. Also of concern was an area for squatters called the Cabbage Patch, just three blocks to the east of their living quarters. A rapidly expanding tent and shantytown, it was occupied not only by outlaws and the homeless but also by derelict drunks and hopheads, including a few former society wives as well as addicted prostitutes who had become too fond of local opium dens.

Fearing for the safety of her daughters, Dolores decided to board them at St. Vincent's Academy in Helena. The place was a snobbish Catholic girls' school that required both business and social references for admittance. With Minnie and Louisa's birth certificates clearly showing they were bastards, the girls did not appear to be likely candidates. But the Stanchfields' Variety Hall and subsequent investments were making enormous amounts of money. Also a factor was Dolores's long tenure in the Helena red-light district because it provided her with enough blackmail material to influence a number of the town's politically important men. So Minnie and Louisa—equipped with their Bibles, rosaries, and the prerequisite wardrobe that included two black cashmere or serge dresses, one white poplin uniform, three sets of underwear per season, and twelve pocket handkerchiefs—embarked on a life of respectability to study with the daughters of Helena's elite. Dolores and Charlie had no intention of joining them, however, until they made their fortune.

———◦———

The basis for the Stanchfield fortune and that of other lucky Butte investors had been assured just a few years earlier by two stubborn miners who were viewed by most as crazy.

William L. Farlin had tried unsuccessfully to mill silver ore back in Butte's early placer days and, in the process, assayed a large copper deposit he thought to be unusual. Because silver was hard to process, and no one knew how to deal with copper yet, most developers gave up on anything but gold. However, when Congress passed a law in 1875 compelling owners to work or forfeit their claims, Farlin was at his Travonia Mine on New Year's Eve to qualify in the freezing cold and pick up twelve other abandoned plots as well. His find included both silver and copper, and, mostly because of those and new processing technology, Butte became the territory's leading mining town within the year.

Then another prospector, William J. Parks, working alone on his Parrot Lode in 1876 long after his partners dropped out, discovered an enormous vein of pure copper. Lying almost directly under the camp at 155 feet, Parks's lode ultimately established Butte as the most successful mining town on earth. Both discoverers profited only marginally, selling out quickly to men who had the major capital required to develop the industry.

The most successful of the opportunists were known as the Copper Kings; they took control not only of the industry but also of the local and territorial government. First among them was William A. Clark, born poor to a large farm family in Pennsylvania, who had made more money in Montana's gold camps peddling trade goods than as a miner and who soon became one of America's richest men through his Butte investments. Marcus Daly, a gifted prospector who escaped poverty in Ireland, likewise gambled on Butte to make his millions. So did Fritz Augustus Heinze, whose scheming was as phenomenal as his mining skills although his New York and European background was decidedly more upscale.

With the backing of the Copper Kings and that of other outsiders, substantial payrolls were quick in coming to Butte and, with them, astonishing prosperity. City fathers incorporated in 1879. Following a devastating fire, they banned wood-framed buildings, and the town was quickly rebuilt. By 1880 the price of copper had risen to eighteen cents per pound, and investors built smelters to take advantage of it. The finished product had to be driven via ox cart to the nearest railhead in Corrine, Utah, but within a year the Utah and Northern Railroad built a narrow gauge spur to Butte, and the town's future was secured.

———

Soon the foundation was being laid for an impressive city hall on Broadway near where Jim Murray, a local gambler turned mine operator, was planning to build an opera house. Several variety theaters attracted vaudeville shows from the East. Even grander theaters were on the drawing board. Butte had two lively newspapers plus a town crier. No one could keep track of the population, which had topped four thousand, but lodging was in such short supply that transients were sometimes forced to spend the night snoozing in Turkish baths or in houses of ill repute they would not normally have patronized. First-class hotels were finally being built, and the town's super rich organized Butte's Silver Bow Club, where they could meet privately and in style to plan for the future.

During this heady period, the Stanchfields—who were not yet rich enough to qualify for club membership, but close—launched a campaign to ensure their financial future. First, Dolores transferred ownership of her Prickly Pear homestead along with all her other legitimate Helena property to her daughters. In addition, she filed a sole tradership declaration testifying to her intent to engage in farming and entered property declarations in her own name, perhaps because she was less than impressed with her husband's business abilities. However, she did appoint Charlie trustee for her girls and joined with him in subsequent business dealings.Shrewdly, she divested herself of all her red-light property in Helena just before the town decided to go respectable and prices fell. Then, with the proceeds and revenues from their Variety Theater, the couple invested so widely that by 1883 they were paying several thousand dollars in property taxes.

In the process, the Stanchfields found themselves in league with the neighboring Nadeau clan, French Canadian neighbors who, despite their highly respectable background, were out to make a killing in the skin trade. Arriving in Butte about the same as the Stanchfields, Delia and Joseph Nadeau and their three young children had settled with Joe's brother, Arthur, and an odd assortment of gamblers, laborers, and wood choppers in the Quebec Boarding House a couple of blocks from the Stanchfields on East Park. Joseph, who had previously made his living as a shoe salesman, opened a French restaurant, which he soon managed to parlay into a legitimate hotel. But he and Arthur also began purchasing cribs and whorehouses, which produced richer returns.

A turning point for both families came in 1884 when city officials voted to banish all tenderloin operations from the heart of the city. Previously streetwalkers had operated so openly on the main drag that newspaper reporters usually referred to them as "Park Street girls," but merchants established in the area wanted them gone. So all red-light operations were consigned to the south side of Galena between Main and Wyoming, one block south of Park, where most of the houses were flimsy one-story shacks or log cabins and there were plenty of vacant lots in which to expand. A number of working girls protested the move, but the central location ultimately worked to their advantage. Their banishment also increased the value of Park Avenue property, which both the Nadeaus and the Stanchfields were holding, while providing great investment possibilities in the sparsely developed restricted district.

Meanwhile, Butte continued to grow at a rapid pace. Marcus Daly's Anaconda mining company had just built a settlement with an enormous copper smelter about twenty miles to the west, but instead of detracting from, it encouraged Butte's expansion: a rail spur between the two settlements allowed Butte miners to process cheaply and increase ore production in the new plant. By 1885 the Black Heart of Montana had become the largest mining camp in the West, with a population of nearly twenty-two thousand.

For Joe Nadeau and his brother, Arthur, who had focused on the fact that the majority of Butte's population were single men, the key to making money lay in gaining a monopoly on red-light real estate and on distributing liquor to the same clientele. Joe's wife, Delia, who had come from a respectable family in Rhode Island, was socially ambitious, not only for her children but for herself. Her goals—which included sending their sons to Ivy League schools, owning a fine house, and making a grand tour of Europe—would take more money than Joe could make running hotels and restaurants, and she didn't much care how he filled the gap.

Butte's recently established high society was ragtag at best. Most of its movers and shakers had come from backgrounds less auspicious than Delia's, and it was easy to buy in. So when son Ovila elected to work with his father overseeing their red-light operations, Delia didn't object. Their youngest, Albert, was a better candidate for Harvard anyway. Certainly the family would have need of a good Harvard lawyer.

In contrast, Dolores Stanchfield missed her daughters, and she was not happy with the way Butte was building. Park Street for two blocks between Main and Arizona remained fronted with beer halls and gambling and billiard houses, and more were going up on Galena and Wyoming, where prostitutes were housed in small frame shacks.

"With a few drinks of the arsenic they sold in those places, a squaw, a Mexican, a nigger wench, or a Barbary Coast blonde, all looked alike," a wary customer reported. "And you could spend your money on one as quick at the other."

Yet despite disturbing evidence of lawlessness, the Nadeaus were making healthy progress on buying up whatever real estate was for sale in the tenderloin. Although the Stanchfields might have aspired to do the same, they did not have access to nearly as much capital, which the Canadians had apparently raised through family connections. Besides, the Stanchfields continued to think of Helena as home. With the arrival of railroad service in 1883 city fathers predicted that Helena would replace Denver as "Queen of the Rockies," and a constitutional convention held the next year gave promise that it might become the capital of Montana on statehood.

A downside to moving back was that Dolores, who was illiterate, was also socially ambitious, and Helena society, which was much longer entrenched than that of Butte and took itself too seriously, did not welcome former inmates of the red-light district or saloon dancers. Still, Dolores's daughters had been accepted at St. Vincent's Academy, and all the Stanchfield holdings in Helena were now strictly legal. It was a perfect time to sell out in Butte. They would invest the proceeds in more legitimate Helena businesses. If the Stanchfields couldn't make it in high society, at least they'd score with the merchant class and their daughters would still marry well.

So the Stanchfields sold. The Nadeaus stayed. And it wouldn't be until a decade later that they would know who had made the soundest financial decision.

3

MILES CITY AND THE WILD WEST

✧ 1880 ✧

The gold had been all but mined out of Virginia City and Bannack, leaving them nearly ghost towns. Helena and Butte, now Montana's only viable cities, were both in the south-central part of the territory, little more than a day's journey apart. In the west, Missoula, of interest because of its timber resources, could claim only four hundred residents. The east remained unsettled for want of gold discoveries and because marauding Indians made quick work of would-be settlers looking for other options.

The Indian liability finally came to the attention of the U.S. government with the massacre of Lieutenant Colonel George Custer and his troops in 1876, and the government decided to fortify the region. Yet, ironically, residents of Deadwood, Dakota Territory, were more aware of the military buildup and the opportunities it offered than those of Montana because Deadwood was just over Montana's southeastern border, and residents who hadn't gotten rich there were looking for new opportunity in Montana.

Maggie Burns, a young and enterprising Deadwood whore, had set her sights on Butte. It was, after all, the most successful camp in Montana territory. The mines had huge payrolls. Where else would a working girl want to go? she asked, looking thoughtfully at the fine-featured prospector who was the new man in her life.

William Bullard, who was fourteen years Maggie's senior, was dead set against the move. Maggie wouldn't stand a chance in Butte, he argued. Neither would he, even though he had more capital than she did. Wealthy investors and mining men already had such a tight lock on that town that working girls could never buy in. Maggie might as well stay where she was.

But "where she was" in the early summer of 1880 was no longer an option for Maggie or for many of her colleagues who had been lured to Deadwood under false pretenses. Al Swearengen routinely recruited girls from back East for his Gem Theater just as if it were legitimate, when really it was nothing but a bordello under the guise of being a variety theater with all-too-private viewing boxes. Wearing abbreviated costumes, would-be actresses called box rustlers were required to hustle drinks and share caresses with their customers behind drawn curtains with the goal of soliciting later visits to their rooms.

Although raised quite properly on an Iowa farm and only fifteen at the time, Maggie was no blushing virgin, unlike singer Inez Sexton, who had to be rescued by the respectable ladies of Deadwood, who bought her a ticket back home. Maggie had not only taken advantage of the illicit job opportunity but excelled. Good-looking, petite, but with red hair and a frightening temper, she had managed to escape the brutal manhandling that Swearengen and his manager, "box herder" Johnny Burns, inflicted on many of her fellow workers. In fact, she had taken up with the box herder until she decided she would do better on her own. Then, early that summer, the Gem had been badly damaged by fire. Swearengen was rebuilding, but Maggie wanted out.

William Bullard had bolted from his family's Missouri farm to work in the mines of New Mexico and then followed stampedes to Arizona and Dakota with lackluster success. Recently he had returned to Deadwood after joining a company of citizen soldiers for a military campaign with Colonel Nelson Miles that ended with the Cheyenne surrender; it had given him a chance to see the potential of eastern Montana. Now Bullard was planning to construct a sawmill there in partnership with army captain Charlie Heintzelman, who was the quartermaster in charge of building Fort Keogh on the lower Yellowstone River.

The military installation was to be one of the country's largest, built to house at least fourteen companies. Captain Heintzelman had just brought five hundred construction workers via sternwheeler up the Missouri and then up the shallow Yellowstone during a rare period of high water to where the Tongue River branched south. There would be great opportunity for an ambitious girl who got in on the ground floor, Bullard insisted, and even more after the fort was completed and some fifteen hundred soldiers arrived.

Maggie was not enthusiastic. Military outposts in the West were usually dismal affairs with camp-following prostitutes officially employed as "laundresses" by the government and living on base in a grim little section dubbed Suds Row. Nor could outsiders hope to make much money even if they could get to the troops: enlisted men made only thirteen dollars a month and higher-paid officers too often brought their wives. In some locations, independent prostitutes attached themselves to hog ranches established near the bases to supply fresh meat. Saloons and gambling dens were often built near the ranches, too, but most were low-class establishments.

Nelson Miles had been named commander of Fort Keogh, and Bullard argued that the highly regarded military hero would make sure that the neighboring town would be worth buying into. In the months that followed, Miles forced a motley crew of saloon keepers, whores, and merchants camped on the outskirts of his military reserve to move two miles distant, and then relocated the fort itself two miles farther away. Undaunted, the tradespeople, along with William Bullard and his fellow veterans, jumped military reservation boundaries to establish a permanent settlement handy to the troops. Commander Miles's nephew, George Miles, though serving in the 5th Infantry under his uncle, built one of the first homes on the new site, and in March 1878 the general grudgingly made the town legal. Citizens named it Miles City in his honor, or perhaps simply to get even.

Presbyterian J. H. Hewett, who appears to have been the first missionary on the scene, wrote the venture off as hopeless, noting there were only five church members in the whole settlement.

"One was a Methodist, who had been a bartender in a saloon," he reported to his superior, Sheldon Jackson. "Two were Episcopalians, ladies a little doubtful in reputation, and two were Baptists not wishing to come in at once."

By late 1879, Tom Irvine, one of Colonel Miles's scouts who had resigned to build a jail and become sheriff, noted in his diary that "Miles Town has about 350 residents, five stores, 20 saloons, about 25 whores, lots of gamblers, and as many thieves as any town of its size in the world." There was no hotel because visitors didn't want a bed or much to eat, he told Granville Stuart, a former prospector who had turned cattle rancher and was looking for range. "They were just thirsty."

But William Bullard opened a hotel anyway. Uncertain as to who might patronize it, he also took a job as deputy sheriff for Tom Irvine, with whom he'd served in the army under Miles. Citizens soon elected Bullard as one of their first aldermen, an unpaid honor but one with real power. Then they promoted him to county sheriff when Tom Irvine resigned to become a federal marshal. Still working closely together, the two successfully pursued horse thieves and cattle rustlers while looking for other business ventures.

Maggie Burns remained dubious about Miles City and Bullard's future, too; she doubted he would settle anywhere for long. However, in September 1879, after a horrific fire destroyed three hundred Deadwood buildings, including Swearengen's newly rebuilt Gem Theater, Bullard's enthusiasm over Miles City began to make more sense.

No one, including Bullard, could quite explain what fueled the new town's economic growth beyond military spending, but business was constantly increasing. Built on an undercut bank just off the Yellowstone across from Fort Keogh, Miles City's streets flooded annually but no one seemed to care. High water, which was brief, meant steamboats from St. Louis, providing relatively low freight rates, could make it through the unusually shallow waters. There were plans to build a bridge replacing the fort ferry. Apparently the settlement had a future if for no other reason than by virtue of being a welcome oasis of at least semicivilization in the middle of nowhere.

The nearest train station was 297 miles to the east through dangerous Indian territory in Bismarck, Dakota Territory, a fact recently brought home when Indians killed the U.S. mail carrier. There was a rough, two-hundred-mile stagecoach trail to Deadwood, and nothing much out there for about the same distance to Bozeman, the nearest viable town to the west. Yet the seemingly unsettled prairies that surrounded Miles City were being invaded. Commercial buffalo hunters followed successful military troops, and once they'd annihilated their prey, ranchers and cowboys took advantage of the

rich grasslands. Congress was talking about opening the land to homesteading, and farmers and sheep men were moving in.

Nelson Miles, who was already being called the frontier's most consistently
successful military commander, ably put down the Cheyenne, the Sioux, and
the Nez Perce. In fact, his troops had pacified the region to a point that the
Northern Pacific was planning an extension of railroad west from Bismarck
to connect Miles City with the outside world.

By the time William Bullard had convinced Maggie Burns to open a parlor house there, Congress had done away with laundry service for its soldiers, forcing unattached prostitutes to move off base and compete with the
town girls. Many now operated out of saloons or from the second floors
of otherwise respectable businesses. Two Suds Row inmates, former slaves
named Annie Turner and Fannie French, had established fairly upscale bordellos on Bridge Street that catered to military men, all of whom were white.
But ranchers and cowboys usually boycotted women who serviced soldiers
because they were considered a lower class than regular working girls, who
could command better wages, and the specialty of the former laundresses
proved an advantage to Burns, who made sure her establishment was more
lavish than theirs.

Maggie did worry about the unusual number of families already established on base and in town. By far, they outnumbered those in a usual frontier settlement, and she knew that an overabundance of respectable citizens
usually meant trouble for the demimonde. Ensuring her success, however,
was her standing as William Bullard's girl. Although he officially lived alone
or with nephews John T. and John W. Bullard, Maggie was rumored to have
moved in with him. Bullard's status as both sheriff and city alderman served
her well. So did the mind-set of most city officials, who were not eager to
interfere with their town's growing reputation as a center of vice, which was
considered a plus in boomtowns.

A district judge who visited in 1881 described Miles City as a "lively little
town of 1,000 inhabitants, but utterly demoralized and lawless. It is not safe
to be out on the street at night. It has forty-two saloons and there are on an
average about a half-dozen fights every night. Almost every morning drunken
men can be seen lying loose about the city."

Maggie Burns's parlor house, which opened with several lovely inmates imported from Deadwood, was welcomed by the city fathers. Her profits were so extraordinary that within a year she helped bankroll Bullard and his partner, Tom Irvine, to build and operate a brewery and bottling plant, which was an immediate success. Bullard was soon selling about a thousand bottles of beer a day. In addition, he was elected to replace Irvine, who resigned as county commissioner. And things got even better.

———◈———

During the Civil War, longhorn cattle originally introduced by the Spanish were allowed to go wild, overrunning Texas ranges and free for the taking. Ranchers there had discovered colder climates produced better grasses on which to fatten this stock, but not until the summer of 1882 did cattle drivers from the Lone Star State begin making Miles City their destination, attracted by the sudden availability of the Northern Pacific Railroad to get their beef to market. Local ranchers, who had raised large herds but previously had no place to sell them, became flush, too. Nor were ordinary cowboys to be overlooked; although they made at best only twenty or thirty dollars a month, working long drives usually meant several months between paydays and a sizable bankroll when they finally hit Montana's easternmost cattle terminus.

To accommodate the livestock, corrals were built among the new business buildings on Main Street. Harness, saddle, and boot shops sprang up on the main drag, along with new saloons, gambling casinos, and restaurants that also thrived with the influx of railroad builders. Major William MacQueen, a genial fort trader, built the 110-room MacQueen Hotel with a barbershop, a billiard parlor, and a fine dining room. The rooms were elegant, with red velvet carpets, marble-topped dressers, huge gilded mirrors, and electric service buzzers, and delighted guests usually forgave the fact the walls were so paper thin it was easy to eavesdrop on conversations next door.

Few were more attuned to the upscale spending habits of Montana's new cattle barons, spree-prone cowboys, and the well-heeled businessmen who dealt with them than Maggie. They had become the backbone of her business, and, sagely, she moved to capitalize on their largess by building a palatial whorehouse on Main Street, conveniently across from Charlie Brown's livery stable (the equivalent of a good parking garage today). To celebrate its open-ing, she not only issued engraved invitations to her clientele but also let it be known that she would name the establishment according to the wishes of the lucky customer who purchased the most drinks during the event. That honor fell to the owner of one of the longest-established spreads in Montana, who chose to name the landmark Forty-Four, after his cattle brand.

Taking advantage of rail connections, Burns provided variety for her cus-tomers by importing girls from around the country with frequent turnover. It was two nontransients, however, who became the enduring favorites of the cattlemen, not just because they were fun-loving beauties. They could ride the range as well as any man and loved the frontier.

On learning a cattle drive was approaching Miles City, Annie McDougal, known as Cowboy Annie, would hire a horse from the livery stable, ride out to meet the herd, and work with the cattlemen until the animals were in the shipping corral. Yet she was otherwise very much a lady and seemed out of place in a sporting house. Her origins remain a mystery, although she proba-bly came from a local ranch, and she proved equally adept at herding herders.

"Oh, Johnny, I've got a sealskin coat and hat coming from Chicago, and there's still $150 against it at the express office," she said one day to John Bur-gess, hard-drinking foreman of the N Bar Ranch, who like many others was in love with her. "Won't you get it out for me?"

When Burgess demurred, saying he didn't have $150, she just shrugged and said it didn't matter. That Jim Green, the foreman of the ST outfit, would spring it for her.

"I've got just as much money as any ST son of a gun in Montana," Burgess exploded, stomping off to the express office to pay her bill.

Annie could be generous, too, quick to loan money to any cowboy in need. She kept a little book with the names of all her clients written with their brands. Usually they didn't all come to town at the same time. If they did, there would be war. Yet they rallied as a group when a cowboy from an outfit up on the Niobrara River spent a week with the girl, then ran out owing her seventy dollars. When his foreman heard about it, he fired the man on the spot. Word spread, and the no-good was blackballed throughout the region. Meanwhile, the boys at the N Bar took up a collection to pay Annie off.

One of the reasons for such dedication was that cowboys were, for the most part, migrants and not well regarded. Maggie Burns had realized early that the social lives of her range-riding customers revolved around prostitutes and hired a number of game girls who would appeal to them. Most cow punchers treated her sporting women better than some men treat their wives, she was fond of saying. As for Cowboy Annie, her success was soon commemorated with a popular song.

> *In Miles City there was a girl*
> *With big black eyes, and long black hair*
> *With her peachy cheeks and her ruby lips that I love to kiss*
> *Oh, Cowboy Annie was her name.*
> *And the N-Bar outfit was her game.*
> *We'll work a year on the Musselshell*
> *And blow it in, in spite of Hell*
> *And when the beef is four years old,*
> *We'll fill her pillow slips with gold.*

Even more successful was Connie Hoffman, raised by an apparently affluent Louisiana family, who somehow managed to end up in Deadwood in her mid-teens with a deadbeat, drunken husband. A singularly beautiful brunette with a stunning figure, the product of a French mother and a father from Ireland, Hoffman quickly found a place in a first-class "boarding house." By 1879 she was recognized as "the leading painted girl," in all of Deadwood, which is why Maggie Burns recruited her for Miles City, where she soon became known as the Cowboy Queen.

Hoffman did not drive cattle, but she was an excellent rider who loved fine horses, which local ranch owners vied to provide her. One also made Hoffman the gift of a lovely dress valued at $500 and embroidered with local cattle brands from the Platt to the Missouri River. The brand of the donor's ranch was positioned strategically in the middle of Connie's back, above the waist. As time went by and the fortunes of her lovers changed, Hoffman relocated a number of the designs, moving favorites to the side of her neck and bosom, while those out of favor were banished to the bottom of her skirt or, even worse, positioned so that they were frequently sat upon.

Other major houses of joy in town—those of Annie McGregor, an Oregon girl working under the name of Frankie Blair, little Willie Johnson, who was so into management she bristled when referred to as a prostitute, and Kitty Hardiman, who ran a large dance hall with a wonderful grand piano on Park Street—were also doing well. So were their black sisters, ensconced on Bridge Street, for nearly one-third of the cowboys who came north on trail drives were black.

Most successful was Fannie French, whose mother was from England and her father from New York. Of mixed race—a so-called high yellow mulatto—French could not only read and write but proved a whiz at finance. Starting at age sixteen as an army scrubwoman who also sold love from a nearly unheatable, vermin-infested shack at Fort Keogh, she moved to manage a house discreetly off the main street, which she expanded as business improved. By 1882, French's bordello, which also hosted dances and gambling games, boasted a ballroom complete with piano plus eleven bedrooms with a mulatto woman in each. She also owned her own livery stable. Like Cowboy Annie and Connie Hoffman, she was a talented equestrian who enjoyed riding the range with her string of fine horses.

Somewhere along the way, French claimed, she had wed, had three children, and been widowed, although children were not in evidence in her red-light operations. No government records found to date connect these accomplishments to Miles City, although French was definitely high profile. Old-timers named her with Maggie Burns as Miles City's most notorious madam.

Running Fannie a close second was black, Tennessee-born Annie Turner, who had no knowledge of her father and who had left home early to learn her trade in Leavenworth, Kansas. In 1878, at twenty-four, she gained celebrity by producing John Turner, who was the first non-Indian child born in Miles City. The lad was no doubt a by-product of Turner's job as a laundress at Fort Keogh. She had hauled Sergeant Eugene Allen into court to charge him with fathering her child out of wedlock. While no settlement is recorded, Allen, who was Caucasian, apparently did the right thing. On discharge two years later Allen settled in as a clerk for a respected Miles City merchant, and Turner invited townsfolk, including "grown people," to a birthday party for their boy, publicly recognized as Eugene Miles Allen for his second birthday. The event was staged at his mother's residence, "in honor of the first child born in Miles City," according to the notice she had published in the *Yellowstone Journal*.

Allen may also have helped fund Turner's successful career, which began with the purchase of a twenty-five by sixty–foot log cabin housing a reception room, saloon, and dance hall near Fanny French on Bridge Street. As the nightly "balls" Turner threw became increasingly popular, she built an addition on the rear and then a string of bedroom-sized shacks in the backyard. According to a review of one of her festivities, the dance was good, with plenty of fights, and the "girls were hot and sweet."

Later Turner built the California Restaurant at a cost of $2,000. According to the opening notice, it was in business night and day near a theater on Sixth, with fried chicken, ham and eggs, and "oysters in every style" on the menu.

Meanwhile, Turner had become engaged in a feud with William Knight, editor of the *Yellowstone Journal*, with whom she had previously been on good terms but whose coverage had grown increasingly hostile.

"Annie Turner's house 'Coon Row' is becoming a very hard hole," he wrote in July 1882. "Not a night passes but what some inmates or visitors indulge in a wild carousal, always ending up in a fight. Wednesday night some of the festive coons became enraged at a white brother who was 'taking in' the sights, and proceeded to jump him, which was accomplished with grand success. This enraged the colored landlady, who, deponent says, lives with the white brother mentioned, and she pulled her 44 and fired into the crowd of Negros, the ball piercing the ear of one of them. This ended the row. The officers should pull this low brothel."

A month later, after Knight referred to her as the "coon queen," the rival *Daily Press* published Turner's letter to Knight warning his "drunken Journal Reporter" to keep away from her dances and restaurant so that she could keep her house respectable. "I pay my debts which is more than he can say," she added as a parting shot.

Yet they were all on a roll. The Miles City population had gone from 550 inhabitants in early 1880 to 2,200, and more were moving in daily. Maggie Burns was rumored to have as much as $100,000 in her account at the newly established First National Bank. Its cashier was quoted as saying one of her certificates of deposit, totaling $50,000, was the largest he'd ever handled. The boom showed no signs of stopping, and most Miles City sisters were out for all they could get.

One exception was Mrs. Harry Keenan, a doe-eyed young woman with elegant taste who was making excellent money as a lady of the evening when she fell in love with a local policeman. John Henry "Harry" Keenan had started his career as a cowboy, developing a penchant for red-light ladies and gambling along with an arrest record. The prostitute with whom he became enamored was so amazing that a photographer would later capture her in a nearly life-size, full-length portrait wearing a gorgeous gown of fine laces and tulle. She appeared to be way out of his league, but Keenan had charm. His father was a decorated Civil War veteran who worked at Fort Keogh as a wheelwright, and his mother ran a large but homey boardinghouse in town. So when the young lovers decided to turn their backs on the demimonde, both were accepted by the respectable citizens of Miles City, who welcomed their reformation.

Likewise, renegade Martha Jane Cannary, famous as a prostitute in boom-towns like Deadwood and at the Openly Lewd Hog Ranch in Fort Laramie under the alias Calamity Jane, picked this time to marry and settle down despite the economic opportunities Miles City offered. With Frank King, a Montana rancher, she established the Rosebud Ranch and Roadhouse on unsurveyed land about twenty miles from Miles City and embarked on what she would later refer to as an idyllic period. The couple added to their income by cutting wood for market. Although the local paper referred to Jane as a "queer freak of nature" because she was earlier reputed to be a hard drinker who had worked as a bullwhacker and Indian scout, she was obviously trying to put that reputation behind her.

Orphaned at fifteen, left to care for five younger siblings with little legacy except the family wagon and livestock to pull it, Cannary had headed with her charges to Fort Bridger in Wyoming Territory, supporting them by doing any odd jobs she could get until she could farm them out. Later she earned better pay as a teamster and, supplementing that income as a prostitute, she had enjoyed real prosperity for the first time. Even then, though, her fondness for alcohol usually kept her broke, and it was not until her acquisition of the Rosebud Ranch that she came close to living a normal life.

"It was said that she was a reckless woman, dressed as a man, but during her stay in Miles City, she won many friends," an old pioneer recalled. "She never dressed as a man and conducted herself with fine manners. The poor people of Miles City knew her only as one of their dearest friends. She bought numerous shoes for children and presents for older people. They often praised her with the expression, 'She had a heart as large as a wagon box.'"

A studio photograph taken of Cannary during this period shows her to be a remarkably good-looking woman, apparently in the prime of health, quite fashionably dressed in an elaborate gown and feather-trimmed hat.

Two years later, in November 1882, she bore a son who died in infancy, and things got rockier from there. According to her own account, she and King returned from a trip to Idaho to discover someone had legally claimed the ranch for which they had worked so hard, and King died shortly thereafter.

Homeless and at loose ends, she followed railroad builders west to the newly founded town of Billings and then on to Livingston, also a fledgling railroad town. Whether Jane went back to prostituting herself during this period is not known, but in March 1883 she was arrested with a partner for selling liquor to Indians, and she was also rumored to be a member of a gang who stole horses.

While Jane stayed clear of Miles City for the next decade or so, a number of personable outlaws like train robber Butch Cassidy (Robert LeRoy Parker) and a fellow Hole-in-the-Wall Gang member Kid Curry (Harvey Logan), who worked at the nearby Circle Bar ranch, went recognized but unmolested. But the influx of hundreds of cowboys, railroad builders, and other transients produced some problems the citizens of Miles City refused to overlook.

Cowboys often faced death, not only from hostile Indians and fellow gunslingers but also from stampeding wild cattle, flash floods, snakebites, lightning, blinding blizzards, and dozens of other prairie hazards. In addition, black cowboys were usually former slaves who had been forced to learn the trade from brutal masters or who had escaped earlier to Mexico, where vaqueros taught them how to handle cattle. So it is no wonder they were tough to deal with on the rare occasions when they hit a cattle town.

Their patronage of Annie Turner's might still have gone fairly smoothly if her establishments had been exclusively for black cowhands, but her steadiest clients were still from Fort Keogh, and cowboys—black or white—traditionally despised military men. Other white customers—railroad workers, ranch hands who liked "exotic" women, and those who believed black women were less prone to carry social diseases—added to the racial strife. Newspaper reports show the number of fights escalated at Turner's through the fall of 1882, as did editor Knight's efforts to close down her operations.

On December 14, Turner ran an ad in the *Miles City Press* to tell Knight off in graphic detail, and that very night her bordello burned to the ground. According to Knight's account, the blaze was caused "by a lamp being upset by one of the children in the house." At that point Annie had two: the very spoiled Eugene, age four, who appears to have been a handful, and his younger brother, William Turner, who was two. But it seems an odd coincidence that the fire followed just hours after Turner's charges against Knight were published. Although her restaurant and the bedroom shacks at the rear of her building were spared, she estimated losses at $2,500.

Fannie French also sponsored a number of dances during this period and, although Knight sarcastically referred to one as a "social hop" and called her place a "coon dive," he failed to attack her as vehemently as he had Turner. While Annie continued to operate and may have eventually rebuilt, she did so without a dance hall, giving French a competitive edge. This may have caused the mulatto madam to become careless. In the fall of 1884, one of her girls knifed a cowboy named Block Lane, angering other patrons—both cowboys and soldiers—so that they joined forces in a rare alliance to pitch bottles and stones at French's house.

In late November 1885, French was indicted for "lewd and boisterous behavior" while running a house of ill fame. Fined $300 and sentenced to county jail for three months with bail refused, she appealed to Montana's Supreme Court, which ignored her case. Newspaper accounts show she attempted to recoup, moving to several new locations in Miles City, but otherwise kept a low profile.

———◆———

Nor was violence solely a problem of minority madams and their customers. Cowboy E. C. "Teddy Blue" Abbott, who was raised in a dirt-floored Nebraska dugout and hired out by his father as a cattle driver at age ten, saw plenty of it and also created his own. It was in a Miles City whorehouse one night that he responded to a woman's screams and the sound of a body falling.

"Someone's been killed, sure," he recalled thinking. "I got up and got my six-shooter and went and stood at the head of the stairs, and there was a woman coming up, slowly. She had on a white nightgown and the front was covered with blood. . . . I heard someone coming behind her, and I called down: 'If you take one more step, I'll shoot you.' And I would have, because I thought I couldn't do less."

The victim was Willie Johnson, who ran the house, although she was just a couple of years older than Abbott, who was twenty-two.

"She came into the room, and I helped her get fixed up," he recounted. "She was in an awful mess, with blood all over her from that cut on her forehead and a black eye that he gave her, this man who was her sweetheart."

"'I don't care for the black eye, Teddy,' she said whimpering, 'but he called me a whore.'"

Later Abbott made a name for himself at Maggie Burns's when, on a bet, he paraded through town dressed with Cowboy Annie's long, lacy ruffled underdrawers pulled over his pants, her scarf draped around his Stetson, wearing her gold chains. Burns went along with the stunt, but Abbott discovered the madam was not nearly so tolerant when he and three comrades began a drunken songfest that threatened to raise her roof.

"If you leather-legged sons of bitches want to give a concert, why don't you hire a hall?" she screamed. "You're ruinin' my piano."

Angered, Abbott got his horse out of Brown's Livery across the street and rode him into Burns's parlor, bent on finishing the piano off. Maggie, right behind him, locked both horse and rider inside and went for the sheriff, leaving Abbott to escape by jumping his mount through a low-lying parlor window and dashing for the ferry with the lawman in hot pursuit.

Although those packing guns were required to leave them with the sheriff, shoot-outs inside and outside favored saloons were not uncommon. Nor were theaters safe, especially those with a balcony containing a row of curtained booths like "Red" Ward's Vaudeville House, where a patron got his throat slit while leaning over the railing to talk to an unknown enemy on the floor below.

Certainly most white owners of bars, brothels, and gambling halls were in league with the city fathers in a town where ethics were generally murky and cover-ups commonplace. No one was much alarmed when one of the city's first elections, which took place on the faro table in the back room of Charlie Brown's saloon, produced seventeen hundred ballots when the total population was just twelve hundred and women and children were excluded from voting.

Two years later, the county commissioners, clerk, and treasurer were all indicted for misappropriation of funds and other irregularities because they had spent $100,000 on building the courthouse, which was budgeted for $30,000. The treasurer escaped to Texas, only to be extradited, but he needn't have worried. No one was ever convicted, nor was the missing money ever returned.

That same year, 1883, when Methodist minister George Stull arrived wearing a long-tailed frock coat and a high hat and carrying an umbrella in the dead of winter—temperature fifty-seven degrees below zero—a kindly cattleman suggested he get rid of the outfit or he would have trouble with the cowboys. Before the easterner could locate a change of clothing, a similarly dressed traveling salesman was tracked down by locals on their pinto ponies who lassoed his hat, threw it in the air, and shot it full of holes. Stull was spared because he abandoned his umbrella and overcoat, stuffing his shirt with newspapers for warmth, and his hotel clerk provided him with a western hat.

But when the preacher spoke out publicly against Miles City's lawlessness, he was given notice to leave town within twenty-four hours. Happily, a would-be parishioner provided him with a forty-five Colt and told him not to be afraid to use it. A fast learner, Stull did so the following midnight, answering a shot that splintered his hotel door, which ended the hostilities.

Still, he was a bit surprised the next summer to see the body of a local ruffian swinging from a bridge trestle, the victim of Miles City vigilantes. The deceased, William Rigney, a part-time bartender at John Chinnick's Cosmopolitan Theatre, had been returning home drunk from a night on the town when he forced his way into the home of Robert E. Campbell, whose family and a boarder were enjoying breakfast. The windows were open, and saloon owner Charlie Brown, also on his way home, heard the drunk making obscene remarks to Campbell's wife and daughter and rushed to the rescue. Rigney, charged with attempted rape, was carried to jail, only to be removed the next evening by a posse of forty men who strung him up bearing a cardboard sign with the vigilante warning "3-7-77," a secret code few understood but everyone in town respected.

According to insider reports, the posse's action actually followed Rigney's death—Brown had clobbered him over the head with the handle of a pickax, probably killing him instantly. The posse pretended to be vigilantes in an attempt to spare the well-liked bar owner from manslaughter charges. But when friends of Rigney burned the Cosmopolitan Theatre in retaliation the following day, the idea took hold. In the hours that followed, a vigilante "committee" issued warnings to several ne'er-do-wells including John Chinnick, whose theater had just been torched and who had helped found the town.

Although Chinnick was personable, well mannered, and quick to respond to civic duty, his ranch house and bar were known underworld hangouts. "Big Nose" John Parrott, with whom Chinnick had purchased the Cosmopolitan, turned out to be a road agent who had relieved a local merchant of $14,000 and was also wanted for several murders in Wyoming. Following Parrott's apprehension and extradition, the highwayman was subsequently hung by an angry mob.

So Chinnick was probably not surprised at his own exit notice and appeared to take it gamely. Still, there was some indication that Chinnick had no intention of going willingly, and when a committee member who was watching his ranch noticed a flurry of activity followed by the arrival of a doctor, he discovered the bar owner had been "accidentally" but fatally shot by his wife, Nell, who successfully claimed she was trying to disarm him. Bereft of Chinnick's leadership and bravado, his underworld cronies scattered, and the community resumed what was referred to tongue-in-cheek as its "accustomed peaceful flow" and a continuing bonanza.

With continued prosperity came a horde of titled foreigners, range-riding wannabes who invested heavily in the region and made Miles City their home away from home. The interest of royalty was nothing new. Prince Maximilian of the German Rhineland had pitched his tent in the area for big game hunting in 1833, and Sir George Gore of Sligo, Ireland, also a sportsman, camped near the site for nearly two years beginning in 1854 with forty employees and 112 horses. By 1881, however, Great Britain alone was importing 110 million pounds of American beef annually, which explains why the new wave of foreigners staked hundreds of acres of Montana range and began ranching in earnest.

First on the scene were the Marquis de Morès (Antoine-Amedee-Marie-Vincent Manca de Vallombrosa), and his wealthy wife, Medora von Hoffmann, who hoped to bypass the Chicago stockyards and ship meat directly to that city in their own refrigerated cars. Claiming 44,400 acres in the North Dakota badlands just over the Montana border, they established the town of Medora, complete with a meatpacking plant, and opened a stagecoach line to Deadwood to promote it.

Pierre Wibaux, the son of a wealthy French manufacturer of textiles, sought de Morès's advice and established a ranch with sixty-five thousand head of cattle near the town of Mingusville, which he ultimately paid to have named after himself.

Then in 1881, General James Brisbin, stationed at Fort Keogh, published *The Beef Bonanza: Or, How to Get Rich on the Plains: A Description of Cattle Growing, Sheep Farming, Horse Raising and Dairying in the West.* A Civil War veteran and Indian fighter, Brisbin knew little about the industry, cribbing much of his material from other sources. But grazing on the open Western range was free if you could keep from being shot by competitors, and the writer insisted that Western cattle could be left to fend for themselves, even in the dead of winter. So how much work could there be? His tome's favorite phrase was "and the profits are enormous," which fueled the cattle boom and proved a major influence on foreign investors.

The majority of new European arrivals were the sons of earls, barons, and other nobility not in line to inherit their family titles but for whom riding and hunting were social obligations as well as sport. Theodore Roosevelt, American royalty of a sort, had also claimed a spread near his friend de Morès in an attempt to recover from the death of his wife, Alice.

Lady Isabel Randall, whose father was a baronet, invested with her husband, James, an Oxford grad, in the Moreland Ranch Stock Company near Three Forks, Montana, and worked hard to keep up appearances. Locals were bemused by Randall's book, *A Lady's Ranche Life in Montana*, which did not view them kindly. "The Natives are very queer, independent, and rough: it is no use trying to make them into servants, and very disagreeable to have half-educated, ill mannered sort of people to eat and sit with you; and if you had English ones, the natives would make them discontented," she wrote. But she also championed the lifestyle of a rancher "where one feels much richer and happier," and her work, published in 1887, brought more Brits in her wake.

Many were remittance men, misfits whose titled families were happy to pay handsomely if they would just stay away from England. A few made good, but the majority hung around Miles City at Sam Pepper's saloon and the MacQueen Hotel, spending freely.

Seemingly typical was Sydney Paget—fifth son and twelfth child of Lord Alfred Paget—who seemed to have endless resources and squandered them like a genuine playboy. Arriving about 1881 at age twenty-four, Paget purchased Nebraska cattle, pasturing them first on Montana's upper Tongue River and later at Otter Creek, about sixty miles from Miles City. Because he was an excellent horseman who quickly adapted to living on the range, no one paid much attention to him until 1885, when Paget took up with Connie Hoffman, Miles City's much-loved Cowboy Queen, who had grown bored with the locals.

Much of what we know about Connie during this period comes from an account by Nannie Alderson, a rancher's wife who had come to town with her new baby and made the acquaintance of the prostitute at MacQueen's.

"I had seen her before, and knew she was staying at the hotel, but had never had occasion to speak to her," Alderson later wrote. "She got down on her knees and began making a fuss over the baby, who was of course delighted. . . . She told me she was waiting for her husband, who was on his way up the trail from Texas with cattle. She didn't know how much longer she would have to wait, and she was so lonely."

Sympathetic, Mrs. Alderson invited Hoffman to help her walk the baby some afternoon, but when she went to fetch the dark-haired beauty a day later she found her in the process of pinning on her hat dressed only in skimpy underwear.

"I must confess I was taken aback, though I could not help noticing she had a very pretty figure," Alderson recounted. "I asked her if she cared to go walking. She explained that she had another engagement. Although my mind did not work very quickly, it did seem strange to me at the time that she should say 'Come in' like that, when she could not know who was knocking at the door. It might have been anybody!"

Later, after it was discovered that Hoffman was "one of the most notorious women in the West" and she was asked to leave, the overly naive Alderson would recall the woman's habit of talking with the men on the porch after dinner and how she often appeared for breakfast wearing a very beautiful satin Mother Hubbard, hand-painted with flowers, which was hardly appropriate for a public dining room. But it was Paget's blatant affair with Hoffman that really shocked the town.

"We heard later that she went straight back to the red-light district. But she did not stay there for long," Alderson reported in a follow-up. "There was a wealthy Englishman, among several such around Miles City at that time, whose brother later came into the title; and this man set her up in an establishment of her own with horses, a carriage, everything, and was seen with her everywhere. She would even appear at the races—for the town boasted a race track in those days—dressed in his cream and scarlet colors. It was the most brazen performance. . . . One day at the height of her notoriety I was right next to her carriage but we never spoke as we passed by."

The establishment in which Paget set Connie up was Maggie Burns's Forty-Four parlor house, which Hoffman operated until it burned to the ground in August 1886. Knowing Connie's low threshold for boredom, former lovers were amazed that she would content herself for such a long period with a remittance man, no matter how rich and handsome.

"Typical of the 'hail fellows well met' was Sydney Paget, a sportsman to the core and ardent lover of horse-racing," one of Miles City's gambling set noted. "As the speeds of his little string of ponies were pretty well known, the town sharpies would promote a match whenever a faster horse came to town. As a result he was 'taken' regularly, but this did not seem to dampen his ardor, and money was not too difficult to secure to meet his losses."

But Paget was not the lightweight locals thought, and Connie Hoffman stayed with him.

These were good years for cattlemen, for beef prices remained high. In the summer of 1884 some one hundred thousand head were driven onto Montana ranges from Texas, and Miles City boomed as never before. British ranchers established a polo circuit, introducing the game to local cowboys, who excelled at the sport. *How to Get Rich* author General James Brisbin, still at his day job with the military, began moonlighting as a broker, negotiating ranch sales between the locals and foreigners, and was generally hailed as a visionary. However, Montana cattlemen were concerned about three problems: invasive cattle diseases, which included bovine pleuro-pneumonia and Texas tick fever being introduced by outside herds, overgrazing of the range, and rustlers, who accounted for 3 to 5 percent of stock loss.

In 1883 the legislature, led by Granville Stuart, who was a stockholder and manager of the sprawling DHS ranch, passed a bill creating a Board of Stock Commissioners to stop diseased cattle from entering the territory, regulate range use, and act against cattle and horse thieves. When it was vetoed by Governor John Crosby—bowing no doubt to powerful opposition from mining interests out to kill the measure because of property taxes voted to fund it—ranchers revived the Montana Stockgrowers Association, which had been organized in Helena in 1879.

Tempers ran short at a Miles City meeting in April 1884 when a number of hotheads, Theodore Roosevelt and the Marquis de Morès among them, advocated an all-out "rustlers' war." Angrily, they accused Granville Stuart of "backing water" after he made a speech warning ranchers against violence. But Stuart, who had nine children to support, was only covering their backs. Having come into the country as a prospector in Bannack and Virginia City in the early 1860s, he had not only participated in vigilante hangings but may have led them, and there was every indication that he was planning to do it again. As president of the cattlemen's outfit, allowing a declaration of war on the record would most certainly have led to the arrest of members for the stealthily executed hanging epidemic of rustlers that followed, and young Teddy Roosevelt would no doubt have missed his chance of becoming president. As it was, the vigilantes—who were rumored to have executed sixty-nine men in eastern Montana and western Dakota—went quietly down in history as "Stuart's Stranglers" with no repercussions.

During the legislative session of 1885, often referred to as the Cowboy Legislature, the cattlemen finally overcame the mining interests to establish their Board of Stock Commissioners and managed to fund it a year later. That summer Kansas entirely outlawed the driving of Texas cattle across its borders, and other states followed suit. Fewer herds from the south managed to detour to Miles City, causing a shortfall in retail revenues. Local ranchers also took a hit when beef prices dropped from $4.40 a pound to $3.90, but, flush with their legislative victories, most remained optimistic. The only disturbing news, in fact, came from a few old weather watchers who were upset at the rare arrival of Arctic owls from the north.

In the summer of 1886, the range was crowded with at least one hundred thousand additional cattle brought north by Texans and stock being held by locals hoping for a Chicago price rise that didn't happen. The problem was compounded by a severe drought followed by such crippling grass fires that one rancher moved his large herd to Canada, but the rest stayed put.

In late October a blue haze lifted to high altitude causing subdued daylight and ghostly moonlight. The first cold front arrived in November, causing the local paper to report, tongue-in-cheek, that the banana crop was a failure. Snow and bitter cold were followed by a brief melt in December and then a sixteen-hour storm that produced an inch of snow per hour. Temperatures plummeted to sixty-three degrees below zero. There were blizzards that lasted almost a week. Left to fend for themselves as usual, between 50 and 70 percent of the cattle died in the eastern part of the state, and most of the ranchers, including Granville Stuart, were wiped out. Roosevelt and de Morès fled the country with a host of well-established cattlemen. Others, like Pierre Wibaux, who had pastured his cattle on western ranges, began buying the holdings of hard-hit outfits and southern trail herds to restock what they had lost. Sydney Paget also stuck it out.

In contrast, the winter of 1886–1887 proved a bitter blow to the majority of locals, who, unlike the wealthy immigrants, had no family or patrons to help them stage a comeback.

"Things in general are at a complete standstill," a local photographer wrote to his father on June 28, 1887. "We are now on the eve of an entire change of methods in conducting the great industry of this country and the sudden change has and is financially annihilating our solidest men."

Those in the Miles City demimonde moved quickly to save themselves. Annie Turner was already in trouble. She was listed as owing a moderate amount of delinquent taxes in 1883. However, the sale of one of her houses and lots to the Northern Pacific Railroad, and her usual industry, must have helped, and she remained entrenched for another two years.

Fannie French was last heard from as "occupying a house" near the corner of northwest Sixth Street and Fort, opposite Drover House, which was a legitimate hotel near the railroad station. During this period, Miles City officials and census takers were careful not to identify houses of prostitution, so French's means of support during that period might be questioned.

Calamity Jane had returned in 1885, considerably worse for wear, to move into a little shack behind Kitty Hardiman's dance hall that had become a tough house of prostitution running under the name of Grey Mule. Shortly thereafter, it took three men to jail her following a drinking spree, and, on release, she left in a huff claiming Judge Milburn had fined her simply "for being a celebrity."

Maggie Burns, having sold her whorehouse just before a major fire destroyed that part of the town, invested well by backing her lover, William Bullard, in establishing a plant to manufacture bricks with which the town rebuilt. Bullard, himself, commissioned a handsome structure at Sixth and Main that he named the Bullard block.

Not so lucky was Cowboy Annie McDougal, who opened her own house in Miles City just about the time the big Texas trail rides ended and compounded the problem by becoming dependent on alcohol. Teddy Blue Abbott recalled she was once arrested for getting drunk and riding her horse endlessly up and down Main Street, and that her fortunes dwindled from there. When Blue saw her last, she was "played out and went to Fort Assiniboine, on Milk River, to a soldier dive," he reported. "The soldiers was the bottom. They used to say out in this country that when a woman left the dogs she'd go to the soldiers."

Blue himself fell in love with the first decent girl he ever had a chance to meet, who happened to be one of Granville Stuart's daughters, Mary. It was just after the grim winter of '87 that Abbott decided to marry her. Cowpunching jobs being short, he worked in a mine, which he hated, and later tried farming to fund their new life. But Blue was a cowboy at heart, and he got back into ranching as soon as the industry reinvented itself.

That unenviable task of rescuing the ranching economy, and with it Miles City, fell to the Montana Stockgrowers Association, which met again in that city in the wake of what came to be called the Big Die-Off.

"Had the winter continued 20 days longer, we would not have had the necessity of an Association," admitted newly elected president Joseph Scott, a replacement for founding member Granville Stuart, who had quit ranching for good. However, Russell Harrison, the organization's secretary, best summed up the enormity of the task ahead. Harrison had just resigned after a five-year stint as head of the U.S. Assay Office in Helena to help run a successful national presidential campaign for his father, Benjamin Harrison. However, the wealthy entrepreneur also owned Montana ranching property and was determined to save it.

"Drought without parallel; a market without bottom; and a winter, the severest ever known in Montana, formed a combination testing the usefulness of our association and proving its solidity," he concluded in his annual report in 1888.

The stockmen would eventually stage a comeback. Miles City would continue to grow because it remained the first stop in the middle of nowhere. But never again would anyone enjoy the wild successes of their pioneering days, when the range was as free and open as the red-light district and the only limit was the sky.

4

———◆———

LAST OF THE
SILVER YEARS

~❧ 1887 ❧~

Although ranches in the Helena region were hard hit by the winter of 1886–1887 that crippled Miles City, the cold was not as severe in central Montana, and most ranch owners were better capitalized to make a comeback. Meanwhile silver production, which already provided the bulk of Helena's income, was on the rise. Just to the south, Helena tycoon Anton Holter was working several ore deposits so large it appeared he would soon attract British investors. Sam Hauser, who had made a killing in silver at Philipsburg, was consolidating claims and attracting East Coast backers. Aging prospector Tommy Cruse, considered for years just a crazy, illiterate old duff, had discovered gold and silver in such quantities that he had founded the town of Marysville around his nearby Drumlummon Mine and purchased one of the most opulent homes in Helena. Then he had staged a magnificent wedding, complete with orange blossoms in January, with Margaret Carter, half his age, whose brother would soon be Montana's delegate to the U.S. Senate.

The economic climate was so good, in fact, that Chicago Joe Airey was planning to go legit. But quietly, because whenever Helena old-timers heard the news, they just about died laughing. She did, after all, have a monopoly on property in the town's red-light district. And she'd been in the skin trade so long, it was hard to think of her any other way.

Her reputation was good as far as that business went. She was a zealous community booster and open-handed. Also well reviewed by revelers was her Red Light dance hall. Even after propriety deemed that she rename it the Red Star, fond memories of it spawned a bad poem:

> *There was music in Joe's hurdy-gurdy,*
> *The polka and waltz in full swing:*
> *Where with full bosomed girls of the dance hall*
> *Gambler, miner, cowboy and judge had their fling.*

But in her two decades as a Helena businesswoman, Josephine Airey had also made some enemies who had friends in high places.

One of them was a crusading Republican district attorney named William H. Hunt, who loudly declared himself for God and motherhood. Inspired by legislation intended to curb "pernicious" hurdy-gurdy houses ramrodded through the 1885 legislative session, Hunt had dispatched the local cops to Josephine's dance hall asking her to close it down. The absurdness of it caused her to laugh in their faces. A similar law passed by the legislature in 1873 had twice been defeated in the courts, and because her club required a cover charge rather than payment per dance, Airey had been operating quite successfully, despite it, for thirteen years. Later that day, however, Hunt sent officers with a warrant to arrest Airey and two of her girls, setting the date for their trial as August 30, 1886, just nine days away. Happily, Isaac D. McCutcheon, former secretary of state and one of the sharpest lawyers in the territory, resided in Helena and was delighted to take on Hunt.

Although it was difficult to locate five men who claimed to be impartial on the subject, attorneys finally settled on a jury composed of a local dry goods merchant, a brick- and stonemason, a builder, and, oddly enough, a policeman named John A. Quirk. Assistant District Attorney Elbert D. Weed opened the trial with purple prose about the "immoral sinkholes wherein men's souls were lured to the shores of sin by the combined seductive influences of wine, women and dance." Then, calling all three arresting officers to the stand, Weed established that Chicago Joe did run what was commonly known as a hurdy-gurdy house.

Attorney McCutcheon countered by asking each of the officers, in turn, if he had actually seen a hurdy-gurdy played at the Red Star. None had. Then, without calling additional witnesses, even though Josephine and her girls were present, McCutcheon addressed the jury, Webster's dictionary in hand. A hurdy-gurdy, according Mr. Webster, was a stringed, flute-like instrument "whose sounds are produced by the friction of a wheel, and regulated by the fingers." Could anyone run a hurdy-gurdy house without a hurdy-gurdy? Chicago Joe had a contemporary orchestra that did very well without one.

The jury, befuddled by retirement so soon into the trial, quickly reported deadlock, but Judge Joseph Davis was determined not to sit through anything that silly again. Mercilessly he sent them back to their chamber, where, with time out for a free supper, they finally pronounced the defendants "not guilty." Righteous citizens were astonished that the new legislation had failed them, and local newspaper editors were incensed. "An Inning for Sin," the *Helena Independent* proclaimed. But Josephine knew the ball game wasn't over. Disappointed to discover that District Attorney Hunt would not be running for reelection, she set out to defeat his Republican successor, throwing her considerable resources behind a Democratic candidate. Her man won, but this would be Airey's last foray into politics. The real problem was that Helena was changing, and she recognized it.

———◦———

The coming of the railroad in 1883 had encouraged the settlement of new classes—affluent investors, unskilled workers, foreigners, and the poor. Few of them showed as much spunk as the early pioneers, who had arrived by foot, horseback, ox cart, or rattling stagecoaches, expecting few amenities. Yet even the toughest pioneers, impressed perhaps by their new connection with civilization and the building of a grand new courthouse, were predicting Helena would soon become the "Queen City of the Rockies." That, of course, would require higher moral standards, and the frontier code of "live and let live" was fast disappearing.

Some fifty millionaires were now in residence or in the process of building on Helena's west side, where the governor's Queen Anne–styled mansion was also enthroned in regal splendor. Given that the population of Helena was something under ten thousand, it suddenly housed more wealthy families per capita than any other town in the United States. The exclusive Montana Club had been established for male members of this social elite society, fostering a new class consciousness.

The first indication that Helena's restructuring might affect its demi-monde came from innocuous complaints that prostitutes were monopolizing the best seats in Ming's Opera House. The opulent theater, built for $20,000 through the largesse of wealthy cattleman John Ming to rival pretentious houses in larger cities like St. Paul and Portland, was considered Helena's cultural center. Although it could seat six hundred, some offended patrons approached manager John Maguire and owner Ming suggesting there was no room for scarlet women.

As longtime residents, Maguire and Ming were keenly aware of the huge economic impact the red-light district had on Helena and sought compromise. While they had no wish to prevent the demimonde from witnessing any performance, they issued a written statement that these women must be content with segregated seating on the main floor. When five well-known prostitutes garbed in the black and white habits of the local Catholic nuns arrived early in the first act a few nights later with tickets for the front row, center, Maguire quietly expelled them. A few years earlier the incident would simply have provided a good laugh, but polite society was incensed.

"This insult to a sisterhood which everyone in the community, irrespective of sect or creeds, holds in the highest veneration, is a matter deserving of severe punishment, and such steps should be taken as will make the offenders think twice before committing such an insult to religion and morality," the editor of the *Helena Daily Independent* raved under the headline "A Shameful Affair."

Heeding the public outcry, the city council passed a lengthy ordinance that restricted "any prostitute, courtesan, or lewd woman" from working on Main Street, effectively creating a centralized red-light district on Wood, Bridge, and Clore streets in the older, commercial section of town. As the measure did more to protect legitimate businesses than penalize prostitutes, that might have been the end of it had not a crusading journalist arrived in Helena to push the *Daily Independent* to greater heights. Twenty-six-year-old

Joseph E. Hendry kicked off his campaign by reporting happenings in police courts, using the sorry stories of hapless criminals to get across his moral message. Then he undertook an exposé of Chinese opium joints, reporting them a dangerous threat to young white womanhood. Hendry's crusade provoked a police raid backed by the newly elected, moral-minded Republican administration. Young white women were not well represented in the raid but, flush with success and press approval, the city fathers crafted an ordinance that banned prostitution from the city in uncompromising terms. "Wood Street Shaken to Its Core" was Hendry's triumphant headline, although it was the collection of fines and not a shutdown that the city fathers had in mind.

Until this time, no woman in Helena had been arrested for prostitution or for keeping a disorderly house, even though police court was located in the red-light district. The next elected city council, also Republican stalwarts pushed by Hendry and his newspaper to deal with "the attaches and the habitués of certain white dens of infamy," ordered the first raid on June 4, 1887, netting sixty-five white and Chinese ladies of the evening. All appeared willing to pay a quarterly fine or "license fee"; the going rate was cheap compared with that of other cities. However, Mayor Richard Howey, a lawyer who also served as Helena's superintendent of schools, voiced the unusual opinion that men were as responsible for prostitution as women. In addition he boycotted city use of prostitutes' earnings, so the city attorney refused to prosecute. Following the untimely death of young editor Hendry that December, the issue languished without newspaper coverage. The city council turned its attention to more urgent civic problems like street paving and the introduction of sewage facilities, while Helena's red-light district did business as usual, and better.

While vocal newcomers might lobby for the moral values they'd brought from their long-established hometowns, the majority of Helena's rapidly growing population was still single males who were in the market for a good time. Few were looking for marriage, and few of those who were could afford to buy a bride, as Tom Cruse had done. So the red-light district was more popular than ever.

Mindful of the town's new wealth, Belle Crafton brazenly mortgaged everything she owned to invest $12,000 in a *maison de joie* so elegant that it would be known as the Castle, while her rival, Lillie McGraw, remodeled her Joliet Street houses in similar style. Both were in so tightly with the city fathers, their classy whorehouse operations were touted by the secretary of the Helena Board of Trade and duly noted on the Sanford-Perris insurance map, while Chicago Joe remained in peril for running a dance hall.

Following the hurdy-gurdy trial, Josephine had remodeled the Red Star as a saloon and then, at a cost of $5,000, built the Coliseum, a small variety theater that she stocked with pretty "waiter girls," and focused on burlesque. Business was so brisk that expansion was in order, but Josephine had it on good authority that territorial politicians—under pressure from a newly formed group called the Women's Christian Temperance Union, led by the mayor's wife, Laura Howey—were planning to take her out. Their crippling legislation, passed in the spring of 1887, prohibited the sale of liquor and the employment of women in variety houses, but by that time Airey was well on her way to a legitimate venture they couldn't touch.

Although vaudeville had come into its own nationally, it had not hit Helena. To introduce it, the savvy madam planned a theater that would top even Ming's Opera House. Funding for it, $23,000, would be hard to raise. In addition to remodeling her dance hall and building the burlesque house, Airey had recently purchased an interest in the International Hotel and picked up several other properties around town. But Joseph Switzer, her longtime liquor supplier, had everything to gain by backing her, and she also turned to Tom Cruse, who had just opened a bank. She had guessed correctly that the Irishman would be a good fit. He had a brogue even thicker than her own and had immigrated to New York City during the potato famine before working his way west. He was the town's biggest contributor to Catholic causes and was one of very few men of wealth there who invested only locally.

Even with financing, however, Airey faced the challenge of completing her theater before the new law went into effect. Her husband, James "Black Hawk" Hensley, had been a real asset when she built the Red Star, but that had been a decade earlier. Since then he'd become prone to drinking sprees during which Josephine published legal notices asking bartenders not to sell to him and declaring she would not be responsible for his debts. Because she just couldn't count on him, she sent to Canada for Phil Weinard. The twenty-four-year-old ranch hand was happily employed in a good cow-punching job, but Josephine claimed he was the only man she really trusted, and he owed her.

———◈———

At a young age Phil Weinard had moved with his family, which included two draft-dodging brothers, from a town on the Rhine in Germany to Minneapolis. There the Weinard business changed from the production of portraiture and fine sculptures to fresco painting, which young Phil came to hate. At fourteen, he ran away to Montana and spent the next three years crewing on riverboats out of Fort Benton. Then, seeking a change of scene, he arrived in Helena without a cent in his pocket and ended up washing dishes at the Cosmopolitan Hotel. Soon he was promoted to pantry manager but quit on the advice of a gambler to peddle fresh fruit in the casinos, which more than tripled his earnings. Somewhere along his route, Chicago Joe spotted Weinard toting his big basket of apples and invited him to peddle them at her dance hall, which proved even more lucrative. Then, when the season for fresh fruit ended, she hired him as a nurse for her husband, Black Hawk, who she explained was sick in bed.

The job was stranger than Weinard had anticipated.

"One night, he [Black Hawk] said there was a Mountain rat chewing his saddle," the former fruit peddler recalled. "When I told him he must be dreaming, he sat up and said, 'No, I'm wide awake. See, there he is now!' With that, he reached under his pillow and brought out his .45 six-shooter and began to shoot at the supposed rat. Before I could do anything, his wife and others appeared on the scene. By this time he had jumped up, and it took several strong men to hold him."

Weinard's calm reaction to the episode convinced Josephine that the eighteen-year-old was unflappable, and she kept him on to help run the small ranch she bought in neighboring Prickly Pear Valley to keep Black Hawk off the streets once he'd recovered from delirium tremens. She also found the boy useful in doing some writing for her and helping with small business transactions, so she encouraged him to stay in the family apartment in town when things got too boring at the ranch. There, much to Weinard's astonishment, he kept finding gold pieces under the sofa, behind the doors, and in

other out-of-the way places. Chicago Joe was casual about it, saying Black
Hawk must have lost them when he was drinking, or Nelly, one of the girls
she sometimes used as a secretary, had carelessly dropped them due to her
drug habit. Later he would learn that Josephine was just testing him, and Phil
Weinard was honest to a fault.

But he was also restless, despite the fact he had grown fond of the oddball
family. In April 1881 he left Helena for a job riding the range in Canada.
Alberta Province charmed him, but when he learned Chicago Joe was in
trouble, he returned to help and was pleased that he had. The main reason
was Josephine's niece, dark-haired little Mary Ferris, just twenty and only one
year in the territory from Ireland. She was pert and fresh faced, looking much
like her famous aunt in her younger days, before Josephine's ample figure gave
way to stoutness. Ferris, as flirtatious as she was hardworking, probably would
have done well at her aunt's trade, too. But Joe, who had paid her niece's passage to America and was hiring her as a part-time maid until the new theater
opened, insisted that the girl tread the straight and narrow.

Josephine had no objection to Weinard's marrying Mary, but she was
vehemently opposed to his moving her niece to Canada, where he had been
hired to ride range after her theater was opened that summer. Then there
was the matter of the company Weinard was keeping. He had befriended a
cowboy named Charlie Russell, who worked, when he worked, in the Judith
Basin but lounged around Helena during the winter.

Russell had been one of her best customers, an enthusiastic patron of Mrs.
Martha Hughes, a lost little whore she employed as a dancer under the name
of Dutch Leina. Russell had been good to the girl, and when, for reasons
unclear to any of them, she committed suicide via an overdose of morphine,
he was badly shaken. He came from a good Missouri family, Josephine understood, and always treated her and her girls with respect. But he drank, sometimes to oblivion, and seemed to devote the rest of his time to drawing little
pictures on the backs of used envelopes and playing practical jokes. Russell
had become Weinard's closest friend, and Joe worried that Phil might follow
his lead, because it was obvious to her that Russell was lazy to the core.

Charles Marion Russell wasn't actually lazy. He was lost. At age twenty-four, success had eluded him on all fronts, and he couldn't catch a glimpse of it on the horizon. Although he had earned his living as a night rider, babysitting cattle on Montana ranges for the last seven years, and enjoyed the work, he was neither a skilled horsemen nor a bona fide cow puncher because he was not much good at roping. The woman he loved had passed him by for some "fancy-assed" St. Louis gentleman and, although he'd been born into St. Louis society himself, he sure as hell did not belong there either.

Russell's wealthy parents, unable to force his school attendance, had indulged his fondest dream by sending him west at age sixteen to work for a family friend who owned a sheep ranch in the Judith Basin two hundred miles north of Helena. There, on the grassy green prairies with their seeming endless blue skies and the ghosts of mountains in the distance, Russell felt at home. Spending the last of the money his parents had given him to buy two horses and a buckskin outfit, he was determined to settle in, but he hated sheep herding. His employer was more than happy to let him go after Charlie lost several flocks while engrossed in his sketchbook. As a result, the boy ended up alone and penniless on the remote frontier. To his rescue came Jake Hoover, a prospector fifteen years Russell's senior, who took him on as a gofer.

Hoover was known as Lucky Boy because of a gold discovery he'd made years earlier in the great rush at Bannack. But, young at the time, he had been too quick to sell his lucrative claim to William Clark, providing the soon-to-be-millionaire with his first substantial capital. To fund a second chance, Hoover had become a trapper and professional game hunter, based out of a log cabin on a remote fork of the Judith River near the small supply center of Utica. Working for him, Charlie had managed to pick up enough survival skills to try out for a job as night wrangler with Horace Brewster, boss of the annual Judith Roundup, who was one of the top hands in the country. When "Kid Russell" had arrived at his camp broke, wearing a dirty Stetson with the crown missing, frayed buckskins, and worn-out boots, Brewster had his doubts, but he sent the greenhorn out with part-Indian Charlie Contway, who could do the job with his eyes closed.

"Brewster, that kid's goin' to be OK," Contway reported a few nights later. "He's a lot smarter than he looks."

It was hard country to stay alive in. Russell's favorite cousin from St. Louis, whom he'd talked into joining him, died of mountain fever just four weeks after arriving in Montana. There were his cronies: Pat Riley, killed while sleeping off a drunk on the grass range; Charlie Bowlegs, killed in a card game; Pan Handle Jack, killed by a Gilt Edge saloon man; Frank Harstel, bushwhacked while peeling potatoes on his ranch. There was Dutch Leina, so quick to make him laugh and buck up his sinking spirits, but who could not buck up her own. Yet Charlie Russell had come to love Montana. He loved being a cowboy, too, although he kept on with his art because it still came first.

In the beginning, Russell painted at the home of William Edgar and his family, who had moved to Utica from Missouri where they had known his parents. It was then that he'd fallen hopelessly in love with Edgar's daughter Laura, and she with him, he figured. It was Laura, just a girl at the time, who'd been watching when he worked on his first commission, a poster for a general supply house in Helena. And she was there, too, for the arrival of the substantial check that came with that sale. But her parents, much against the match, sent her back to St. Louis. She had written Charlie wonderful letters, which he'd read and reread by the light of a cigarette when he was night hawking. But, although he had finally followed her to the city, he was outmatched by other suitors. His only chance was to become a famous artist, and that just wasn't happening.

As for the little pictures he was always drawing on any handy blank surface, friends told him they were good, and he sold quite a few, but always at low prices. After twice entering his work in competitions without success, he'd grown discouraged, although he had garnered some local fame during the deadly winter of 1886–1887.

At the time, Russell was working for Jesse Phelps on the OH Ranch, about a mile or so east of Utica, where Phelps was looking after a herd owned by two Helena butchers. Facing the prospect of writing the Helena men that most of their five thousand animals had perished, Phelps asked Charlie to draw something to make them understand just how tough the "Die Off" was. Using a piece of cardboard from a box of detachable shirt collars, Russell dashed off a watercolor of a dying steer facing hungry wolves. The little watercolor was so grimly graphic that Phelps decided no letter was necessary. The work, later publicized by its recipients, who survived the disaster, became symbolic of the near-demise of the ranching industry.

It was also because of that painting that Phil Weinard had sought out Charlie Russell. Because many in his family were professional artists, Phil recognized Charlie's special gift and urged him to perfect it. Almost the same age, and temporarily exiled to Helena from their preferred cattle ranges during the late fall of 1887, the two became fast friends. Always going for laughs, they dressed as Indians for a masquerade ball at the opening of Helena's Labor Temple—Weinard as the chief with Charles as his unsmiling squaw—to win first prize for best costume and also for best sustained character. Phil did a war dance. Charlie thumped a tambourine. War paint intact, they had their photo taken to commemorate the event. Weinard, who was thinking of going into vaudeville, was much encouraged by their success, but his focus quickly changed after Mary Ferris agreed to marry him in early May.

Neither Mary nor Phil wanted to wait. Chicago Joe insisted that their plans be postponed until after the all-important opening of her New Coliseum Theater on July 4. But she was also counting on them to help her run the thing. No way would she allow her underage niece to move to Canada, which, after last year's cattle die-off in Montana, was Weinard's best chance of getting work as a cowboy.

Elopement was the obvious answer. Knowing the primitive trail north would be too rough for his bride, Phil decided Mary should travel by train to stay with his parents in Minneapolis until he could send for her from Alberta. Charlie had long wanted to see Canada, so he agreed to keep Weinard company on the trip north after serving as best man. Under cover of darkness he helped Phil smuggle his belongings out the window of the upstairs bedroom where he was staying at Chicago Joe's.

Phil set the date for May 16, making arrangements with the Episcopal minister for a 7:30 A.M. service to accommodate Mary's train schedule. When Charlie failed to muster—too drunk to walk after an all-night farewell appearance at Auntie Fat's House of Joy—Phil enlisted their hack driver as a stand-in and managed to deliver the new Mrs. Weinard to the train station on time. Charlie finally arrived—trail ready, complete with a pack horse, but suffering a monumental hangover. With him he brought B. J. "Long Green" Stillwell, a young Southern rebel who had been doing poorly in his career as a professional gambler. Stillwell had no horse and neither he nor Charlie had any money, but Weinard, who was glad for their company on the dangerous, three-hundred-mile trip, staked them both.

Two weeks later, despite heavy rains and flooded rivers, they made it through to the village of High River, Alberta. Weinard found Russell and Stillwell free lodging with an English ranch owner about five miles outside of town and bought them supplies before pushing on to the nearby ranch where he'd agreed to manage the spring roundup.

Delighted with their new surroundings and their neighbors, who were mainly Blackfoot Indians, Russell and Stillwell settled in for a lazy summer when no jobs materialized. Their host, who was an amateur painter, provided some paints, brushes, and canvases, but Russell didn't produce much. He and Stillwell lived mainly on fish they caught in a nearby creek and the generosity of their neighbors, one of whom offered his daughter to Charlie as a bride.

"I expect if I ever get married it will be to [t]his kind as there is a grat many fo [of] them here and I seem to take well among them," he wrote. "I had a chance to marry Young louses daughter he is blackfoot Chief[.] It was the only chance I ever had to marry into good family but I did not like the way my intended cooked dog and we broke off our engagement[.]"

Later Russell would confess that he had contracted a venereal disease while living with an Indian woman. He seems to have made no complaints about the cure, which at that time was a bitter dose of mercury, but there was also the fact that the Alberta government prohibited the use of alcohol, which posed a greater hardship. Within three months, he and Stillwell headed back to Butte without notice to the Weinards, to whom they owed considerable money.

Meanwhile, Chicago Joe struggled to get her theater ready for its Fourth of July deadline, at which time she would have to pay the cast of a hugely expensive vaudeville company whether they performed or not. Had she not been so motivated, the defection of Weinard and her niece would probably have fractured her heart. Earlier she had supported the education of two younger sisters, another niece, and a half brother in Chicago so they never knew her trade, but all had eventually drifted off and now she was completely without family.

Yet to her surprise Black Hawk finally came to her aid as he had in times past, sobering up to oversee the builders while Josephine hired a top-flight theater manager who also proved an excellent master of ceremonies. The *Helena Independent* predicted failure for the venture in the face of the new legislation. However, Josephine dismissed all her female employees and switched to serving temperance beverages while making alcohol discreetly available via a hole cut through the wall to her bar next door. The theater's lavish interior, plush boxes, comfortable seats, fine paintings, heavy velvet curtains, and modern stage, plus the novel and exciting programs Josephine offered, soon made the New Coliseum a family favorite. Even the once-skeptical *Independent* favorably reviewed her shows.

———◆———

This heady period would be the high point of Chicago Joe's checkered career. Famous as a party giver in her less reputable days, special entertainments like her Valentine's Day grand masquerade and fancy dress ball of 1889 became standouts in the town's social history.

"Orgies were the order of the evening," observed a reporter for the *Helena Daily Record*. "Frail coquettes in silken tights and decolletted bodices, their symmetrical limbs and snow white arms revealed to the public gaze, glided to the enchanting numbers of melodic music over the glassy floor, forming a picture pleasing to behold."

Josephine, garbed as usual in velvet with an array of diamonds, fluffs, and laces—graced with a huge pink silk-lined Elizabethan collar and wide gold and jewel-studded belt encircling her large girth—presided as usual, but now with the town's upper crust in attendance. She paid taxes on more than $200,000 worth of Helena property, and her theater payroll alone was said to be $1,000 per week.

Josephine reinvested her earnings in additional local property including another ranch, where she found herself the neighbor of her former colleague,

Dolores Jarra, back from Butte and masquerading under the name Laura Stanchfield. With her husband, Charlie, Dolores had returned from her dance hall venture with enough money to join Helena's economic elite, enrolling her two daughters in an expensive Catholic school and effectively burying her beginnings as a refugee from the red-light district and an unwed mother. Josephine wished her luck, especially after Charlie was arrested for getting drunk and raising hell in a local whorehouse, but that didn't seem to mar their social standing. Their property taxes were $12,630, Dolores complained by way of a boast, and Chicago Joe understood where she was coming from.

Josephine's ventures were so successful, in fact, and her spirits so high that she eventually welcomed back Mary and Phil Weinard with their fast-growing covey of children. Eventually she even forgave Charlie Russell, who seemed to be on the verge of a meaningful art career. On his return from Canada, the *Helena Weekly Herald* claimed Russell was planning to study painting in Europe, but he soon had too much going on the home front to consider it. Russell Harrison, who was back in Montana following his father's successful campaign for U.S. president, had purchased an interest in the famous national magazine *Frank Leslie's Illustrated Weekly*, determined that it would better represent the West. Harrison was negotiating to purchase a paper in Helena when Charlie's work came to his attention, and a spread of the cowboy's sketches titled "Ranch Life in the North-West" appeared in *Leslie's* shortly thereafter.

Charlie continued to work seasonally as a night rider, and his art, which he often used as currency, was more likely to be found decorating the walls of the local bordellos and bars than in legitimate galleries. But most, including Russell, figured if he could just stick with it without drinking himself to death he was headed for sure success.

———◆———

Success, of course, was considered a given for Helena. There was no reason to doubt it. In 1882 the self-elected "Queen of the Rockies" was the first city in Montana wired with electricity and phone service. Six years later citizens could boast the first electric streetcar system in the territory, and an elegant new courthouse as well. The ornately decorated, three-story stone building with a turreted clock tower almost as high was featured on the cover of *Frank Leslie's Popular Monthly* in February 1889 under the heady caption "Our Would Be States." Statehood followed within weeks, so imposing federal and capital buildings were added to the drawing board. Then transportation tsar Charles Broadwater opened the fifty-room Hotel Broadwater and Natatorium, a spectacular Moorish-style complex with the world's largest indoor pool that he had built at a cost of $500,000 on forty acres of carefully manicured land just out of town.

Broadway, the main business section, was lined with imposing stone and brick buildings, and the town's landmark fire watchtower was connected by phone and an electric alarm system to Helena's well-equipped fire department. Two competing hospitals had been built. A group of nuns of the Convent of the Good Shepherd arrived from St. Paul, Minnesota, bringing with them one wayward girl, Veronica, who would be the first to find shelter (or be imprisoned, depending on one's point of view) in their Home of the Good Shepherd. And the Helena red-light district was expanded.

By 1890 the property of the town's eight proprietor prostitutes was being assessed at $102,560, and they contributed nearly $1,000 to the city budget in personal taxes in addition to healthy "fines" levied through the city's unofficial "licensing" system. Only the railroads, a few lucky businessmen, and the now legitimate Chicago Joe contributed more to Helena's well-being.

The silver boom was at its peak and, although it had attracted plenty of outside investors, the majority of owners remained local, which was viewed as a plus. Helena was Montana's largest city, with 33 percent of the state's population as opposed to Butte's 31.2 percent share. Helena had led by 3,827 votes over second-place Anaconda in an 1892 statewide ballot for the capitol site. That was not enough for the needed majority but city fathers had no doubt they'd win the second election scheduled two years hence.

National politics also seemed to favor the town. Although America stopped coining silver in 1873, Western mining interests won passage of a law that required that the U.S. Treasury purchase domestic silver bullion to be minted into legal tender. Montana's silver boom had coincided with a global increase in silver production at a time when many nations were switching to a gold standard, causing silver prices to fall. In response, the Free Silver Movement, (a coalition of miners, farmers, debtors, and William Jennings Bryan) engineered passage of the Sherman Silver Purchase Act in 1890 requiring the federal government to buy all the silver produced in the Western states in exchange for treasury notes redeemable in gold.

This prosperity would be short-lived, however. Although Helena residents hailed passage of the Sherman Act as a victory, it depleted gold reserves to undercut national finances and local businesses as well. In 1891 Helena's cherished streetcar system went on the block, while most of its grand hotels announced failure or were hastily sold. Gone was the Merchants Hotel, while the owners of the Cosmopolitan transferred title to its head clerk and a local caterer. Josephine feared for her holdings at the International. The manager and a major stock holder insisted it would soon reopen under the name of the Mineral Hot Springs Hotel, but Josephine's husband, Black Hawk, took up residence there to see if he could turn things around.

In June 1893, banks and big businesses failed across the country, ushering in America's first full-scale depression. The New York Stock Exchange was rattled by the biggest selling spree in history and the market collapsed. Within a year, nearly three million people, one in five, were unemployed. "Mills, factories, mines, nearly everywhere shut down in large numbers," the *New York Commercial and Financial Chronicle* reported in August.

After the price of silver dropped from sixty-five cents an ounce to fifty-five and then to fifty, there was no hope. In Granite, Montana, three thousand people fled the mining camp in a twenty-four-hour period, converging on the Philipsburg bank to withdraw their savings. It "was the most incongruous procession ever seen," one witness recalled. "No one had stopped to pack. The mine whistle at Granite, tied down by an engineer, wailed on in diminishing tones as the steam pressure lowered and finally vanished." Most banks appeared about to fail, and the panic spread to Helena, which had six.

First to go were Sam Hauser's First National Bank and the Montana National Bank, owned by Sam Broadwater. Because Hauser and Broadwater had long been considered the town's most successful capitalists, they had earned the trust of the local elite, who went down with them. At one point Chicago Joe appeared before the city council to ask for a reduction in the variety theater tax from seventy-five dollars to forty dollars per month, claiming that the closure of her New Coliseum Theater would throw thirty or forty people out of work, but that too would soon become a moot issue.

During the bank run that followed, Tom Cruse ordered his staff to pile $600,000 in the gold bullion he had in reserve by his cashiers' windows, and he noted the names of anyone who closed out an account. Buoyed by the gleam of the cagy Irishman's assets, many former customers tried to redeposit, but Cruse curtly turned them down. Nor did he show mercy to fellow bankers who came to him as a group, "earnestly pleading" that he tide them over. Patiently, he listened to their desperate presentation and then rose from his chair triumphant.

"One fall in partic'lar I needed a grubstake to see me through the comin' winter," he thundered in his rough brogue. "I went to you an' you an' you (pointing a gnarled forefinger at the bankers in turn) and begged ye fer a little help, jest a little help. An' what did ye do fer me? Nawthin; not a dom one of ye's lent me a doim. All roight, me dandies, it's me turn now; as fer as I'm concerned, ye may all go t'hell."

Josephine made the mistake of underestimating the old man, who was quick to bail out the less arrogant. Assuming he would sink with the rest, she sold off property, including some that she had mortgaged to him, to meet the debts of other creditors. Cruse went after her, throwing the disputed properties into receivership and causing her financial collapse.

Chicago Joe and Black Hawk were not alone. Neighbor Charlie Stanchfield had just mortgaged everything, including the family ranch, to capitalize a new venture. He and Delores lost it all. Many others struggled to survive.

The majority of Helena's demimonde had overextended during the silver boom. Loans on Belle Crafton's Castle went unpaid until 1895, long after they came due. Lillie McGraw failed to repay the $3,000 she had borrowed from Cruse, although Tom eventually released his lien, perhaps for services rendered. Others sold out after their customer base eroded.

As dozens of silver mines locked their gates, many miners moved on to Butte, which was booming with the copper market. The Klondike gold rush lured others, and more men left to fight in the Spanish-American War. By 1900 Helena's population had dropped from 13,854 to 10,770, and it would be slow to come back. Also within that decade, the number of Helena's prostitutes decreased radically. But even more telling is the fact that in the end, not one woman owned property in the red-light district, which had, from its founding, been the only capitalist venture in which females had enjoyed an edge.

Chicago Joe managed to rescue only her New Coliseum, but she could no longer afford to bill first-class acts, and as the novelty of her entertainments faded, so did attendance. Yet she continued to enjoy presiding nightly, dressed in her long-outdated velvets and laces, flashing the few jewels she had been able to save. She also had the pleasure of learning that her first husband, Al Hankins, had been strangled to death by a folding bed following an adulterous tryst at his plush Chicago gambling casino while his wife awaited his appearance for supper—confirmation that she'd done well to dump him early.

Reduced to near poverty, she sponsored no more grand balls, but she was in attendance with Black Hawk for the biggest party Helena would ever see. It was the night of November 6, 1894, after the town finally won the viciously fought election that made it the capital of Montana. The bar bill alone was $30,000, cheerfully paid by William Clark, who had championed Helena's cause to spite his mortal enemy, Copper King Marcus Daly, who had unsuccessfully backed his own remote company town, Anaconda.

Any hangovers that materialized following this unforgettable event were countered by new hope for the Queen City of the Northwest, but Chicago Joe would not live to see its comeback. She died following a brief bout with pneumonia in October 1899.

Chicago Joe Airey's passing was marked with a huge and uncritical front page spread in the *Daily Independent*, and her funeral procession from the cathedral of the Sacred Heart to the Catholic cemetery was impressive. Her husband, Black Hawk Hensley, was in attendance with most of the town. So was former governor Joseph K. Toole, riding unashamed in an open carriage. Chicago Joe Airey had helped him, as she had so many others, in time of need, the lifelong bachelor explained.

No reporter felt moved to question him further.

5

THE CELESTIAL
SEX TRADE

~⟨ 1900 ⟩~

It is not surprising, in the wake of the Great Potato Famine, that the majority of Montana's early settlers—including Chicago Joe Airey, most of its governors, the Copper Kings and their workers—had roots in Ireland. Yet Chinese immigrants played a near equal role in pioneering the territory with virtually no recognition because they purposely kept a low profile.

For this reason, officials were startled on the afternoon of November 3, 1881, when Butte's police court was interrupted by the entrance of a pretty young Chinese woman, supported on both sides by fellow countrymen, all talking excitedly in their native tongue. Celestials, as Asians were called by American journalists, were rarely if ever seen in American halls of justice, preferring to settle their disputes in their own mysterious ways. However, this young woman was discovered to be bleeding badly from a wide cut made through her silk cheongsam into her back, about one inch to the right of the spine.

"About at the point where President Garfield was shot," an official estimated. "Had it been made with a little more force it doubtless would have been a mortal wound."

With the help of an interpreter, the court learned the young woman, Yow Kum, had been the property of Gong Sing, a man well known in Butte's Chinatown and also in nearby German Gulch, where he had apparently done

very well as a miner. Some time earlier he had purchased the girl in California
for an undisclosed sum and was in the process of selling her to Ah Kum for
$1,100 when there was a dispute over her price. Sing demanded an additional
$300, which Ah Kum insisted was not in their original agreement. Enraged,
Gong Sing seized a hatchet and deliberately chopped her in the back as Yow
Kum sat patiently in front of him, waiting for the outcome of the transaction.

The wounded woman, aided by her supporters, had fled directly to the
police court. Judge W. J. Wilcox, who, with the prosecuting attorney, witnessed the gory damage firsthand, immediately issued a warrant for Gong
Sing. Jailed on the charge of assault with a deadly weapon, Sing sent for Dr.
George Beal, then serving as Butte's mayor, for whom he had worked "as a
valued employee" for the past three years.

Beal was an important businessman who owned the Centennial Hotel
on Broadway as well as about half the mining interests in German Gulch,
a rich gold producer with one of Montana's largest populations of Chinese.
Beal's medical specialty, allopathy, was looked down on by many as being too
alternative and oriental in approach, so it was his mining operation, which
employed nearly one hundred Chinese miners, that had made him a wealthy
man. But even Mayor Beal could not spring Gong Sing, who was bound over
for an appearance before the grand jury.

A week later Yow Kum was returned to police court by Jim Hong, who
married her following what seems to have been the resale of discounted goods
by Ah Kum. According to an account in the *Butte Miner*, Judge Warren
O'Mara tied the knot after bemoaning the fate of scores of other slave girls he
said he knew were living prisoners in this section of camp. Since the paper did
not report further on Gong Sing, it can be assumed the grand jury decided
not to indict him, perhaps under pressure from his powerful employer, Mayor
Beal. What is known for certain is that Beal was not reelected and that the
candidate who was, livery stable owner William C. Owsley, used the winning
slogan "Cheap Chinese Labor Must Go!"

<hr/>

While prostitution was considered "necessary" to protect respectable women
from the baser appetites of men during the morally strict Victoria era, there

was growing alarm over purported "white slave traffic," the kidnapping and enslavement of white women for that trade. The tabloid press, Hearst newspapers, and fiction writers had convinced the public there were international rings of white slavers kidnapping as many as sixty thousand women a year. Even the august *New York Times* bought into the myth until well after the turn of the century, when it was proved beyond a doubt to be untrue. There were plenty of enslaved prostitutes like Yow Kum, for sure. But since they were Asian, not white, and their Chinese kidnappers were as secretive as they were clannish when living abroad, it was extremely difficult to rescue these desperate young women, even in a small town like Butte.

In fact, the story of Yow Kum was the first of its sort to appear in the local press and would be the last for several years. Although officials like Judge O'Mara were aware both of enormous profits being made there by Chinese slave masters and of the miserable conditions under which Butte's Chinese prostitutes worked—often with scant nutrition, caged in filthy cribs no larger than four by six feet—there were no complaints from the victims. Should one be desperate enough to attempt escape, she could be almost certain of being recaptured or murdered by Chinese henchmen called highbinders, paid by vengeful masters, but physical force was seldom needed to keep these women in check. Most, abandoned by their families, were in the country illegally with no resources. Illiterate, they spoke only Cantonese and knew little of local laws or customs. Their intercourse with customers was usually brief and often brutal, and customers were their only contact with the outside world.

Most of Montana's Chinese had come from the province of Kwangtung (Pinyin Quandong today), which had been economically spent by natural disasters, civil wars, and corrupt governments. They began immigrating to America just after China lost the Opium War, and the discovery of gold in California six years later made mining their primary goal. In droves they came, poor farmers and laborers mostly, seeking their fortunes on the "Gold Mountain," following the mining strikes wherever they led.

They were in residence in Bannack almost immediately after gold was found at Grasshopper Creek, and between 1864 and 1869, when more than $30 million was taken from Alder Gulch, as many as five hundred Chinese were working claims there at one time. Sometimes they labored alongside white miners, filing or buying claims on their own, but more often they hired out in well-organized gangs through contractors to rework claims left behind by American miners who had moved on to richer ground.

They were officially welcomed in 1868 with the signing of the Burlingame Treaty, which accorded them all the rights of any person in America except naturalization. This was no drawback because the majority of these immigrants wished only to get rich and return to their homeland. From the beginning, Chinese established their own system of governing via highly organized gangs called tongs, clans, and families while keeping to their traditional dress, diet, and a value system that was often at odds with western culture.

For these reasons, many westerners came to hate them. Some even wondered sincerely if, with their alien ways, the Chinese could be classed as human. The *Butte Miner* concluded in one editorial that "a Chinaman could no more become an American citizen than could a coyote." But the major grievance was the fact that these immigrants had come from circumstances so dire that they would work under dismal conditions for considerably less pay than the average American.

Anticipating the problem, the first Chinese immigrants in California formed a brotherhood for their own protection called the Six Companies, so when working in groups they were generally safe from physical harm. Those who prospected alone in remote camps, however, were sometimes imperiled, especially if they proved more successful than white neighbors. Historical accounts are sketchy yet persistent that one Chinese prospector was hanged at Rocker, Silver Bow Basin, on July 4, 1868, pretty much for the hell of it by an American miner named Don Faffie.

"It was not a judicial execution," the *Anaconda Standard* reported much after the fact. "It was simply the cool, premeditated act of a disheartened, yet patriotic and Fourth-of-July conscious miner who hanged the Chinaman to a cottonwood tree just for the devilment and in the hopes that it might bring luck."

Nor could Chinese count on help from locals, even when an American justice system was in place. Even after Helena was well established, the fiendish murder of a prostitute called Chinese Mary sparked no reaction from camp lawmen and only brief notice by the *Helena Weekly*. The killing had apparently taken place because the girl defied orders given by the company or clan for which she worked. Her funeral did not receive the backing of her male countrymen, who refused to send her body back to China so her spirit might rest. Only four Chinese women turned out to mourn her, the paper reported.

More widely respected was Hing Lee, who not only prospered as a businessman at German Gulch but was trusted as a translator by English speakers and his Chinese countrymen. Yet his 1878 murder, following which the culprit made off with $7,000 in gold dust and thirty cases of opium (legal at the time), was never resolved.

In 1865 Charles Crocker of the Central Pacific Railroad imported a Chinese labor force of twelve thousand to California after Irish workers went on strike, and he pronounced the Chinese workers superior. One of his associates, Leland Stanford, argued for their expulsion when he became governor of California, but cost-cutting American capitalists continued to import them, even after public outcry caused passage of the Chinese Exclusion Act of 1882, followed in 1885 by a law forbidding the importation of contract labor.

Montana mining interests, noting one-third of all placer mines were in the hands of Chinese by 1870, began legal action culminating with a ruling by the Montana Supreme Court in 1883 that effectively denied the right of the foreigners to own claims. This left Celestial entrepreneurs with just three options for making real money in a hostile society: investing in opium dens, investing in gambling halls, and investing in prostitution. By then all three were illegal, but with a population overweighed with single males, importing whores promised the most exciting profits.

Initially, "decent" Chinese women were not allowed to travel abroad, which meant that Chinese men working overseas by the thousands would provide a good market. So would Caucasians in early Montana, where white prostitutes were almost as scarce as respectable white women. Also a plus was the fact that young Chinese women were easy to obtain cheaply in times of economic stress. Because the labor of daughters was considered less productive than that of sons and they could not carry on the ancestral line, impoverished families considering infanticide or abandonment could easily be convinced to sell their girls instead. There was a strong tradition that daughters must sacrifice themselves for the good of the family. And kidnapping was also an option, even from wealthy families that didn't volunteer.

According to most sources, the Chinese American slave trade was pioneered by a Hong Kong prostitute named Ah-choi who came to San Francisco with a patron who died en route. Through the generous help of her ship's captain, she set up business in San Francisco during the California Gold Rush. Within two years she owned her own brothel and was making trips to the Orient to import more women, whom she soon began wholesaling. Early recruits worked under contracts that, though heavily weighted to favor their employer, might be paid off with luck in about four years. But Ah-choi also targeted illiterate candidates, tricking them aboard California-bound vessels and encouraging the ship's crew to "break the girls in" en route until they became submissive.

Learning of Ah-choi's success, other prostitutes with capital followed her example as free agents. However, there were few women with enough money for American passage, and by 1854 the trade had fallen under the control of Chinese secret societies. Most prominent was the Hip-Yee Tong, which organized the market so well that it circulated up-to-date lists of the going prices for captives in San Francisco to its Asian recruiting agents. Between 1852 and 1873 this organization, which controlled close to 90 percent of the trade, sent about six thousand Chinese women to America.

A number of them found themselves in bordellos after being misled by a promise that they would work as domestics or were destined for matrimony as mail-order brides. And even those who were given promised employment were little better off than kidnapped slaves. The terms of indenture were so tightly structured that volunteers were required to serve much additional time for sick leave and needed services. None was provided protection from a physically brutal master or husband. Few had access to medical treatment. Many employed in gambling and opium dens became addicted to one or both, further indebting themselves, while about 90 percent of those forced into prostitution are estimated to have contracted venereal disease.

Passage of the 1875 Page Act, which allowed the commissioner of immigration to prevent certain classes of people including "lewd or debauched" women from entering the United States, did little to curb traffic. As a follow-up, the Chinese Exclusion of 1882 allowed no women to enter the country except those born or married in the United States or born overseas to domiciled merchants. Families of Chinese men outside these categories were denied, and single men were no longer permitted to send for Chinese wives.

Spurred on by these new incentives and by the fact that there were about two thousand Chinese men in America for every Chinese woman, slave importers provided candidates who did not qualify with "coaching papers" listing answers to the standard questions asked of returning daughters and wives by immigration authorities. Elaborate systems were established to bribe both Chinese and U.S. officials who oversaw the traffic and local police who patrolled Chinese American districts. In fact, the clandestine trade became so lucrative, not only to Chinese slavers but to those elected to thwart them, that relatively little is known about their dealings even today. Writer Lucie Cheng Hirata noted that only four indenture contracts have been discovered. However, she did estimate that even a low-grade prostitute could earn her master about $3,400 during a four-year period, while the higher classes would gross about $7,650 plus resale value.

Those destined for Montana were usually purchased in San Francisco, either by special order or selected from the latest shipments of women, who were housed in temporary quarters called barracoons. Here women designated for the skin trade were stripped and inspected like cattle. When sold, each was made to take her purchase price in hand to the seller and to sign a contract if one was included in the bargain.

One cruel agreement read:

> For the consideration of [whatever sum had been agreed upon], paid into my hands this day, I, [name of girl], promise to prostitute my body for a term of _____ years. If, in that time, I am sick one day, two weeks should be added to my time; and if more than one, my term of prostitution shall continue an additional month. But if I run away, or escape from the custody of my keeper, than I am to be held as a slave for life.
>
>   (Signed) _____

Since menstruation was usually regarded as an illness, sexually transmitted diseases most certainly were, and pregnancy traditionally added an extra year of servitude, the chances of a prostitute working her way to freedom were slim.

Beautiful women had a better chance. They were reserved as concubines or second wives for wealthy Chinese men. Especially favored were girls from upper-class families with purposely deformed feet no more than four inches in length, referred to as yellow lilies. Such "small-footed women" walked slowly with a swaying motion that pleased Celestial patrons. Beauties who weren't reserved for the exclusive use of these wealthy men usually ended up in high-end brothels patronized by them.

Since it was considered degrading for any daughter of China to have sexual relations with a Caucasian, girls who didn't make first or second cut were consigned to servicing both white and Chinese laborers, sometimes working in teams of from two to six in a barn-style crib behind a barred window set in a narrow door off a dank alley. Management generally required such low women to advertise their wares loudly to any male who might stop to peer at them.

"China girl nice! You come inside, please?" was the standard pitch, followed by announcement of the going prices. "Two bittee lookee, flo bittee feelee, six bittee dooee!"

Recruits and captives considered less than beautiful and those hard to discipline were sent to remote mining camps, sometimes as the only available woman where nonstop duty was required. For this reason, the threat of Montana service was enough to discipline all but the most unruly of slave girls waiting in San Francisco for distribution.

The first official census taken in Montana, in 1870, reported 1,949 Chinese. This number is more impressive when one notes that it represented at least 10 percent and possibly one-third of the entire population and that census takers were as notorious for underestimating "Orientals" as the Orientals were for avoiding them.

Only 123 Chinese females were recorded during this period, but it is clear that the majority of prostitutes in early mining camps were Chinese. In 1880, when only eighty females were listed out of Montana's Celestial population of

1,765, twenty-one of Butte's thirty-five women of the evening and about 50 percent of fifty-three enrolled for Helena were Chinese. It is believed about 90 percent of those who worked as prostitutes were physically forced to, so clearly slaves made up the majority of all Celestial females in the state. Yet their business was conducted quietly. None was well known by name, and their remarkable pioneering has been all but written out of history.

There was some concern over the opium dens they frequented, but Celestial welfare was not at issue. In 1879, the *Butte Miner* breathlessly reported that there were between "75 and 80 *white persons* in Butte addicted to this horrible habit," with the only interest being in the danger posed to Occidentals.

"Nightly bleary-eyed males and lewd girls, creatures of the town, congregate at these places, and the debauching they indulge in is too indecent to describe in print," the editor lamented. Opium, available in numerous patent medicines at the time, was legal under federal law, yet the city responded by passing an ordinance against using the drug and then raiding Oolu Jack's, the most popular of Butte's dens. The only patrons arrested, however, were Annie Northcutt, "a woman well and unfavorably known in Helena," and a local named Charlie Cummings. Testifying against them and Oolu Jack before Judge Wilcox was Nellie Linwood, whose qualifications were not cited, although she seemed to have a good grasp on the workings of Jack's place.

"She said that men and women would go into Oolu Jack's den, give him two bits or four bits, or more, and lie down for a smoke in one of the four loathsome bunks provided for that purposes," the *Daily Miner* reported. "She illustrated with the opium kit, pipes, etc., which were still in court, the method of preparing the gum opium for consumption; how it was rolled and roasted on an 'anhawk,' or short, pointed wire, and then pushed it into the bowl of the pipe, ready for use. Her testimony was quite interesting and provoked some applause as she facetiously alluded to the opium den as a 'Joint,' and the wire roaster as the 'anhawk.'"

After Judge Wilcox fined Northcutt twenty-five dollars plus court costs, the newspaper made one additional plea for "rigid and persevering punishment" before abandoning its crusade with the doors of Oolu Jack's still open. Those who knew Butte's Chinatown watched it expand over the next decade to include a number of "female boarding houses," the designation for brothels on insurance maps, but little more would ever be learned about Celestial prostitution.

Suspected opium dealer Ah Fok did inadvertently provide some insight into the slave trade in the summer of 1882 when Butte police were drawn to Chinatown by his outcries of anger and the obvious alarm of his neighbors. Lucy, the youngest and prettiest of six women with whom Ah Fok was living, had been kidnapped, he reluctantly explained. Knowing that polygamy was common among rich Chinese residents, police asked if Lucy was Ah Fok's wife. She was not, he assured them. Nor were the other four who "belong alle same to my wife No. 1."

According to his account as reported by the local paper, Lucy had gone out in the alley, where she was seized by one white man and two Chinese men, who "stuff a pole of lags" in her mouth so she would not scream. And, since Ah Fok had inadvertently summoned the American authorities, he decided he wanted something done about it.

Investigation led police to the conclusion that the kidnapping was "apparent rather than real." Lucy, they suspected, objected to being only one-sixth of a wife, especially after meeting and becoming attached to Lem, the dishwasher at the St. Nicholas Hotel. Later there were reports that she had fled with him to Virginia City, but whether Ah Fok sent the highbinders after them was not known. Since it was learned that Lucy's market value was about $1,500, the answer was probably yes, but Chinese henchmen worked in secrecy and were so clever at disposing of bodies that there was no evidence on which to prosecute. Nor did any of Ah Fok's remaining wives dare testify against him for bigamy.

The only similar Chinese foray into the American justice system was noted about a decade later in the form of a complaint made to the city marshal by Way Ching Foo that his wife had run off with a former Butte store owner. Foo, it seems, had been so taken by the wife of One Lung Sing that he offered to purchase her along with Sing's small variety shop for $750 in cash. Sing agreed. Inspired to make a fresh start, he handed over all the promised goods and moved to Moscow, Idaho, where he landed a job as a hotel cook. The former Mrs. Sing, however, who apparently had not been involved in early decision making, fled Butte for Moscow, where she moved back in with husband number one.

At Way Ching Foo's request, Marshal Langdon journeyed with him to Idaho to confront Sing and the wayward wife, who did not seem inclined to return. After what Langdon reported as considerable "rag chewing" among themselves—not including him—the threesome decided to settle things in the traditional Chinese way. Langdon had no follow-up to report for the *Moscow Star*, which took an interest in the case.

***

While impressive Chinatowns with more than a hundred residents grew up in mining camps like Marysville and German Gulch, and Chinese eventually took over the abandoned Silver Bow camp of Rocker, renaming it Foochow, Butte's district eventually became the largest in Montana because it proved the state's safest haven. The census of 1890 had recorded 602 Chinese living in Helena and some 400 in Anaconda, but by 1900 most had fled.

Resentment against the Celestials in Montana had been indulged early on by holding them responsible for major disasters like the great Helena fire of 1869, officially "started at a Chinese gambling house," and a fire in the Anaconda that originated in the establishment of two white whores yet was credited to "the carelessness of a Chinaman." George Crofutt, editor of the Butte city directory of 1886, blamed the number of typographical errors appearing in his final text on "John Chinaman," ending with the conclusion that "The Chinaman Must Go."

Ignored was the fact that Chinese workmen were roundly praised for the difficult task of building Montana railroads over the Great Divide in the dead of winter to Butte as well as the celebrated Mullan Tunnel into Helena. Or that nine of Butte's trusted physicians were Chinese. Or that Chinese farmers produced most of the state's fresh vegetables and ran countless popular restaurants and noodle parlors and laundries. Or that Montana-based Chinese endeavored to coexist in white communities in peace, heard from only during their noisily happy New Year celebrations and occasional funerals. In fact, between 1900 and 1918, only six Chinese residents were sent to the Montana state penitentiary, four of them for the same crime.

Yet a growing number of citizens wanted them gone. Laws discriminating against Asians encouraged many to act on their prejudices. The strengthening of unions, followed by a nationwide depression, caused these foreigners to be suddenly pushed from the job market via boycott and violence.

In April 1892 employers in Helena were urged to dismiss their Chinese help, and a public meeting was held to make the point. Critics ignored the fact that the tax revenues of Helena's Chinese population had grown from $38,900 in 1870 to $80,905 annually by 1890. Union members blocked doorways to discourage customers from entering Chinese restaurants and laundries. Members caught patronizing them were fined.

During this period, the foreigners feared violence, which had already erupted in riots in Washington, Colorado, and Wyoming, and Montana citizens did not disappoint. They began with the dynamiting of a "wash house" on Anaconda's Front Street in 1890. In 1891, three Chinese were beaten to death by an elusive gang of hoodlums in Butte. Then, under the headline "A Chinaman Departed," the *Anaconda Standard* reported that the decaying corpse of a Chinese man had been found hanging from a tree and that authorities had finally gotten around to investigating the accident several weeks after it was reported. Although the subhead for the article read "A Dose of Poison, A Leaden Bullet and a Slipknot Transported Him," the reporter concluded the man had taken his own life because he could borrow no more money with which to gamble. With brandy and poison in his pocket, the deceased had climbed a tree, tied a noose around his neck, drunk the brandy and poison, then shot himself in the heart, thus hanging as he fell, the writer suggested.

Given that the congressional passage of the Gary Act of 1892 not only extended restraints already in force against Chinese for another decade but also eliminated their day-to-day legal protection such as bail and legal redress through the courts, it is not surprising that many fled Montana for the relative safety of large Celestial enclaves on the West Coast.

In 1893 the Citizens Anti-Chinese Committee of Anaconda published a resolution in the *Anaconda Standard* demanding residents boycott Chinese businesses, "resolved that they should not live amongst us." A mass meeting was held where the names of those employing Chinese were publicized and white ranchers were asked to begin supplying vegetables to replace those farmed by the Chinese. Members of a similar committee in Butte visited the red-light district demanding the madams fire their Chinese help. When the women responded by directing said help to throw out the committeemen, astonished members left in haste promising a boycott.

What they had not considered was that Butte's white prostitutes, whose district abutted Chinatown, patronized its noodle parlors, which offered good meals at low prices plus twenty-four-hour-a-day delivery service. They also relied on Chinese doctors and herbalists to supply them with birth control and cures for venereal disease, neither of which were available through white practitioners. Opium, carefully administered, could produce an abortion, a method certainly preferable to the knife. And most of the town's affluent parlor houses were staffed with trusted and efficient Chinese cooks, butlers, maids, and bouncers.

Nor was the Butte Labor and Trades Assembly much more successful in punishing members who employed or patronized Chinese, for respectable citizens in Butte had long relied on Chinatown's merchants, and its leaders were well respected, so much so that four of them successfully protested the union boycotts to both American and Chinese governments and filed suit against the organizers.

There was negative press when reformers again crusaded against opium dens. This time the target was the upscale establishment of Yung Lee, who offered mattresses and pillows on his bunks and silk trappings much appreciated by his upper-class white clients. His prices, from ten to twenty dollars a pipe, were at least one hundred times higher than what Oolu Jack had charged a decade earlier, but Lee offered privacy and was proud of his services.

As a Writers Project of Montana scribe reported—in what one can only assume was a good-faith effort at capturing the speaker's dialect—Lee explained to police judge Warren O'Mara (who had recently married a prostitute known as Lilly the Lush in a public ceremony): "Yung Lee sell dleams—velly nice dreams—if China boy or Melican boy or girl want have nice, pletty dleam—Yung Lee, he fix 'em up. They pay Yung Lee money, he bling 'em one-two-hour dleam—pletty dleams—no distlurbance—no botha anybody—just lay down—sleep—dleam. Much blettah than spend money for Ilish whiskey and want to kill evlybody. Much blettah dleam—no hurt anybody."

Yet surprisingly, as Anaconda's Chinatown became a ghost town, Butte newspaper readers were regaled with a society page account of how Dr. Huie Pock had introduced his bride, recently arrived from China, to the town's elite including mining magnate James Murray and U.S. senator Tom Carter. The contemporary society wedding of Hum Fay to a Spokane Celestial was also covered in detail, with additional space given to the fact that the restaurant mogul had passed every English course offered at Butte's Chinese Baptist Mission and reached a point where instructors had to admit they could teach him nothing more.

"He had wanted to take calculus, having finished trigonometry and analytical geometry," the reporter added.

Still, a number of preachers continued to harp on the Chinese vices of dope, gambling, and prostitution as if this race alone indulged in them. Most ambitious was the Methodist Reverend Dr. A. D. Raleigh, who embarked on a series of lectures advocating the exclusion of Celestials until they became civilized. Moralists agreed that it was the slave trade of young Chinese women that provided the most negative image, but it was the consensus that nothing could be done for these unfortunates. The only solution offered was expulsion of all Chinese so the women would suffer elsewhere.

Ah Oie knew better, however. She would not have been honeymooning in Butte in 1902 had it not been for the efforts of an organization of women who had boldly taken on the highbinders to bring hundreds of slave girls to safety.

It had become increasingly difficult for slave traders to import girls from the old country. Their price on delivery in San Francisco had risen from $1,000 to as much as $3,000 in gold over the last decade. Orphaned between her third and fourth birthdays in Fat Son, China, Ah Oie had been sold by her grandmother to a woman named A. Tie for $130. As punishment for small faults, this unkind mistress would make the child fall on her knees and place a bucket of water on her head, then demand she rise without spilling a drop. If the child failed she was beaten but left unscarred.

Ah Oie grew into a very pretty girl with a fine singing voice. When she reached age fourteen in 1884, A. Tie sold her to a female slaver called Pock-Marked A. Que, who took Ah Oie to San Francisco, where she had presold the girl to a whorehouse for $2,730. Que was also considering an offer from a wealthy Chinese man who promised $500 if Ah Oie would sing at a feast he was planning when immigration agents refused to allow her to land her "chattel."

Que went to court, but, despite the fact that Ah Oie obediently insisted the slaver was her mother, the girl was placed, kicking and screaming, in the Occidental Board Presbyterian Mission Home. The problem was Fahn Quai, a name that translated as "a white devil," which was how slavers referred to a young and beautiful Caucasian woman named Donaldina Cameron, who headed the rescue mission. Inmates of the home called her Lo Mo, or "the mother," because they knew the barred windows of her home were not to imprison them. The mission's goal was to protect the young women from recapture by former owners and their highbinders.

Ah Oie had not requested saving, however, and Pock-Marked A. Que had told her horrible things about Cameron. Finding herself in the White Devil's house so terrified the girl that she refused all food for two days. She realized Que might kill her or worse if she returned to her, but she had also been warned that if she became sick, Fahn Quai would throw her out. Finally, both desperate and starving, she joined the other girls for meals and discovered how lucky she was.

Remaining in residence, studying English, exploring the Presbyterian religion, and learning homemaking skills, she met Dr. Wah Jean Lamb, who was looking for a wife to help him raise his daughter by an earlier marriage and assist in his Butte, Montana, practice. To Ah Oie's relief, neither Lo Mo nor Lamb tried to push her into marriage, and it took her some months to make up her mind. Lamb was older, but he was also a gentle Chinese man and so skilled as a physician and as a speaker of English that many of his patients were white. She wed him in a Christian service at a meeting of the Women's Occident Board in April 1901, wearing white Swiss trimmed with pink and carrying pink roses.

Ah Oie's move to Butte the following August must have been traumatic. The town was primitive in comparison with the big cities she was used to, but she settled comfortably into living quarters behind Dr. Lamb's office at 9 West Galena in the heart of Chinatown.

"It rain pretty hard this few days and most every day so it gets very muddy in the street," she wrote to her friends on the Occidental Board. "Since I came to this city I have been attended the church nearly every Sunday and Sunday school; here has only one Chinese Mission; it belongs to the Baptist." She also noted she was teaching a Sunday school class, which included a very bright little boy and a girl, ages five and twelve.

The Chinese Baptist Mission had been established in 1892 by eighteen Chinese "sojourners" under Mrs. J. G. Pullman, a missionary who focused on teaching them English rather than religion. Early classes were held at a branch of the Young Men's Christian Association until the church built a two-story structure to house them, with basement quarters used as a dormitory for six converted Christians.

Although women could not attend, female missionaries were allowed to teach them at home, which is probably how Ah Oie dealt with the girl in her Sunday school class. This may also have been how she learned of the plight of twenty-three-year-old Choy Gay and her small servant girl Lon Ying. Or perhaps since they lived just a few doors down at 21 West Galena, Ah Oie paid them a neighborly visit.

Choy Gay had been just thirteen in 1890 when Quong Tuck Wing made her his second wife and settled in Butte with her, leaving wife number one to carry on the family name in the old country. Successful as a purveyor of Chinese merchandise, Wing also purchased Lon Ying, then a small girl classed as "mooie jas" (below the age of puberty), for their household slave. Then, with an eye to broadening his business, he enrolled in English classes offered at Chinese Baptist Mission and allowed one of their women missionaries to teach Choy Gay and Lon Ying at home.

Over time the wife, who was sweet and seemingly docile, became unusually attached to Lon Ying, who was quick to learn and a good, hardworking little girl. Things went well with them until Wing, who was forty-six, began to suspect that Choy Gay was not capable of producing an heir and considered making Lon Ying wife number three. The girl was becoming a beauty but she was only eleven, and Choy Gay, who had come to think of her as a daughter, refused to allow the marriage. Wing was determined, and Choy Gay's insubordination provoked so many beatings that she considered suicide.

Records of the Occidental Mission Board do not explain how their rescue worker, Mrs. A. F. Browne, got involved, but it was probably through Ah Oie that Choy Gay and Lon Ying requested help. Browne, substituting for Donaldina Cameron, who was on vacation at the time, was dispatched to Butte in the winter of 1902. Well experienced at rescue work, she stashed the dress of a schoolgirl and a Salvation Army uniform at that agency's Butte headquarters and then walked by Wing's store on Galena. There she loitered until she spotted Lon Ying with a bucket headed to fetch water nearby and followed her, quietly calling her name.

"I have come for you," she whispered. "At 10:30 this evening both of you meet me at this spot."

Enlisting the help of the local police chief, Browne reappeared with a carriage at the appointed hour to swoop up Gay and her young accomplice. Then, stopping only long enough for Ying and Gay to change clothes at Salvation Army headquarters, they hurried to a station seven miles distant, where they had to wait three hours in bitter cold for the arrival of a train. Finally aboard, they were confronted by a sheriff who attempted to arrest Lon Ying until the Butte police chief, who was escorting them to the next stop, told him her story.

At every station, officers boarded to search for runaways, but Browne hid her charges in the ladies dressing room, bringing them safely to San Francisco, where they successfully challenged Quong Tuck Wing in court. Two years later Lon Ying wed Jin Soo Fong in a successful Christian union that produced eight children. Choy Gay, who also embraced Christianity but not another marriage, remained at the home until she developed enough sewing skill to support herself.

———◇———

About 350 Chinese fled Butte between 1886 and 1901. Despite the fact that others replaced them from more turbulent towns like Anaconda and Helena, this population continued to drop. While just a decade earlier Chinese prostitutes had made up the majority of the camp's red-light district, only one, a forty-one-year-old veteran named Du Toy, was listed there in Butte's 1900 census. A prostitute of the same name had been living with a household of pimps in Helena in 1880. While in Butte she headed a family of one, which may mean Toy had worked her way to independence before relocating. Meanwhile, the slave trade appeared to have vanished without a trace. Although it would remain in operation for many years, the only hint of it was to be found in a description of Butte's Chinatown that ran in the *Anaconda Standard*, May 20, 1906.

"Butte's Chinatown is peculiar in many respects," the reporter noted. "Some fine-looking, two-story brick buildings are found upon its streets. Nestling by the side of these are often found frame shacks which are propped up from without and girded within to keep them from falling to pieces.

"It is said that there are underground places beneath some of the squalid structures which look so dingy and dirty to the casual passerby, and that these are fitted up with magnificent and costly furnishing, but whether or not this is true cannot be proven . . ." the writer speculated. "But it is still one of the traditions of the people below the line, and some say that its sacredness is reserved only for the swells among the Chinese populations."

Not until 1936, however, did proof of such a mysterious world come to light with the dismantling of a yawing Chinatown fire hazard owned by Tom Lin between Galena and Mercury in Chinatown bordering the old red-light district. Its ground-floor cribs were no surprise, although they had been vacant so long that the outdated female undergarments displayed in one "show window" had fallen apart with age. What did give pause was an odd labyrinth of apartments with secret tunnels and passages and a concealed basement.

"On the second floor the puzzle begins in real earnest," a reporter for the *Montana Standard* wrote. "The rooms fronting on the streets had little anterooms that connected with closets, that connected with hallways, that led into other rooms that had closets that opened into other hallways that led a winding course—to one of the floors upstairs or down in the basement [which] wasn't really a basement, but a hold dug in the ground."

So many questions!

"Why the tunnel to the basement? Why the light wires passing through closets where they could be—and have been apparently—cut to throw the house in darkness?" the reporter wondered. "Why the electric plug box outside the window of a closet—inside the building and within easy reach of a stealthy hand which knew the location of the box, a location invisible from inside the closet? Why the buried bedroom with three beds, a room so cleverly concealed that the workers did not know of its existence until they tore up the floor of an adjoining room and exposed the filthy quarters to light and air?"

On one of the beds in this subterranean hide-out lay a worn old photograph of two Chinese boys, one in American dress and the other wearing traditional silk. It had been taken against a drawing of Chinese buildings by S. K. Sate, whose shop was located on Fifth Street in Oakland, California. And it was badly faded, although it had laid in darkness for many years.

Intrigued, the editor ran the photograph, wondering who the boys were and who had left the photograph behind. No reader response was ever published, and Tom Lin, who had last been listed in the city directory of 1927, was not heard from. So the building's use remains as much of a mystery as the slave trade it probably harbored.

6

RESPECTABLE
PURPLE PATHS

~ 1900 ~

Mamie Cruse, Mary MacLane, and Anna LaChapelle saw themselves in peril at the end of the nineteenth century, almost as surely as if they'd been kidnapped by evil slavers. All were white. Mamie was rich. Mary's family had been, and still was, fairly well off. The LaChapelles were poor but hopeful. Yet all three young women were desperate to escape the dead-end, mind-dulling future they saw in store for them. And, while there were no highbinders to stop them, none saw a clear path to safety.

Anna Eugenia LaChapelle was born April 1, 1878, in Calumet, Michigan, of newly immigrated French Canadian parents seeking a better life. Her farm-reared father, Peter, the fifteenth of nineteen children, had somehow managed to study medicine in Montreal. Her mother, Philomene, was sixth in a brood of nine. With no inheritance, Peter supported their family, which soon included five children, by running a small tailor shop and, on the side, selling a popular eye lotion he'd developed. In 1889, hearing that Butte was a wide-open town, LaChapelle decided to reinvent himself there as a physician and surgeon while Philomene operated a boardinghouse with the help of Anna, then eleven, her sister, Amelia, thirteen, and their two younger brothers.

The property they rented at 133 East Park was three blocks from the school but even closer to the theater district, both legitimate and otherwise, and the town's burgeoning tenderloin. The fact that "Park Street girl" was Butte's euphemism for a prostitute during this period proved a social handicap. Philomene was strict with the girls, bringing them up with a fine set of manners and making sure they applied themselves to their studies, but against increasing odds.

When the boardinghouse did not work out, they moved around the corner to Wyoming Street, where Philomene again took in boarders and Peter struggled to maintain his practice. Hoping for better walk-in trade, he opened an office at North Main and, that failing, finally moved to 300 East Park. In 1892, however, medical authorities discovered LaChapelle had neglected to apply for a license and forced him to pull in his shingle because his Canadian training didn't qualify. Ever hopeful, trading on the success of his eye medicine and a loophole in the licensing rules, LaChapelle sought to reestablish himself as an oculist.

Anna, now fifteen, was bright enough not to share her father's optimism. The whole country had tumbled into something called a financial panic. Unemployment was huge, even in Butte where jobs were usually plentiful. The situation had become desperate, and so had she and her sister. She would truly rather die than continue to watch her parents work themselves to death.

Amelia's solution was to sign up for secretarial courses at Butte Business College just down the street, but Anna had broader vision. She had spent considerable time observing the town's well-dressed streetwalkers and dance hall girls, eavesdropping when she found herself sitting next to them in the town's noodle parlors and restaurants. She had no inclination to go that route, which she saw to be a hard one, but she thought there might be middle ground. Beautiful and musically talented, she had made a name for herself in school plays and community theater. She'd been told she was an excellent actress, and she decided to put her talents to a real test.

Her target was mining man Jim Murray, one of the founders of Butte's elegant Grand Opera House, who also owned a successful Butte bank. Murray was not only one of the richest men in the state but also among the handsomest: a tall, dark, highly sophisticated bachelor few women could resist. After studying him appreciatively during a number of theater intermissions when they were both in attendance, Anna lightened her already blond hair, dressed in her best, and approached him at his desk at the bank without an appointment.

Murray would later describe her as "a little golden haired girl of prepossessing appearance" who asked him "without much ceremony" to bear the expense of her education. He was wealthy. The expense would be infinitesimal, she reasoned. She possessed the ambition to become an actress, adding that she had acquitted herself well in a few local entertainments and that she could attain "histrionic honors in the world."

Murray, who had never heard of the girl, declined but—gentleman that he was—suggested that she might accomplish her goal through William A. Clark. Clark was unmarried, had plenty of money, and would undoubtedly help her along the road she desired to travel, he said. Anna asked Murray if he would introduce her. Again he declined, explaining that his introduction would do her more harm than good, since he and Clark were not on good terms. But if she laid her case before Clark as she had done with him, the banker believed she would succeed.

A lifelong bachelor, James Murray was fifty-one at the time, easygoing and full of fun. Clark was fifty-four and dapper but a remote, grasping little man who was not well liked. He had recently lost his wife to typhoid fever, and he was richer than Murray and had a place on the New York social register. He, too, had been a founder of Butte's Grand Opera House.

Discovering that he had a genuine interest in the arts and all things French, Anna tailored her approach accordingly. Clark would later recall that he first noticed her at a Fourth of July celebration in a crowd of gaudily costumed young people, where she stood out dressed elegantly as the Goddess of Liberty. She was still blond, but a subdued, mellow blond, and her toga-draped figure was outstanding. Instead of acting lessons, she was hoping to become a virtuoso at the harp, she confided. But her family was in peril because the gifted physician who was her father had lost his medical practice when the government licensing agency refused to accept his perfectly adequate Canadian credentials.

Intrigued, Clark met with her family. It just so happened he had recently helped establish the College of Montana at Deer Lodge and now served as president of its board of trustees. The school had the finest music department in the territory, and, since it was obvious the girl had talent, he would be pleased to fund her board and tuition.

When her parents hesitated, perhaps because Clark's reputation as a womanizer was well known, he hastily added that the girl would be housed in the school's new dormitory, which, of course, would be well chaperoned. And finally he extended his generosity to Peter LaChapelle, offering to pay his expenses to a Chicago medical school.

The LaChapelles accepted, but Philomene, who had long regarded Anna simply as a sweet, obliging little girl, looked at her daughter calculatingly after Clark made his offer of support. As far as she knew, the fifteen-year-old had never even had a serious beau, while her older sister was always falling in love. *Had Mr. Clark suggested . . . ?* He had not, Anna interrupted, noting her mother's awkward hesitation, but she figured he soon would. Then with a confidence borne of her recent success, the girl added boldly that she could keep Mr. Clark interested. However she did pay attention when her worried mother, once a beauty herself, suggested it might be easier and safer to keep the old man waiting.

The LaChapelles saw little of their benefactor in the months that followed. He was fully engaged in a battle with his business rival, Marcus Daly, who was campaigning to move the state capital from Helena to his remote company town of Anaconda. Clark had once made Helena his home, spared no expense to thwart the move, and prevailed in the statewide vote on the issue that November. Anna and Peter, both buried in their respective classes, wrote Mr. Clark grateful progress reports, and after the election Clark occasionally visited Anna at the college—fatherly visits, he explained, standing in for Peter while he was away.

In June, the LaChapelles reunited for Anna's graduation, during which she performed piano and violin solos and, finally, a charming violin duet with a classmate. Clark, as president of the board, addressed the class and conferred degrees. Then he invited the LaChapelles to lunch at a local hotel to present Anna with a graduation gift.

It was obvious to everyone who had just attended that she was a very accomplished young lady who had learned a great deal in a very short time, he acknowledged proudly. But it was her dream to play the harp, something their newly chartered college was not equipped to teach. In fact, no really qualified teacher could be found in the entire West. Consequently, he had contacted Belgian-born Alphonse Hasselmans, a noted composer who had recently established the French school of harp playing and was a professor at the Paris Conservatory. Clark had been assured that the talented girl would be accepted there, and of course he would be delighted to sponsor her.

Anna could scarcely believe her ears. Hasselmans's solo performances had created a sensation in Europe. He was the most famous harpist in the world. She would have killed just to hear him in concert. The idea of becoming his pupil thrilled her.

Philomene knew little about world-class harpists, although she had recently learned on good authority that Clark's wife had left him long before her death because of deviant sexual practices in which he indulged on his frequent trips to France. Thoughtfully, Clark had anticipated parental concerns. Assuming the family could spare Anna for a year or so, he had arranged for his sister, Elizabeth Abascal, herself a mother, to accompany the girl to Paris, where respected matron Madame de Cervellon would serve as her chaperone. Peter had one more year left in medical school, which, of course, Clark would continue to fund. And perhaps, during a vacation break, Amelia might join her sister for a little tour of Europe, to keep Anna from becoming too lonely.

It was an offer too good to refuse, especially when Mr. Clark's philanthropy appeared to delight him almost as much as it did his recipients, for he seemed a lonely man. One of his twin daughters had died early, he explained. Four of his remaining five children were grown with lives of their own. The youngest, Francis Paul, fifteen, was in Massachusetts studying to enter law school, so he saw little of him. It was good to have a talented young family in Butte again, Clark insisted.

Lizzie Abascal, as Clark called his sister Elizabeth, was an original. The only one of his four sisters brave enough to join him out West, she had waited until she was past thirty to marry, settling on a charismatic Spaniard named Joaquin Abascal, who had operated a pack team to the gold camps in competition with William. By the time their daughter Mary was born in 1879, they had settled in Deer Lodge, where Joaquin established himself as a merchant. There, along with his brother-in-law, he was elected a delegate to the

Constitutional Convention and became focused on politics, twice winning election to the state legislature. Neglect of his wife may have resulted; Lizzie was more than ready to take leave from him to accompany Anna to Paris. Adventurous, she prodded her young charge to take in all the sights, but Anna also worked hard at her studies, which included French and German as well as music.

In the early spring of 1896 Clark arrived to discover his sister and Anna had planned a wonderful tour of Paris for him and that Anna had perfected her French to a point that she could be quite useful. Knowing he had become serious about collecting fine art, she introduced him to several valuable contacts, endearing herself well beyond appreciation of her musical talents and the lure of her natural charms. Clark was inclined to linger, but the idyll ended horribly with the news that Clark's young son had died of heart failure in Massachusetts.

Just two months later, Anna's world wavered when Peter LaChapelle died of a sudden paralytic stroke while vacationing from medical school in Butte. There was no insurance and seemingly no hope of a brighter future. Philomene continued to take in boarders. Amelia got a job as a stenographer. Clark continued to support Anna's studies and her chaperone, Madam de Cervellon. His trips to Paris became more frequent, and he came to depend on Anna's language skills and Parisian contracts. At twenty-one she was an elegant beauty, but there apparently had been little change in their relationship when her benefactor absented himself to pursue a longtime dream.

Clark had twice been defeated in his attempts to hold a seat in the U.S. Senate. When, in 1894, he finally got the legislature to appoint him, his quest had ended in a federal investigation for bribery so humiliating that he resigned and decided not to try again. But in 1899 he formed an alliance with Fritz Augustus Heinze, Butte's youngest Copper King, who had built a remarkable grassroots political network that stacked the legislative vote in their favor. Clark finally was seated legally for a six-year term in the U.S. Senate in 1900.

Enter Kathlyn Williams, a doe-eyed little beauty with ripe, Cupid's bow lips and a mop of blond ringlets, who sought the multimillionaire's help to finance the theatrical career her mother boycotted. Williams probably knew that Clark was funding LaChapelle. Certainly the Senate appointment had made him high profile, and his weakness for pretty young women was common gossip in Butte, where the girl had been born and raised.

Whatever the case, Williams had a readymade sad story. Her Norwegian father, a Butte pioneer and successful hotel operator, had died six years earlier, and her Welsh mother was struggling to keep the girl in Wesleyan College in Helena, believing that the religious influence would curb her wildness.

Interested but cautious, Clark discovered Williams had already debuted at Sutton's, the local legitimate theater, two years earlier with astonishing success. That she had shaved four years off her age was a woman's prerogative, but it also meant she was over the age of consent, and Clark need not deal with her mother. If Kathlyn would first acquire her college diploma, Clark promised he would sponsor her at the American Academy of Musical Arts and Sargeant Dramatic School in New York City. Which is exactly what he did following her graduation ceremony on May 28, 1901.

About this time, Anna arrived back in Butte. It is not known whether she came because she was concerned about Clark's relationship with Williams or because Clark asked her to live closer to home, since his Senate appointment limited foreign travel. She was listed in the 1902 city directory as an "artist," living with her sister, Amelia, practically next door to Clark's thirty-room mansion on Granite Street, while their mother, Philomene, resided in fine new digs, also in the "swell" part of town. Later that year, Amelia enrolled at St. Mary's Academy in Salt Lake City, an excellent girls' school, followed by a stint at National Park Seminar in Washington, D.C., one of the most progressive women's colleges in the country. Brother Arthur, still living at home, got to attend Butte Business College, which led to a good job in a company owned by Clark where brother William was already employed.

Cause for the LaChapelles' improved status became clear in August 1902 when Anna moved again, this time in the company of her faithful chaperone, Madame de Cervellon. Their new address was a sumptuous villa overlooking the beautiful Bay of Algiers on the Mediterranean, where Anna gave birth to Wilhelmina Louise Amelia "Andree" Clark. The child's father appeared well pleased with the little charmer but, mindful of scandal, not to mention the potential wrath of his legitimate children, Clark demanded her birth remain secret.

Anna proceeded cautiously, pleading only that he ensure her ability to raise the girl. Clark was accustomed to treating personal and financial problems in a dispassionate manner or not at all, but he did eventually provide a modest sum for Anna and set aside $75,000 for their daughter. The birth of a son who lived less than an hour in 1903 changed little, although that event might have made it more apparent that serial secret pregnancies involving the former ward of a sitting U.S. senator could eventually become a liability.

Four years after the fact, the aging lothario formally announced his marriage to Anna and the subsequent birth of their daughter. Clark had earlier required Anna to sign papers that prevented her from tapping his fortune. However, the storm of newspaper coverage in July 1904 seems to have caught him by surprise and may well have been triggered by the LaChapelles.

Clark's story was that he had made the talented girl his ward following the death of her father, then married her in a private service in Marseilles, France, on May 25, 1901, in the presence of her chaperone, Madame de Cervellon, and two unnamed witnesses. No records of this marriage were ever found, which may be explained by the fact that the newspaper Clark owned in Butte reported his arrival in New York City on June 1, 1901, placing him at sea during the alleged ceremony. Even more damaging was a follow-up story by the *Anaconda Standard*, a paper owned by Clark's rival, Marcus Daly, with a detailed account by James Murray on how Anna had originally propositioned him before he handed her off to Clark.

Clark's first family was so angered that the old man promised he would never allow Anna to occupy the palatial mansion he had recently built on Fifth Avenue in New York City at a cost of several million. He referred to their relationship as an "alliance," never as a "marriage." Yet he insisted Anna was a virtuous woman, that she was sweet and unselfish and wanted nothing beyond a competency for "herself & child."

Anna followed suit, never demanding, bowing quietly to the wishes of the children of Clark's first wife even after they floated the rumor that her second daughter, Huguette Marcell Clark, born the summer of 1906, was not actually Clark's but the result of their stepmother's affair with a New York doctor. This was, however, a theory to which William Clark apparently did not subscribe, and Anna Eugenia would remain his wife until she became his widow, for better or for worse, twenty-one years later.

After a suitable lapse of time, Anna returned to Butte to serve as hostess at Clark's Granite Street mansion, where they entertained, among others, actress Sarah Bernhardt following her performance of *Camille* at the local roller skating rink, and Mary Haldron, the former wife of a New York attorney and a spectacular-looking woman whom James Murray had taken as a bride.

While Anna LaChapelle waged a brilliant campaign to better her own fortunes, she had also proved as dedicated as any traditional Chinese daughter to improving the lot of her family. Mary MacLane—close to the same age and equally desperate but totally self-focused—chose a different path. Like LaChapelle, MacLane saw entrapment in Butte as her major problem. She also loathed her upper-middle-class family and others she judged inferior.

She was born in Winnipeg, Canada, on May 2, 1881, the third child of James and Margaret MacLane, with the birth of a younger brother to follow. Her father, a highly placed government worker who had initially prospered during the California Gold Rush, moved the family to Fergus Falls, Minnesota, when Mary was four. His death in 1888 appeared to have made little impression on her. However, she did not welcome the remarriage of her Canadian mother to Henry Klenze, administrator of her father's estate, under whose management the family fortune soon diminished.

A mining man, Klenze moved the family first to Great Falls, Montana, and then to Butte, where Mary found herself encamped without servants in a cramped little house high up on the northwest edge of the city, with a defunct mining company in view from the dining room window. The town below was locked in a smoky pall produced by dozens of ore refineries. Just sixteen, MacLane felt she had been dropped into an alien world. Fergus Falls had been lush and green, and Great Falls at the very most offered occasional blue skies.

Worse yet, Mary felt absolutely alone, having grown to loathe her stepfather and her mother, too, for saddling the family with him. She had nothing in common with her brother John, twenty, who was a mining engineer. Her sister, Dorothy, called Dolly, eighteen, was too much the dutiful daughter for Mary's taste. James, thirteen, was too juvenile.

To escape, she amused herself by wandering the streets; Butte, with a population of well over thirty thousand, was more than twice the size of Great Falls and open for almost anything. The legislature had just passed a bill closing down its colorful gambling casinos, but there were still more than 250 bars, seven theaters, and nearly as many dance halls, most of which seemed to run twenty-four hours a day.

Someone was building a stylish new batch of cribs named the Blue Range in the red-light district. Just a few blocks north, the Catholics had invested $25,000 in an ornate cathedral, a theater entrepreneur had begun construction on the New Grand Opera House, and cornerstones had been laid for a new high school and the Montana State School of Mines. There were giant boarding homes accommodating hundreds of single miners, dozens of hotels, eight grammar schools, twelve churches, almost as many union halls, and about a hundred shops where one could buy anything in the world one wanted, if only one had the money.

Even more fascinating to MacLane were the citizens. Butte, by virtue of its huge labor force, had become one of the most ethnically diverse towns in America with dozens of colorful neighborhoods. Walkerville, in the area where Mary's family lived near the Lexington and Alice mines, was populated by folks pretty much like them. So was the newer settlement of Centerville, south and slightly to the east on their steep hillside. To the south, an ugly sprawl around Anaconda Hill called Dublin Gulch was a preference for the Irish and recently the Slavs, who were even poorer. Across the hill and to the east was Meaderville, home to Welsh and Cornish smelter men and their various clans, more Slavs, and Little Italy. That was a great spot, too, for restaurants and nightclubs, as was the Flat, an open area near the racetrack, just south of the city. And there were dozens more enclaves for the French, the Finns, the Germans, and the Chinese. Most of them preferred to live among their own but mixed and mingled for holiday events, payday weekends on the town, rallies, and riots triggered by unhappy circumstances.

A big explosion had recently killed and injured scores, and a man who lost his leg in the blast had shot dead a banker who owned the warehouse where

Bannack, 1863. COURTESY OF MONTANA HISTORICAL SOCIETY RESEARCH
CENTER—PHOTOGRAPH ARCHIVES, HELENA

A rare photograph of a Butte prostitute. COURTESY OF JAY MOYNAHAN

Hurdy-gurdy dancer, entertainment
particularly popular in the 1870s.

COURTESY OF TIM GORDON

Molly Welch, aka Mary Welsh, aka Josephine Airey, best known as Chicago Joe.

Either a theater company or prostitutes and clients in this 1890s house of ill repute in Helena. PHOTO BY EDWARD REINIG, COURTESY OF MONTANA HISTORICAL SOCIETY RESEARCH CENTER—PHOTOGRAPH ARCHIVES, HELENA

Main Street, Miles City, circa 1890s. PHOTO BY L. A. HOFFMAN, COURTESY OF MONTANA HISTORICAL SOCIETY RESEARCH CENTER—PHOTOGRAPH ARCHIVES, HELENA

Miles City red-light district, thought to be documented by Robert Morrison, whose office was nearby at the turn of the century. COURTESY OF MONTANA HISTORICAL SOCIETY RESEARCH CENTER–PHOTOGRAPH ARCHIVES, HELENA

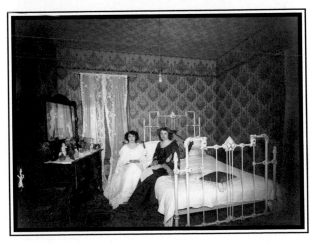

Martha Jane Canary, known as
Calamity Jane, who took time
out from a rough-and-tumble
life to settle tranquilly near
Miles City in 1880. COURTESY OF
MONTANA STATE ARCHIVES

Butte postcard, circa
1890–1900, that job seek-
ers showed immigration
officials to get directions
to the West. COURTESY OF
THE DENVER PUBLIC LIBRARY

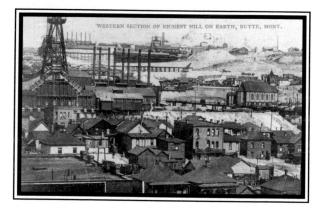

Anna Clark's wedding announcement
in the *Butte Miner*, July 13, 1904.

Wilhelmina Louise Amelia "Andree" Clark (left) and her little sister, Huguette, on a rare outing with their father, William Clark. Hugette, age 103, was still alive in 2011. COURTESY OF MONTANA STATE ARCHIVES

Mary MacLane, a Butte girl who wrote a bestselling, "shocking" book in 1902, and at right a 1917 clipping publicizing her movie, *Men Who Have Made Love to Me.* PHOTO BY J. E. PURDY & COMPANY, BOSTON, 1906, COURTESY OF MONTANA HISTORICAL SOCIETY RESEARCH CENTER—PHOTOGRAPH ARCHIVES, HELENA; COURTESY OF MICHAEL R. BROWN

Mary Cruse, who rechristened herself
"Mamie," circa 1894 and 1898. COURTESY
OF MONTANA HISTORICAL SOCIETY RESEARCH
CENTER—PHOTOGRAPH ARCHIVES, HELENA

Missoula's Jeannette Rankin speaking before a group of suffragettes before
being installed as the first female member of Congress, April 2, 1917.
PHOTO BY C. T. CHAPMAN, COURTESY OF MONTANA HISTORICAL SOCIETY RESEARCH
CENTER—PHOTOGRAPH ARCHIVES, HELENA

the dynamite had been casually stored. An election judge was killed trying to protect a ballot box at a Dublin Gulch precinct, provoking another mob scene. There were battles and bitterness as a number of concerned citizens tried to stop giant Amalgamated Copper from gaining a monopoly on area mines. And silver-tongued William Jennings Bryan drew a huge crowd when he came to defend the silver standard in his campaign to become America's president.

MacLane had no interest in politics but delighted in the street scenes they often provoked.

> There are Irishmen—Kelleys, Caseys, Calahans, staggering under the weight of much whiskey, shouting out their green-isle maxims; there is the festive Cornishman, ogling and leering, greeting his fellow-countrymen with alcoholic heartiness, and gazing after every feminine creature with lustful eyes; there are Irish women swearing genially at each other in shrill peasantry, and five or six loudly vociferous children for each; there are round-faced Cornish women likewise, each with her train of children; there are suave, sleek sporting men just out of the bath-tub; insignificant lawyers, dentists, messenger boys; "pluggers" without number; greasy Italians from Meaderville; greasier French people from Boulevarde Addition; ancient miners—each of whom was the first to strike a claim in Butte; starved-looking China-men here and there; a contingent of Finns and Swedes and Germans; musty, stuffy old Jew pawnbrokers who have crawled out of their holes for a brief recreation; dirt-encrusted Indians and squaws in dirty, gay blankets from their flea-haunted camp below the town; "box rustlers"—who are as common in Butte as bar-maids in Ireland . . .

The opening of the new high school provided MacLane with a chance to broaden her literary skills, which she employed as an editor of its school magazine, and—though considered a bit odd—she managed to make a few friends. Not until her senior year, though, did she find the experience rewarding, and then only because she had fallen in love with her English teacher, a pretty, progressive young woman with steady nerves named Fannie Corbin.

MacLane had never had a boyfriend, nor had she ever been in love before. She was enchanted. She renamed Miss Corbin the "anemone lady," for the "dear blue anemone that grows in the winds and rains of spring." MacLane hung on her every word.

"She used to read poetry in the classroom in a dear, sweet voice that made one wish to stay there forever and listen," MacLane recalled, although she realized her beloved was decidedly different from herself. Corbin believed in the Bible. "Her life is made up mostly of sacrifices—doing for her fellow creatures, giving of herself." She was straight. Yet, miraculously, Fannie became Mary's friend.

"She knows the heavy weight of my unrest and unhappiness. She is tenderly sympathetic," MacLane observed gratefully, not realizing quite how right she was.

At age thirty, Fannie Corbin had grown weary of supporting her widowed mother on the slim salary of a high school teacher. Born and raised on the East Coast, Corbin wanted out of Butte as much as MacLane did. For some time she had been saving every dime she could get her hands on to study at Harvard and would soon earn a degree that allowed to her to become a full professor at the University of Montana.

Corbin's departure, immediately following MacLane's graduation in 1900, nearly broke the girl's heart, and there was worse to follow. Both Mary and her sister, Dolly, had been planning to attend Stanford University. Stoked by Fannie Corbin's literature classes, Mary could hardly wait. But at breakfast on the morning they were ready to depart, their stepfather confessed he had gambled away all their funding. It was a blow from which Mary MacLane would never recover.

Dolly, as usual, did the practical thing, qualifying for a job at the Butte library. Mary applied for another position there but messed up the required exam, ignoring most of the questions to write a clever essay. Rejected, she was disinclined to apply elsewhere. Were she a man, she would have been encouraged to challenge the world. A woman was expected to wait until life came to her, most generally in the form of a family-approved suitor. So, homebound, occupied by only a few modest household chores her mother assigned, Mary lived vicariously through books borrowed from the very same library that had rejected her, investing her restless energy in long, solitary hikes. The surrounding landscape, unsettled buttes and valleys, treeless, defoliated by the fetid air, came to fascinate her. Their near desert state—"sand and barrenness," she called it—seemed to match her weary little soul.

It took just three months of this odd existence for a new option to occur to MacLane. The idea presented itself at the library, where she discovered the diary of Marie Bashkirtseff, a talented Russian-born painter who became the toast of Paris before her death of tuberculosis at twenty-five. *I Am the Most Interesting Book of All: The Diary of Marie Bashkirtseff*, published just two years earlier, was a highly egotistical boast focused on the author's desire for love and a magnificent career. Bashkirtseff's work was bold, often unflattering, and harsh toward men.

"Let us love dogs, Let us love only dogs!" she had insisted. "Men and cats are unworthy creatures."

MacLane, who thought along the same lines, wondered if an American variation on the book might also be as popular, and on January 13, 1901, she sat down to write one.

"I, of womankind and of nineteen years, will now begin to set down as full and frank a Portrayal as I am able of myself, Mary MacLane, for whom the world contains no parallel," she began in a startling preview of what the reader was in for.

"I am convinced of this, for I am odd.

"I am distinctly original innately and in development.

"I have in me a quite unusual intensity of life.

"I can feel.

"I have a marvelous capacity for misery and for happiness.

"I am broad-minded.

"I am a genius . . ."

She was up-front about her reasons for writing the book, too.

"I wish to acquire that beautiful benign, gentle, satisfying thing—Fame. I want it—oh, I want it!" she confessed in her second entry. "I wish to leave all my obscurity, my misery—my weary unhappiness—behind me forever. . . . I want to write—to write such things as compel the admiring acclamations of the world at large; such things as are written but once in years, things subtly but distinctly different from the books written every day."

With a sophistication well beyond her years and the tolerance of the stifling world in which she was trapped, she explored everything from kinky sex with the devil and bisexuality to suicide, providing provocative detail on her faltering struggle to find happiness in a backwater.

"My waiting, waiting soul burns with but one desire: to be loved—Oh, to be loved," she pleaded in an adolescent wail. Yet so subtle was her depiction of a typical bathroom scene to illustrate her family loathing that the vitriol of it goes to the gut.

"The sight of these tooth-brushes day after day, week after week, and always, is one of the most crushingly maddening circumstances in my fool's life," she wrote following a cunning little description of each of the six brushes hanging in her family's bathroom, and concluding:

"But I live in a house with people who affect me mostly through their tooth-brushes—and those I should like, above all things, to gather up and pitch out the bath-room window—and oh, damn them, *damn* them!"

Equally startling was the beauty she was capable of creating, as when she discussed her thoughts of the anemone lady.

"There were skies of spangled sapphires, and there were lilies, and violets wet with dew. There was the music of violins, and wonderful weeds from the deep sea, and songs of troubadours, and gleaming white statues. There were ancient forests of oak and clematis vines; there were lemon-trees, and fretted palaces, and moss-covered old castles with moats and drawbridges and tiny mullioned windows with diamond panes."

MacLane ended her journal entries on April 13, edited the mass, and on October 28 added "L'Envoi" (a conclusion) explaining that this represented her "three months of Nothingness."

Totally dependent on her stepfather for support, she had also written that she longed for the power and resolution to take her life into her own hands.

"What else is there for me if not this book?" she concluded.

Thirty-six-year-old Lucy Monroe, a manuscript reader for publisher Herbert Stone in Chicago, had already taken her own life in hand when MacLane's bulky manuscript landed on her desk. For starters, Monroe went by her mother's maiden name. Her father, a lawyer, was a well-recognized intellectual, but it was her mother, a poorly educated Chicago socialite, who had seen to it that her three daughters received the best schooling available to women despite the family's dwindling fortune. With a successful journalistic career already behind her, Monroe had been responsible for Stone's publication of Kate Chopin's novel *The Awakening*, which graphically depicted female sexuality and its freethinking heroine's fight to live on her own terms in their stuffy Edwardian society. Monroe knew a bestseller when she saw one, and, although she was about to give up her job to become wife of the American ambassador to China, she was determined to add MacLane's book to the list.

While publisher Stone vetoed Mary's blasphemous title, *I Await the Devil's Coming*, he agreed with Monroe's assessment of the book's selling potential. Renaming it *The Story of Mary MacLane—by Herself*, but making few other major changes, he immediately sent the book to market, creating a firestorm of controversy. H. L. Mencken, one of the nation's foremost critics, saw the author as a "puritan wooed and tortured by the leers of beauty." But he also recognized her extraordinary skill, noting that he knew of no other woman writer who could play upon words more magically. A snippy *New York Times* reviewer observed it was scarcely surprising that such trash would come from a Chicago publishing house, New York being the only civilized site of such endeavor. Yet the public purchased one hundred thousand copies in the very first month of publication.

MacLane received scant praise in her hometown, where most were incensed at her grim portrayal. She had, after all, proclaimed Butte so ugly it was the "near perfection of ugliness. . . . For mixture, for miscellany—variedness, Bohemianism—where is Butte's rival?" she had asked.

"And so this is Butte, the promiscuous—the Bohemian. And all these are the Devil's playthings. They amuse him, doubtless. Butte is a place of sand and barrenness. The souls of these people are dumb."

The *Butte Miner* found her pathetic, decrying the "insane craving for sensationalism manifested by some of the eastern press in the case of this unfortunate Butte girl," and adding that the town "ought to offset the popular impression by proving that freak productions of a doubtful character do not constitute our highest ideals."

The Butte Public Library, which had unknowingly inspired the book, banned it. The author's only defenders were theater owner John Maguire, writing for the *Anaconda Standard*, and the *Red Lodge Picket*, which protested the library ban, noting that "in the same way Shakespeare could be expurgated, many of the poets condemned, and even the Bible kept from good society."

Dozens of desperate young things, eight in Butte alone, were reported to be writing similar tell-all tales. Taken by MacLane's lengthy references to suicide, the national press linked the book to several attempts by young girls with similar frustrations. But MacLane, who had earned $17,000 in her first month of royalties and was suddenly swamped with offers of jobs on theater and lecture circuits, and money for endorsements, voiced no concern. With unexpected support from her much maligned family, she embarked on an eastbound train on July 5, 1902.

Untraveled, unaware of the differences in cultures between East and West, and only nineteen, MacLane was a prime candidate to be broadsided by the press. But she chose to camp in safe havens, beginning as a guest of Lucy Monroe in Chicago. Unexpectedly homesick, she displayed little interest in sightseeing, in talking with her brilliant hostess, or even in viewing the fine paintings proudly displayed in the family mansion. In fact, MacLane spent most of her time in the kitchen with their Irish cook, whom she would later claim was the most interesting person she met on the trip.

She was, however, romantically overwhelmed by Lucy's forty-one-year-old sister, Harriet, a striking beauty and highly successful poet. Originally shy and retiring, Harriet had found her stride while a student at Visitation Convent in Washington, D.C., and was soon to launch *Poetry*, one of the most successful literary magazines in America. Her knack for spotting and nurturing literary talent would eventually earn her the title Patron Saint of American Poets, and she quickly put their disoriented guest at ease. In thanks, MacLane dedicated a poem to her that read in part:

> You were so fascinating that day. You were so strong. You were so true,
> Particularly you were so true.
> I loved you.

I had infinite faith in you.
And you were kind . . .

Nerves somewhat bolstered, Mary visited Fannie Corbin's younger sister, Clara, who had also been a teacher in Butte before escaping to Buffalo, New York. Then, proceeding to Boston for a reunion with Fannie at Harvard Summer School, Mary broached the possibility of her own admission to Radcliffe. Their relationship was somewhat dampened when Fannie later told reporters she didn't think the girl was quite ready for the Ivy Leagues, but that became a moot point when Montana papers reported Radcliffe had closed its doors to Mary. The rejection "was no insult to Miss MacLane [but] rather an admission of the excessive stupidity which educated asses display upon the slightest provocation," a Missoula journalist observed. "Miss MacLane needs no more education except that which can be secured by travel and observation."

Meanwhile the public was clamoring to learn more about the young writer, so the *New York World* sent Zona Gale, one of its top reporters, to Cambridge to spend two days with Mary.

"First, she is exceedingly pretty—far prettier than her pictures," Gale began. "Mary MacLane, alert for the coming of the Devil, looks like a Madonna, and a pot of sweet lavender and a fall of old lace. Mary MacLane is not little. She is tall—5 feet and 6 inches, really—and she has a pretty figure and a well-set head."

Her hair, dark with brown shadows, was her chief glory. She was blue-eyed, her features small and delicate, Gale observed, adding that she had a childlike charm.

"Her eyes alone are old, and 'her eyelids are a little weary.' Yet, curiously enough, her sudden far-away look, the droop of her mouth sometimes, and even her direct gaze, are more childish tiredness than ennui."

For the most part, Gale let MacLane do the talking, congratulating herself on her talents as a wordsmith in a nonstop brag, reading her favorite passages from *The Story of Mary MacLane*—the parts about the Gray Dawn and an Italian woman peddler.

Asked what she would do if given any choice in the world, MacLane replied she would like to be a happy wife and mother, but added that she never would be. Nor did she look forward to a long life, she said. But even more unsettling was the dialogue Gale recorded at the end of their luncheon after the server arrived with their check:

"Waiter," said Miss MacLane, "will you match me for the tip?"

"Madam?" said the waiter.

"Will you match me for the tip?" she asked.

"But yes, Madam," he complied. The first quarter he lost; the second time he won them both.

Like her stepfather, who had gambled away her college tuition, MacLane was addicted to the thrill of a coin toss, although no one except Zona Gale seemed to take much notice at the time. Impressed with the interview, as well as *The Story of Mary MacLane*, the *New York World* hired the Montana girl to write a series of features exploring the East Coast—everything from wealthy Newport, where she attended a posh wedding, to Coney Island and its anything-but-posh delights. Settling in Greenwich Village, Mary enjoyed the work, her notoriety as a writer, and running with famous people.

But her second book, *My Friend Annabel Lee*, though written in the same style as the first, was considered tame by comparison and failed to generate much enthusiasm in 1903. Two subsequent attempts failed to pass Mary's inspection, so she tossed them, meanwhile wasting her time and resources by living high.

MacLane's return to her family in Butte after nine years on the East Coast was viewed with puzzlement by the press of her day, but her motivation in light of subsequent research seems clear. She had squandered more than $30,000 in book royalties and freelance money, much of it at a favorite gambling casino in St. Augustine, Florida. She had also developed a taste for gin and broadened her sexual horizons to include men, dozens of them. If the devil she earlier claimed she yearned to marry had ever appeared, it was only to steal the creative muse who had been her liberator. MacLane hoped that by returning to the place where she had done her best work she might recapture it.

—————⊷—————

In contrast to both MacLane and Anna LaChapelle, Mary "Mamie" Cruse was born into a life of endless silver spoons on December 15, 1887, in Helena,

Montana. Her father, fifty-one at the time, was the nouveau riche mining man Tom Cruse, who would soon become one of the wealthiest men in America. Although he had immigrated from Ireland dirt poor at age twenty, he had an innate sense of style and was determined to have nothing but the best once he could afford it. This included Margaret Carter, the twenty-four-year-old sister of Thomas Henry Carter, who was a high-profile Helena lawyer with a real political future.

Despite their age difference and the fact that the blue-eyed girl was charming, Margaret was more than just a trophy bride. She had met Tommy when she first arrived in Helena to live with her brother, in the days when the prospector was desperate for funding to develop his claim northwest of town. It was his habit to spend three months at a time out there digging exploratory tunnels, returning to town only briefly for supplies. He'd been at it so long with no results, most residents, knowing nothing of hard-rock mining, figured he was unbalanced.

What they didn't know was that he was negotiating to sell his mine to a huge British company for millions with the help of Colonel Hugh McQuaid, editor of the *Helena Independent*, as his agent. McQuaid had never done anything of the sort before. In fact, the newsman's chief claim to fame was that he had been the reporter who broke the story of Custer's massacre to the nation. Yet the two were confident they could pull off the sale. Margaret, who had recently attended college and was interested in geology, actually took the time to listen to Cruse and offered to help. She was, in fact, the only one besides McQuaid who had faith in him.

Although the girl's family appeared to be well off, Margaret had a keen appreciation of poverty. Her parents had been Irish patriots who escaped to a farm in Illinois. When she was only eight, for reasons unexplained, they left her and her eleven-year-old brother, John, in the care of their sister, Julia, then fourteen, while sixteen-year-old Thomas undertook their support by working on the railroad, teaching school, and later selling books. Finally successful as a lawyer, Thomas Carter had managed to save the $5,000 he needed to move them all to Helena, Montana, in 1882. Like Cruse, the Carters were Irish and ardent Catholics. Thomas Carter was a Republican, while Cruse was a Democrat, but Carter had recently allied with Cruse and Copper Kings

Marcus Daly and William Clark, and Margaret decided to make a democratic alliance of her own.

The wedding of Tommy and Margaret, staged March 2, 1886, at the cost of $30,000 under the direction of Hugh McQuaid, was boycotted by many of the town's society matrons. Elizabeth Fisk, wife of an editor for the *Helena Herald*, explained she was offended by the age difference in the couple, but in truth they were nobodies. Not only the Carter girl and that old derelict Cruse, but the best man was a store clerk, and the matron of honor lived on a farm. But Tommy and Margaret could not have cared less as they pledged their troth before Bishop Brondel in the Cathedral of Sacred Heart—she in cream-colored silk trimmed with Spanish lace and he in his Prince Albert cut-away. City officials had declared a holiday in their honor, closing banks, courts, and offices. The lavish reception at the Cosmopolitan Hotel was open to what the Fisk's paper referred to sarcastically as an "unexclusive" guest list. Anyone not a guest was invited to drink on Cruse at a local bar of their choice, resulting in a public bacchanal so spectacular that Mrs. Fisk briefly revived the temperance crusade she'd pioneered earlier to address such problems.

Cruse postponed their European honeymoon to successfully launch a bank that spring, but the couple continued to entertain in style. Superstitious about living in a house he had built for himself, Cruse had purchased a twenty-two-room mansion from one of the town's leading merchants in the posh section of town, although their guest lists remained "unexclusive." The celebration lasted until December, when Margaret gave birth to daughter Mary in a seemingly easy delivery but lapsed into an unidentified illness that took her life eleven days later. According to one newspaper, she had succumbed to "intense nervous prostration," something those who knew her tended to doubt. Another account said that an overdose of medicine had sent her on her way. Cruse was reported to be "almost prostrated" with grief, but could anyone be sure? Was he disappointed not to have had a son?

Mary Cruse grew into a winsome little blond girl with a stubborn but sensuous mouth, wide eyes, arched brows, and a profile any Roman would have been proud of. Smitten, Cruse took her with him whenever he could, including visits every evening to the Montana Club—the millionaires' haven to which he had been admitted even without elite society approval— where he let her dance on the bar and gave her occasional sips of crème de menthe. He also allowed her to raise hell in church, much to the consternation of other parishioners. But Cruse was too busy running his mining ventures, overseeing his bank, buying ranchland, and investing in oil exploration to give the child as much time as she needed. Then, worried that Mary might be kidnapped, he installed a high iron fence around the mansion to keep her from others, including her mother's family.

Since she was not allowed to attend school, the only companions Mary had during her early years were Tommy's two nieces, both in their twenties, for whom she appeared to bear little affection. Mary Cruse Rae served as the family hostess. Rose Sheehey filled the post of governess and jailer. Two nephews in their thirties, sons of Cruse's brother William, kept them company along with the cook, a maid, a housekeeper, and the coachman. When the girl was about ten, Cruse finally invited neighboring youngsters over to play. One of them, Lester Loble, who grew up to become a judge, recalled that the beautiful little child had everything he'd ever dreamed of for toys, including a pony and cart, but that she was anything but happy.

Finally, in 1891, Cruse took her to New York City to show her off to the world at large. Camped at the Waldorf-Astoria Hotel, he fielded half a dozen interviews, garnering headlines like "'A Little Girl,' but Heir to Millions" and "She Is but 13 Years Old, but has $10,000,000—Will Inherit $40,000,000 More—She Has a Number of Relatives Residing on Washington Hill."

"That little girl is the richest heiress in America," a *New York Times* reporter observed in awe. "Yet she is scarcely known in New York."

Mary's uncle Thomas Carter, now a senator, and her mother's sister, Julia Carter Larson, made cameo appearances but were quite outnumbered by the children and grandchildren of Cruse's two brothers. It was Mary, however, who was the focus of interest, despite the fact that she uttered not one quotable word.

She looked mature for her age, with her golden curls mellowing to brown, but Cruse had outfitted her as a juvenile with short skirts, frills, ribbons, and silly flowered hats. He didn't approve of "little girls dressing too old before their time," he explained. Nor was he about to let her make her own mistakes.

Once Mary reached high school age, Cruse did let her out of the house to attend St. Vincent Academy, a few blocks away. It was, however, a girls' school, and, as the Catholic Church's biggest donor in Helena and perhaps all of Montana, the worried father was certain the nuns would keep a firm hand on his restive daughter. Yet despite his best efforts, Mary Cruse renamed herself Mamie and began to make friends on her own. She became an expert equestrian, riding like a cowboy instead of sidesaddle and winning local competitions. Named Floral Queen for Helena's Fourth of July parade, she presided with grace and charm garbed in a ridiculous dress decorated with three thousand pink roses. And, somewhere along the way, she fell deeply in love with an upstanding citizen who adored her. She was only seventeen, and he was young, too. Realizing it would be futile to seek permission from her father, they eloped but got no farther than Elliston, about twenty miles from Helena, when Cruse dragged Mary back home.

Since the last thing the old man wanted was for Mary to marry a local, he consigned her to Visitation Convent in Washington, D.C., the very same college where poet Harriet Monroe had found her voice. But Mamie was looking for love, something she couldn't expect to find in another Catholic girls' school. Eventually she kicked up such a fuss that Cruse sent her to Miss Finch's School, much favored as a hunting ground for husbands by New York's debutante set, where she met Alvar De Comeau O'Brien at a reception. A Princeton graduate who had played quarterback for his college team, Alvar was the son of the former president of the Mercantile Trust Company of New York and a partner in a Wall Street brokerage firm until he quit to follow Mamie back to Montana because he was crazy about her. He was Irish. He was Catholic. He was twenty-four, and she, at twenty-two, was over the age of consent, so her father couldn't just say no. According to one report, the wedding was performed in the cathedral at St. Paul, Minneapolis, and the heiress was worth about $10,000,000.

Following a two-month honeymoon in France, Italy, and Switzerland, the couple settled into New York's Waldorf-Astoria and then the Knickerbocker after Tom Cruse cut off Mamie's $250,000 annual allowance. There were, it seemed, two problems. Alvar refused to get a job, and his father-in-law hated him. Within a year, Cruse made it clear that he would cut his daughter out of his will unless she divorced O'Brien.

"It was following a series of discussions at the Waldorf-Astoria that Mrs. O'Brien accompanied by her uncle, William Cruse, left this city on Feb. 14 to go home to her father," the *New York Times* reported on March 31, 1911. "Mrs. O'Brien had been ill for a week before her departure and Dr. Hill, a nerve specialist, and a nurse went west with her."

Whether Cruse had the girl drugged for the homeward trip is not known. He would later testify that Mamie had a drinking problem, but it seems odd that after just a few months of marriage she went from being a strong, healthy championship horsewoman to someone who required the assistance of a doctor and nurse for a cross-country trip. O'Brien followed her, securing a job as a cowboy on a neighboring ranch, but to no avail. At the divorce hearing, which he did not protest, Mamie dutifully testified that O'Brien had refused to support her, thus saving her inheritance.

In October of that year Mamie made one more attempt at respectability, eloping with Harry C. Cotter, a well-liked thirty-five-year-old Butte miner who came from a wealthy family. Cruse refused to recognize the union, however, on the grounds that a divorced woman could never remarry in the eyes of the Church and that the ceremony was also illegal because Mamie had failed to wait two years after the divorce as required by a law few others had heard of. Eventually the old man forced her to abandon Cotter as he had O'Brien, at which point the emotionally battered twenty-five-year-old fled to Butte, where she embarked on what later was described as a "life of dissipation."

"She would take the side of Hell against me any time," her father declared.

Although vastly different in background and temperament, Anna LaChapelle, Mary MacLane, and Mamie Cruse had three things in common:

Each defied the restrictive standards of their times to pursue a seemingly impossible dream and won, happily escaping Montana in the process.

Each prostituted herself—Anna to an old man who was cold, Mary to a lifestyle she couldn't handle, and Mamie to her father's wealth.

And each found herself back in Montana within five years, seeking a new way out.

The unexpected death of Anna LaChapelle's mother in 1896 added to the bitterness of her return to a town that paid token homage to her talents and wealth while snickering behind her back. Worse, Butte meant long nights under the erotic paintings that her aging but still super-active husband had commissioned on the ceiling of his master bedroom. Having gone public, calling their marriage "a pretty romance," the senator could hardly patronize Butte's better whorehouses with his former zeal, and he demanded sexual novelty. Nor would there be much respite when Anna convinced him to purchase a seacoast villa in Santa Barbara, California, or even in residence at the New York mansion where Clark finally allowed her to visit when his first family boycotted it as an ostentatious monstrosity.

Kathlyn Williams, the beautiful young woman Clark had sent to school in New York City just before he fathered Andree, had become one of Hollywood's most successful actresses. Then there was the pain of watching her sister Amelia marry for love—twice—with plenty of action during the intermissions. Still a beautiful woman herself, Anna also had ample chances to explore, but she was forced to consider her spying stepchildren and the possibility that William Clark might one day confess publicly that he had never honored her with a marriage certificate. Cautiously, it would appear, Anna LaChapelle Clark invested all her love in her daughters, so that the death of Andree, the oldest, at nineteen was nearly a mortal blow. The girl had been William Clark's favored child. Her death lessened whatever fragile bond the couple had. From that point on, Anna turned to Hugette, her youngest, babying the girl to the point that Hugette refused to consummate her marriage to a socially prominent New York man. Instead she fled back to her mother, at whose side she remained until Anna's death in 1963 at age eighty-five.

Anna LaChapelle Clark departed this earth a very wealthy woman, eulogized for her devotion to the arts and for her philanthropy. Among other good causes, she had subsidized the Paganini Quartet with its Stradivarius violins in Santa Barbara and the Loewenguth Quartet of Brussels, and she also dumped $700,000 into the Corcoran Gallery of Art in Washington, D.C. Butte, Montana, never made the list.

True to her prediction, Mary MacLane never wed.

"[L]ove of any kind (except the long-suffering affection of one's own family) is a thing of countless cross purposes of corroding and cankering self-torture," she explained, "and an endless chain of jealousy—jealousy in every possible form and hue; so that each love that comes into one's life is like, despite its encompassing fascinations, a wan little bit of hell."

Nor, despite nine more years of trying in Butte, did the writer ever recapture her muse. While her third and final book, *I, Mary MacLane*, was better received than the second, it never came close to her bestseller, perhaps because her life had paled. When not attempting to eke out a living as a freelance writer, Mary spent much of her time seeking amusing company at local roadhouses and—if rumors are to be believed—at dens of prostitution, where her role was not clearly defined.

Finally she abandoned Butte for Chicago, then host to a healthy motion picture industry, where she wrote and starred in a film titled *Men Who Have Made Love to Me*. At thirty-seven she was a sultry beauty. Her director praised her acting ability and the Ohio Board of Censors cooperated by banning the film. But it would be MacLane's last public appearance aside from her arrest for stealing some dresses in 1919. She beat that rap but not rumors that she had become a prostitute following her court appearance wearing nothing but an embroidered Japanese kimono and a feathered hat. How she supported herself thereafter is open for conjecture, but she was alone when she died in a rented room on the fringe of Chicago's poorest district in August 1929, surrounded by her press clippings. Her stepfather had committed suicide four years earlier, and there was some thought she might have followed the same course.

"It's not Death I fear, nor life," she had written in her last book. "I horribly fear something this side of Death but out-passing life a little: a nervousness in my Stomach—a very Muddy Street—a lonely Hotel Room."

Like MacLane, Mamie Cruse sought solace in Butte's roadhouses and bordellos, finding grim joy in the knowledge that her father and his entourage of Catholic bishops would hear about it and become apoplectic. What she hadn't counted on was Cruse's violent reaction to the damage he perceived she was causing to their family name. A hero to many, Cruse had guaranteed the building of the new state capitol by purchasing $350,000 worth of bonds to help pay for it, and he had recently donated more than half the money needed for completion of an ostentatious new cathedral for Helena. Then there was the even more pressing matter of saving his daughter's soul, which would surely be doomed if he couldn't get control of her.

So it was with a perfectly clear conscience in the fall of 1912 that Cruse hired night sergeant Jim Barnes of the Helena police department to kidnap Mamie from Butte and take her to Helena's House of the Good Shepherd, the Catholic facility for wayward girls and prostitutes. Barnes would later testify that he located Mamie early in the morning at a roadhouse about a mile out of Butte and took her to a hotel in that city and later to the police station, although he had no warrant for her arrest. She caused him no trouble on the return to Helena but made "strenuous objection" when he delivered her to the church facility where the nuns imprisoned her.

The Good Shepherd staff and numerous cousins employed by Cruse tried to pressure Mamie into signing a will leaving all her worldly goods to her father, but she refused.

"Tom, here is my will," her second cousin Tom Sweeney quoted her as saying. "I want you to sign it." Yet the document was finally signed in her hand, with Tom Cruse insisting he knew nothing of it until after her death of undisclosed causes a month later.

Police officer Barnes, who had captured Mrs. Cotter, recalled "she had declared emphatically that she never wanted to see her father again." But even that wish was denied when, ten days before her death, Cruse dragged her home where he could keep an eye on her.

One year later Mamie's widower, Harry Cotter, sued Tom Cruse over the will, testifying he looked frantically for his wife following her mysterious disappearance and had been told by the mother superior of Good Shepherd that Mamie was not there. The good mother insisted she was just following convent rules, and Cruse slammed the widower with the testimony of half a dozen nieces and nephews, all on his payroll, who claimed the girl had been happy with the sisters. Cruse had placed her there because Mamie was addicted to drink and a frequent visitor to roadhouses, he told the court.

Mary Cruse Rae, once the family hostess and still in Cruse's hire, testified at length about how she had journeyed to Reno with the girl to help her obtain a quickie divorce, although only Rae had visited the lawyer. But it was probably Miss Catherine O'Shea, billed "a nurse and companion" of Mrs. Cotter, who won the case for the old man.

Ignoring testimony of Tom Sweeney to the contrary, Catherine claimed that Mrs. Cotter had asked her to sign the will for her in the presence of Tom Cruse and that she had been a witness. The dead girl often spoke in harsh terms when referring to her husband, Catherine added. In fact, "the favorite expression of the late Mrs. Mary Margaret Cotter was 'dog,' when referring to her husband," the newspaper noted in its lead, covering the final day of the hearing.

Only later, in reading over the inventory of the jewelry that Tom Cruse inherited from his daughter's estate, might one pause to rethink the real meaning of O'Shea's final charge that Mamie referred to her husband as a "dog." Keeping in mind that the deceased, a beautiful and sophisticated woman, aged twenty-six, had a low threshold for boredom, one might note that the most expensive piece of jewelry in her collection was a diamond and platinum dog collar valued at $25,000. And that next on the list were a five-foot platinum leash and a braided coral rope measuring four feet, six inches, serving the same function.

7

REFLECTION

1900

The new millennium was off to a splendid start; anything was possible. Morning sun pushed through the leaded crystal skylight of the Dumas, causing the dark wainscoting of the bordello's open inner court to gleam and spotlighting the magnificently crafted central stairway that descended to the ballroom below. Not bright sun, of course. On the best of days, smoke from the roaring smelters of Butte muted the light.

"The ladies are very fond of this smoky city, as it is sometimes called, because there is just enough arsenic there to give them a beautiful complexion," William Clark, the industrialist, maintained with a straight face. It was also smoke that had the potential to make everybody rich, just as it had the Copper King. Which is why they all put up with it.

Grace McGinnis, the Dumas's German-born manager, had been considering her relationship with Clark, a definite friend of her establishment, and with the Dumas's owner, Joseph Nadeau, a French Canadian who had risen from pimping to become one of Butte's wealthy social lions. Both had helped make the town's red-light district America's second largest, and Grace was in a key position to benefit. She had just turned thirty-seven, but no one would guess. Maybe there was something to the therapeutic value of the arsenic haze. With luck, it would ensure her future.

Butte, incorporated twenty-two years earlier but still rough hewn, remained starkly isolated despite its connections with three major railroads. Perched on a sky-high volcano cone in the Rockies, it was blacked by excessive open-hearth smelting and political corruption. Nevertheless, it had become the largest urban center between Spokane and Minneapolis–St. Paul, with a population of nearly fifty thousand taking home about $1 million a month. Since men outnumbered women by a wide margin, prostitution was a given. And since many of those men had suddenly become rich well beyond the wildest American dream, Butte offered unprecedented opportunities for a high-class madam with guts enough to tackle the frontier.

The Dumas had been built a decade earlier in the very best section of the town's tenderloin. The exterior of the two-story brick structure was cleverly designed to look like a high-end boarding house, a protective façade that belied both use and content. The interior's embossed and gilded plaster walls with expensive wood paneling were worthy of a mansion, as were its trappings—satin and velvet upholstered furniture and draperies, fine paintings, statuary of tasteful nudes, sparkling mirrors, and recently electrified Tiffany lamps.

The four nubile goddesses in residence occupied elegantly seductive bedrooms on the top floor, each with a splendid bed and an armoire bulging with expensive Parisian gowns. Each room had its own plumbed washstand, with easy access to a communal but state-of-the-art bathroom accessible via the open court. Each had electric communications with which to summon servants bearing champagne and caviar for guests who sought more privacy than the silver- and crystal-embellished dining room on the first floor, or who tired of dancing and conversation in the well-appointed parlors that led to it.

The madam's airy ground-floor sitting room, graced by tall bay windows, was strategically placed near the front door, with an excellent view of Mercury Street, which often proved useful. This morning, however, she'd secluded herself in a small adjacent alcove that featured the little Queen Anne desk where she kept the books. Usually she attacked the job wearing a lacy silk dressing gown, but today she had chosen a stylish morning suit of fine blue wool with a fitted bodice, a high neck trimmed with modest frills, and a plain but elegantly gored skirt. Her hair was dressed in a tidy chignon. The matronly fashion made her look older than she was, but that would be a plus in talking business.

Receipts from the night before had been near record due in part to William Clark, who was making his second try at Montana's U.S. Senate seat and had been entertaining important constituents. The legislature had voted him in earlier, but when the election was contested in Washington on the grounds that the Montanan had bribed his way to victory, he'd prudently resigned, figuring he could make another run at it.

"I never bought a man who wasn't for sale," he argued.

Clark was a cool, tough, immaculately groomed little man. A former schoolteacher from the East, he made his Western stake laboring in Colorado mines and driving a team of oxen over the rough trail between Salt Lake City and Bannack to peddle trading goods to gold camps. He was as ruthless as he was ambitious, with scant sense of humor. Most people disliked him including the Dumas girls, who were uncomfortable with some of the sexual habits he'd picked up in France, but he had befriended Grace when she first came from Chicago to work for Nadeau two years earlier. She valued his support, and she actually felt sorry for him.

Although Clark would soon become one of the richest men in America, if he wasn't already, he'd lost two of his six children and his wife within the last few years and his lot did not seem to be a happy one. He wanted to be liked and could be generous. The previous night, with considerable flourish, he had presented her with an exquisite painting of a nude that he'd just picked up in Europe. Clark had long hoped to be recognized as a discriminating art collector, and his taste was certainly improving. She'd hung the treasure with equal ceremony in the main parlor. Now she added it to her listing of the establishment's business assets, wondering how best to thank him. Perhaps with the darkly beautiful Anna King, whose parents came from Asia. She was from New Orleans, and her erotic skills certainly provoked more interest than those of her peers.

For some reason, perhaps because he had the humor Clark lacked, Joseph Nadeau had put the name of his social-climbing wife, Delia, on the deed of the Dumas, although Grace had never met the woman. In addition to a number of respectable enterprises, the family owned more red-light property than any other landlord in Butte, including some low-class "female boarding houses" and a smattering of thoroughly disreputable cribs. But at least the Nadeaus were honest about it. Other owners usually acquired title through some front man, while the Nadeaus appointed their streetwise son, Ovila, and Harry Adams, a German bartender, to make theirs a quasi-legal operation by personally paying off city officials. It was Ovila, known as the "Tsar of Butte's red-light district," with whom Grace mostly dealt, but this morning old Joe himself was coming to discuss her operation's future.

Happily, she should be able to convince him it was assured. Of course the Dumas didn't gross as much as the neighboring Richelieu, a small castle that rivaled Butte's handsomest private mansions, boasting three stories and twenty-four rooms. But that establishment had recently acquired a new madam, a thirty-nine-year-old veteran of French descent from Louisiana named Bertie Leslie, and changed its name to the Windsor in a thinly veiled attempt to shore up a tarnished reputation. But because Bertie had eight inmates to support, plus a lover at least ten years her junior, Grace suspected the Windsor was showing a smaller profit than the Dumas, with a greater potential for management disasters.

The Victoria, run by Lou Harpell, was their toughest competition. In fact, Lou's place was the only other high-class house that worried McGinnis. Like herself, Harpell limited her inmates to four and charged outrageous prices. However, trading on her legendary reputation from Chicago, where she'd once been queen of the tenderloin, Harpell successfully billed her harlots as "the most beautiful women in the world," openly advertising in theater and race track programs. In addition, she had the backing of Marcus Daly, who, having sold his huge Anaconda Mining Company in a cozy deal to the Standard Oil monopoly, had become the most powerful man in the state. Next to William Clark, he was also the richest, but that proved a plus because the two men hated each other. Clark was not about to patronize any Daly operation, and Augustus Fritz Heinze, the newest of Butte's Copper Kings, was of a like mind. The Dumas was their first choice, although the handsome young Heinze was a real womanizer and also bedded occasional high-society women along with girls from the cheaper houses and cribs.

Still, Butte was producing one-fourth of the world's copper. With the growing popularity of electricity and the telephone, there was a seemingly endless demand for copper wire and no lack of rich speculators in Butte trying to get in on the action. More than enough carriage trade to go around, Grace McGinnis decided, although she hedged her bets and she was guessing Joe Nadeau was of like mind.

Back of the Dumas was Pleasant Alley, long the trawling spot for overage prostitutes and Butte's few Japanese and black women who had no place else to solicit. Now dozens of independent prostitutes, some of them young and good-looking, were settling into the grim little street in flimsy cribs built by enterprising businessmen. Rent was generally about five dollars per day, not much but it would add up if Nadeau wanted to add some more impressive rentals onto the back of the Dumas. He would do better yet if he allowed her to staff them. Grace didn't think it would damage the Dumas's reputation. In fact, it would be a plus for patrons who yearned to go slumming in safe places.

Considering her percentage of additional revenues, Grace figured that if Nadeau agreed, she might get out of this god-awful city a year earlier than she had originally planned, but she didn't have time to do the math this morning. Checking the gold Tiffany watch she wore pinned to her bodice, she noted he would be there in half an hour, and she needed to make certain the house was in order.

Everything was quiet on the top floor, where the girls were getting their beauty rest while their overnight guests slept off their hangovers. A glance out the front window showed East Mercury to be almost as dull, with only a couple of servants out on errands. Foo Lee and Yse Chung, laboring over breakfast in the big basement kitchen, greeted Grace with the happy news that Yse had managed to repair the dumbwaiter, which had broken the evening before ferrying an overload of Montana steaks and fine wines. She collected some stray wine glasses in the parlor and two outrageous masks with dangling beards of human hair. Gentlemen hoping to remain anonymous often requested them and then abandoned them along with all caution as the evening heated up. These were lipstick-smeared but otherwise undamaged. She set them aside for Foo Lee to clean before returning them to their glass display case. Everything was in order. Everything was golden.

Finally, checking her watch, Grace headed slowly to the sub-basement to welcome Nadeau, who was due to arrive via one of the underground tunnels that networked beneath the city to house steam-heating mains. How she hated to go there! To open that door into that eerie, subterranean darkness broken only by a string of small, bare lightbulbs.

It wasn't the tunnel—which provided Dumas patrons with much-needed privacy—but the doorless, open-mouthed caves dug in along the sides, where girls who could afford no better plied their trade on squeaky iron cots. Some brought their pimps to shill for them. Usually, though, they propositioned the passersby themselves, baring most of what they had for sale. The contrast of the Dumas's sunlit rooms and the disgusting degradation of the tunnel whores was unsettling to McGinnis, who so seldom gave thought to the hazards brazened by her sisters in sin.

Joe Nadeau, dressed in his dapper Homburg, dark frock coat, stiff boiled collar, and newly fashionable bow tie, ignored them as he approached her door. As a businessman, he saw the derelict women simply as merchandise. Big on family values and a pillar of his Catholic church, he personally believed a whore was a whore no matter where she worked. But, ever the gentleman, he tipped his Homburg to Miss Grace and followed her up the stairs to his favorite spot in the house, the Queen Anne desk just off her parlor.

"Ovila tells me we're doing well, Miss Grace," he began, dropping his Homburg onto a convenient chair.

"Ovila knows this business. Wait till you see yesterday's books," she said excitedly. "Still, I've thought of a plan that will grow the business, even if copper prices should slide."

And suddenly she had Nadeau's full attention.

8

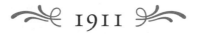

THE BEGINNING OF
THE END

1911

Few women had acquired as much business acumen as Grace McGinnis by the turn of the century, and those who chose legitimate ventures often failed because of legal roadblocks. On paper, Montana's "weaker sex" had gained an impressive number of rights since statehood, including protection against male brutality and mental cruelty. However, getting to court—mustering the money for a fight or surmounting physical restraints like the ones that ended the life of Mamie Cruse—remained a serious problem. Then there was the challenge of actually winning a court case in a corrupt legal system dominated by good old boys. The only fair trial in Butte was one where the fix was in on both sides, a veteran attorney explained.

So there was surprise when Ella Driggs Bordeaux, thirty-one, stood up to her husband, John Bordeaux, forty-seven, when he filed for divorce against her, charging desertion, in 1899. Denying his claims, Mrs. Bordeaux filed a cross complaint citing extreme cruelty and abusive and intimidating behavior and claiming John had walked out.

Ella's father, A. E. Driggs, was a pioneering Butte farmer, and her uncle was none other than William L. Farlin, a tenacious miner who had helped put Butte on the map as a silver camp, which made the family socially prominent. Bordeaux, a relative newcomer from Mississippi, had started his career

with a shabby restaurant on Park Street before becoming rich through mining investments, so he filed an amended complaint adding adultery to his
charges, assuming Ella would back down rather than face the shame of his
accusations. Instead she froze his assets, which she claimed were valued at
$100,000, and asked for $1,500 per month. He hired lawyers that also represented Anaconda, which was busy taking over every mine in town. She hired
the firm that represented Fritz Augustus Heinze; up to that point he had
successfully challenged Anaconda. The judge was William Clancy, a lawman
of questionable ethics who tended to fall asleep unless properly entertained.
The twelve-man jury was made up predominantly of Catholic blue-collar
workers.

According to the first witness, John's friend Robert E. Campbell, Ella had
rendezvoused with Lyman Sisley, a mining broker, in September 1897 at an
unfinished building on West Broadway. Campbell had spied on them because
her husband had requested it, he added.

"They were enjoying each other's company," Campbell testified. "He laid
her down on the bench there, and pulled up her clothing; she had on a
dark suit of underwear; it looked to me like a dark suit of combination
underclothing; from where I was I could see they were in the act of sexual
intercourse."

Then Campbell said he had seen Tom Bordeaux, John's brother, jump up
from under the carpenter's bench to claim he had them dead to rights. At that
point, according to Campbell, Sisley ran from the building while Ella arose,
put on her straw sailor hat, and headed home.

Two other witnesses told a similar story, which Ella's lawyers blew out
of the water by proving that the Broadway house where they claimed the
assignation had taken place had not been built at that time. Unfazed, John
Bordeaux and his troops amended their testimony to say the event had happened in December of that year when, according to the current owner, the
house was finally standing.

Then Bordeaux continued with damaging testimony about what a lacka-
daisical wife Ella had been. The jury agreed. John may well have intimidated
Ella, even beaten her on occasion, but he had provided her with a servant,
jewels valued at $1,350, and a generous allowance and had let her sleep until

11:00 A.M. They ruled against the ungrateful young matron. Her stubborn appeal—all the way up to Montana's Supreme Court, where she lost again—only showed what an obstinate woman she was.

But even the Supreme Court justices conceded that the charges of adultery were pathetic. What upper-middle-class Butte matron would wear dark underwear with a straw sailor hat in September, much less in wintery December, as the amended testimony claimed?

————⊙————

Happily, out of court, women were encountering new freedom because fashion had finally given them increased mobility. Considered shocking just a decade earlier, split skirts and bloomers allowed females to enjoy sports like bicycling, playing tennis, and riding horses astride. Even swimming was condoned as long as there was no vulgar showing of bare flesh, which meant wearing a swimming skirt that fell to the knees and long dark stockings. Corsets were still required, of course. American women were spending $14 million on them annually, and not just for the sake of modesty. Despite the fact that progressive doctors declared them dangerous to the lungs and internal organs, favored artist Charles Dana Gibson depicted the ideal turn-of-the-century woman with a tiny-waisted, amply bosomed hourglass figure that only tight-laced stays could accomplish.

Large leg-o'-mutton sleeves puffed above the elbow, sweeping skirts, at least two petticoats, and drawers below the knee were also required for respectability. Gloves and enormous hats trimmed with flowers, feathers, and stuffed birds were added for outings, although shop and factory girls might resort to easy-to-wash shirtwaists with simple skirts for every day.

And respectable women in the workforce were suddenly high profile. Lured from farms to mill towns and factories with the promise of proper chaperoning and respectable boardinghouses in the early 1800s, armies of them bolstered by waves of immigrants began flooding into urban areas as moral standards relaxed. While only thirty-eight hundred single females were living on their own in Chicago in 1880, more than thirty-one thousand were so engaged by 1900, and government agents—disguised as traveling salesmen, pimps, and madams—scouted major cities including Butte to see how they fared against the forces of evil. The answer in Butte was better than most. Salaries below the cost of living usually drove such women to a life of sin, not white slavers as government agents had feared. Butte boasted the highest wages in America because it had thirty-four trade organizations representing eighteen thousand professions. Women were members, too, for the first time in American history.

In fact, about the only calling not represented was prostitution, a serious oversight. Although it paid considerably better than the rest and ranked as one of Butte's top female livelihoods, it would soon become clear that women who chose it were vulnerable on three fronts. Prostitution was tolerated only on the whim of the city fathers. If women worked without a pimp or madam to protect them, the clients they solicited might also prove dangerous. And, finally, Butte's working girls were at the mercy of their landlords, the vice kings, and liquor distributors whose pricing guide was "all that traffic would bear." The bargaining power of these women lay solely in the need for their services, which grew along with Butte's huge workforce.

But appearances were suddenly a consideration, too. Still very much a mining camp, Butte reveled in its wide-open reputation, but when its predominately male population grew from about ten thousand to more than thirty thousand between 1890 and 1900, and the number of resident whores increased at about the same rate, even the most tolerant citizens became uneasy. While streetwalkers had always had free run of the town, Butte had recently incorporated. The Salvation Army, the Women's Christian Temperance Union, the International Order of Good Templars, and a platoon of local preachers were demanding propriety. Irate businessmen, especially hotel owners, claimed provocatively dressed young women soliciting on or near their premises scared away respectable customers. As for the many whorehouses, dance halls, and ramshackle cribs located in the heart of town, anyone capable of simple math could see the financial gain to be realized if legitimate business replaced them.

The death of Pete Hanson, one of Butte's pioneering vice kings, helped bring the problem into focus. Born in Denmark, Hanson had arrived on the scene from Florida in 1887 with enough capital to open the Clipper Shades, which soon became known as the most dangerous "concert hall" in town. Although genial, Hanson acquired a reputation for drugging and robbing patrons imprudent enough to flash a good wad of cash.

"Ridiculous!" Hanson defended. "If a man drinks intoxicating liquors, you don't have to drug him to make him blow his money. Get him drunk and he'll blow it himself."

But drugging was the least of the offenses lawmen suspected; Clipper Shades came equipped with many bedrooms, and Hanson's reach extended beyond its Park Street location. While his partner, James W. Kennedy, kept a low profile, declaring himself a "miner-promoter," Hanson became known as the King of Galena. His mistress, the beautiful Edith Sommers, was described by local newsmen as "one of the most vicious grafters that ever struck this city." Yet the only successful arrest involving this couple was for running a dance hall.

Even Hanson's death was a disappointment to lawmen. Considering his reputation, his physician refused to sign a death certificate without an inquest, but the cause of death turned out to be natural. Also a shock was the reaction of Hanson's supposedly hard-boiled mistress.

"She has been a woman of rare beauty, but she looked greatly changed as she made her appearance on the witness stand, dressed in deep mourning," the *Anaconda Standard* reported.

"She bore such marked evidence of having experienced a great grief that her good looks seemed gone, and bad as the notorious creature's reputation has painted her, she must have been greatly attached to the former 'King of the Row.'"

City fathers were not. Nor could they tolerate other flesh purveyors over whom they never managed to gain control. But a new breed of vice tsars like Joseph Nadeau and Thomas Stephens were also legitimate businessmen who had everything to gain by limiting prostitution to a restricted district. With increasing property values on Arizona and South Main, the town's two main streets, resulting vacancies there could profitably be exploited.

In April 1901 the *Butte Miner* tackled the subject head-on with the headline "Red Light District Must Find a New District . . . A Festering Sore to the Public Gaze." In case readers missed the point, there followed a subhead:

"Popular Demand That the Denizens of This District Be Ordered by the Proper Authorities to Remove to a More Secluded Quarter of the City."

Since the paper was owned by William Clark, long rumored to be an eager patron of Butte's ladies of the night, the exposé was amusing. However, Clark, more than most, was aware of the growing value of downtown property, and his paper's crusade made economic sense.

"The so-called red light district in Butte, an idea of which can be gained by the accompanying illustrations, occupies a prominent place in the very heart of the city," the editor began. "Its wooden shacks adjoin the business blocks on the main street and half-clad women can be seen skylarking on the sidewalks in plain view of those whose business calls them south of Park Street on Main, Wyoming and Arizona Avenues.

"These women are, as a rule, attired in very abbreviated skirts, and the waists worn by them are so diminutive that a person has to look twice to make sure that it is there," he reported, discussing occupants of the street-facing cribs on Galena. "With an abandon that has no trace of modesty in it, these women lean out their windows and address the vilest kind of language imaginable to people passing on the street, or else boldly make their appearance on the thoroughfare and visit from one crib to another."

Public reaction was mixed. City councilmen began experimenting with ordinances including a decent dress code, required gates for crib-filled alleys, and shaded windows for cribs facing the streets, but they lacked the town's wholehearted support.

Finally, on January 19, 1902, the *Butte Miner* treated residents to a Sunday edition on the issue. While conceding that the social evil could not be eliminated by law, the editor insisted it was still possible to protect the home life and rising property values of Butte's citizens.

"Has Butte—progressive, enterprising, growing city that it is—reached a point when municipal authority crouches in terror and indecision and hopelessness before the influence and self-assertion of the slums, ready to acknowledge—with knees knocking together—that nothing can be done to remove the red-light district from the heart of the city?"

Then, with unusual boldness, the paper featured interviews with local prostitutes who universally refused to move.

"They do not object to being clothed from neck to heels, and do not pro-test against the drawing of blinds during the daytime, but they do object to having the curtains down at night," the reporter noted. "They are willing to obey the mandates of the police department and submit to all restrictions, so long as they are allowed to remain where they are."

As for monthly fines, a system instituted by most other cities but new to Butte, one leader, speaking for the "French colony," offered no objection.

"All of the girls make money, and there is no sporting woman so poor that she cannot afford to pay a fine of $5. It is so small that we do not think of it," she bragged. "The sporting women bring a lot of money to the town and they spend it freely. If it was not for them there would be many stores on Park and other streets which would be unable to dispose of their delicacies. We pay high rent, and it is bosh about our presence depreciating the value of property."

But finally, ignoring all protests, in 1903, city fathers moved all red-light activities out of town to a semi-settled outback between East Galena and Mercury, bordered on the west by South Main and to the east by South Wyo-ming. Already the site of several high-class parlor houses and the Blue Range cribs, the area also included the Copper block, which served as headquarters for Joseph Nadeau, and the Silver Queen block, owned by Thomas Stephens, who—between them—already controlled the bulk of red-light rentals. Addi-tional cribs, sponsored by nameless investors, were quickly built in Venus and Pleasant alleys and several walkways at the back of the buildings.

Also included in the restricted district was the Casino, known as the Fairy Palace because of the number of prostitutes who worked the premises. A one-stop shopping mart for vice, it included a dance hall, a bar, a gambling joint, a boxing ring, and a variety theater that seated one thousand patrons, some of them in private boxes where anything went.

———※———

Stanislaus Kiecalis, one of its soon-to-be most famous residents, arrived in the new district in 1901 after living as a hobo for a couple of years. Raised on a farm in Grand Rapids, Michigan, by Polish immigrant parents, he had fled because he mistakenly believed he had killed his father, a suspected murderer, in a fight. Always a scrapper but just 140 pounds and five foot, nine inches tall, with unusually small hands, the lad was not imposing until he took off his shirt to reveal a brace of muscles that appeared to be made of solid steel. At age fourteen he landed a job as a bellboy at Joe Nadeau's Empire Hotel in the Copper block but quickly tripled his salary by becoming a bouncer at the Casino just across the street. Happy with the arrangement, he changed his name to Stanley Ketchel and settled into room number fifteen at the Empire, which also served as home base for whores who were delighted to have the handsome young womanizer as a neighbor. With these basics covered, Ketchel then signed up at the gym of Freddie Brogan, an old boxing pro, to learn that trade.

Charlie O'Connor, a local photographer who managed a string of fighters as a sideline, recognized the championship potential in the small greenhorn who kept splitting his punching bags and called for help. Pete Stone, a Billings man who had earned a mean reputation as a bare-knuckle boxer before gloves became mandatory, became Ketchel's trainer. O'Conner stayed on as his business manager.

Boxing was huge in Montana, and the bouncer discovered that a number of resorts in the lower section of town known as the badlands would pay a fighter twenty bucks to knock around an opponent as part of their variety shows or backroom entertainment. Soon Ketchel was doing so well he quit his job at the Casino, raising police suspicions that he was a pimp because he had no visible means of support. A big spender and a hard drinker, addicted to fine clothes and newly popular ragtime music—making the rounds nightly in the company of one or two beautiful women—it was rumored that the young fighter never slept. He drank, smoked cigars, and occasionally used opium. Yet he was much more careful of his health than it appeared and dedicated to his sport.

Within a year he had made a name for himself in the lightweight division. On June 13, 1905, he fought the opener on Miner's Union Day at Butte's Grand Theater, knocking out Young Peacore in the fifth round of a six-round event. Taking on Frenchman Sid LaFontise at the Casino, he flattened him in the twenty-fourth round, leaving spectators spattered with blood. Shortly thereafter Ketchel came close to annihilating Kid Lee of Havre, as he did Kid

Fredericks of Miles City, where officials stopped the fight in the eighth of a twenty-five-round match to save Fredericks's life.

Ketchel's speed, headlong charges, and the fact that he was absolutely fearless made him almost impossible to beat, even by opponents who towered over and outweighed him. Sportswriters would later agree that pound-for-pound he packed one of the hardest punches in the history of the sport and was utterly ruthless in action.

Yet outside the ring Ketchel was a gentle and unusually thoughtful young man. A soft touch for any street bum, he also made it a point to visit any opponent he vanquished to offer him a part of the winning purse. He kept a diary, wrote to his mother regularly, was shamelessly sentimental, loved animals, and enjoyed photography as a hobby. He also loved scarlet women, and it was mutual. By 1906 he had become a Butte favorite, but he had made at least one well-placed enemy.

Ketchel was still growing and now classed as a middleweight. He'd just taken on Montana Jack Sullivan, the town's most famous homeboy, in a brutal twenty-round battle at the Broadway Theater that had ended in a draw. Sure he could eventually beat the local hero despite the fact Sullivan was two inches taller and packed considerably more pounds, Ketchel was in the process of negotiating a rematch when he was arrested during a high-voltage night in the badlands. Herded before the judge with a group of overdressed pimps and charged with vagrancy, Ketchel protested. The fact that he was a prizefighter apparently kept him out of jail, but the judge gave the boxer just twenty-four hours to leave town.

Though humiliating, the eviction proved the turning point in Ketchel's career. Between 1903 and 1906 he had lost just two of thirty-nine bouts. Manager Charlie O'Connor, who followed him to California, knew Ketchel was ready for the big time and helped make it happen. But it would be two years before Ketchel got his rematch with Montana Jack Sullivan, who was by then middleweight champion of the world. As before, they hammered away at each other for twenty rounds, but finally Ketchel knocked his old adversary cold to take the title. Ketchel's attack had been so furious that Sullivan's manager at first thought his fighter was dead, and he darned near was.

———✥———

The era of Stanley Ketchel's coming of age was also golden for Butte, which had become a world-class city. Streets remained unpaved, and the clock on the fine new city hall never worked properly, but it wasn't needed anyway because residents were in the habit of telling time by the whistles signaling the changing mine shifts. The New Grand Opera House was even grander than the Old Grand Opera House. The elegant red brick Silver Bow Club had been recognized as one of the leading private clubs in the West—so impressive that city fathers had hired its architects to design a courthouse and jail to fill the rest of the block it occupied on the corner of West Granite and Alaska. Modern high-rises had replaced the tottering old cribs and shanties once occupied by good-time girls in the downtown area.

Even whores who had protested moving were pleased with their new working area because customers found it much more convenient than chasing all over town to check out the merchandise. Gated, fenced, and accessible from the downtown area via underground tunnels, the district offered patrons privacy. Wealthy tycoons who spent much time discussing business in the drawing rooms of fancy parlor houses particularly appreciated access that screened their visits.

Traffic was particularly heavy on a December night in 1907 when Ruth Clifford, the youngest of Butte's upscale madams, threw a soirée for the opening of her Irish World. The twenty-four-room vice palace, which took up two lots on East Mercury, was the largest and the oldest of Butte's fancy parlor houses. Formerly known as the Richelieu and then the Windsor, it had been rechristened and refurbished under new ownership that, like past ownership, was well hidden behind front men. Miss Clifford, who was just twenty-two and new to management, apparently bribed newsman Warren Davenport in hopes of garnering free publicity. The jaded, thirty-year-old bachelor had recently founded Butte's only independent newspaper, the *X-Ray*, with the goal of coming to "death grips with the subtle poisons that rise from the rotten swamps of political corruption and the cesspools of social life." Who better to cover the grand opening of a whorehouse?

Guests were received in an ivory and gold room with a rich bottle-green carpet, yellow flowers, and Japanese silk particolored portieres (curtains hung across the doorways) "producing an effect that on clear nights can be heard as far as Anaconda," Davenport began. Miss Ruth, "Butte's common mother-in-law," was a Junoesque maiden—a bit on the "Oleo margaramic" side. "Her ample figure was attired in a glove-fitting, plum-colored Princess suit, trimmed with lace, with a bellyband of untanned leather fastened with a massive buckle, hammered into shape in Harry Couter's blacksmith shop." Her accessories included golf stockings and scarlet garters embroidered with seed pearls, tan-colored shoes with pointed toes and six-inch French heels, and $25,000 worth of diamonds including a scarf pin at her breast "as big as the headlight of the Meaderville [street]car at midnight."

Verbose to the point of sounding Shakespearian, Davenport covered the attire of the twelve beautiful and accomplished young ladies of the house in considerably less detail while making it clear they were elegantly done up, displaying plenty of cleavage. Guests, who immediately took to the dance floor for cotillions with a dose of ragtime, were diverse—everything from military officers to a Wyoming ranch owner. Also represented were members of the Elks, the Silver Bow Club, and Butte's Miners Union and owners of two of the town's finest hotels. But it was Davenport's description of Miss Ruth's "supper of 127 courses," served at 3:30 A.M., that provided the best feel for the event. Its serving—by "colored garcons wearing yellow silk suits and red hollyhock boutonnieres, powdered wigs and dress swords"—appeared most impressive until one hapless waiter tripped over his sword and dumped soup down the neck of a new city alderman. Maintaining her composure, Miss Ruth explained to her guests that the soup had cost a dollar per pint. The dance caller whacked the careless waiter on his powdered wig. Undeterred, guests reveled on until dawn, and Davenport speculated that Miss Ruth made enough by providing extra services to open a bank.

Oddly, the journalist did not report on the seamier side of the red-light district, perhaps because it failed to provide much sport. Under the pressure of new restrictions, tiny cribs had been jammed into back alleys and terraces to a point that second and third tiers were being built. Just large enough to accommodate a bed in one corner and a stove and coal hod in the other, most were also equipped with a small dresser and washbasin. Linen customarily included a strip of oilcloth or a rain slicker at the foot of the bed so customers who were rushed need not take off their shoes. Plumbing, if any, was of

a primitive nature. Arty pictures—pastoral scenes and calendar art, not por-
nography—provided the decor, while the mixed odors of disinfectant, hair
oil, and cheap perfume permeated the entire district.

"It was a tough hole if there ever was one," one patron recalled. "T'was
sin and virtue crawling through the stinking street—where Salvation Army
girls were passing the tambourine and trying at the same time to convert the
painted hussies in the dives. And where sneakin' pickpockets were waitin' in
dark corners and doorways to give the drunken miners a knock on the head
and take their money."

Some of the girls roomed elsewhere, but the majority lived where they
worked because crib rental was between two and five dollars per night and
city fathers required a ten-dollar monthly license fee with jail as its alternative.

———◆———

Irish born, fun-loving Mattie Mems had been the reigning beauty of her day,
operating out of Lou Harpell's Victoria Hotel, but her day had been in the
1890s, and it ended because she didn't age well. Gamely, Mems had taken
demotion in stride quite literally by hitting the pavement when streetwalk-
ing was still allowed. But she was at least thirty the year that prostitutes were
confined to the restricted district, and not earning enough to afford a well-
located crib. Revolted at the idea of working a dark alley or among the rats
in a cave dug into one of the city's underground tunnels below the Dumas or
the Blue Range, she quit to support herself as a chambermaid with occasional
quickies at a hotel on the outskirts of the district.

Her death, just before her fortieth birthday in 1911, was attended by a
Catholic priest and a few former colleagues. Someone sent flowers. There was
no family. The only thing of practical value to be found in her Spartan room
was a picture of a strong young man set in an old-fashioned locket. Friends
defrayed the burial expenses.

In contrast, Lizzie Hall, who claimed to be forty but was probably at least
a decade older, not only set up shop in Paradise Alley but took out an ad in
the Butte city directory to let old customers know she was there. Because she
was black, in fact known as the "darkest black in Butte," she found herself segregated for the first time in her long Montana history, shuttled to the back of

the dank street with a couple of young Japanese whores and a Frenchwoman even older than she was. But Lizzie had seen worse working conditions when she pioneered the gold camps of Bannack, Virginia City, and early Helena. She remained a friend to her former customers, who often looked her up, and much present in the police courts, where she was famous for lifting customers' wallets.

"I's got a million dollars wofth of chawm, but Ah can't get a nickel fo hit," she complained, but, half blind and toothless, she kept on working and paid her own way.

———◦———

In 1898, Butte reported 2,500 men working underground in 260 mines. By 1910 that number had grown to almost 7,000 men and 344 mines. To meet the demand for additional workers, the industry had began to hire unskilled immigrants who would settle for lower wages than experienced hands, even though it was miserable, dangerous work. Some died of pneumonia making the transition from the hundred-degree temperatures far below ground to Montana's subzero winter temperatures. Many were killed or injured in tunnel collapses, rockslides, failures of the elevators that ferried the miners to and from their work, and a general carelessness with safety precautions. Slower but surer was silicosis, death from silica dust, which increased with new drilling technology and lack of proper ventilation. During a six-year period, 675 Butte miners were known to have died of this silent killer, which could have been stopped had mining companies invested in water drills, which kept down the dangerous dust.

But Anaconda, the Standard Oil–backed operation, owned almost all of Montana's copper mines, plus the power sources required to operate them. In addition it controlled both local and state governments charged with regulating and taxing its operations. Company shutdown of its mines threw at least twenty thousand Butte residents out of work, threatening the economy of the entire state. This was the powerful bargaining tool that Anaconda had used to stymie F. Augustus Heinze when he opposed it in 1903, and from that point on the mere threat of similar action brought to heel any union or government agency that tried to buck the mining giant.

Nor was the general public safe. In November 1902, men on the outskirts of Butte began finding the carcasses of dead horses and cattle with increased regularity due to pollution from industry smelters. When negotiations with Anaconda failed, one hundred ranchers banded together to sue for damages only to have the case dismissed by a judge who favored the monopoly.

The Copper Kings—Marcus Daly, William Clark, and finally even scrappy Augustus Heinze—sold out. Other independent tycoons followed suit, producing an exodus that changed the extravagant nature of the town.

"Soirees were no longer staged in the elegant Dumas parlors, and the luxurious upstairs suites were no longer a playground for the wealthy, most of whom by this time had gone back east," Ellen Baumler, coordinator of Montana's National Register of Historic Places, wrote. "For those who remained, elaborate social pretense was no longer a marketable commodity."

Butte had become "just about as dirty and disagreeable place as the average mining camp," a visiting trade union representative observed. "There are some buildings of skyscraper dimensions, and some of the parasites have quite elaborate residences, but the average wage slave's home is a miserable, dingy, dirty board shack, and the main feature is the numerous boarding and lodging houses, dirty crowded and unsanitary."

Yet the population kept growing, bolstered by ever-increasing numbers of immigrants streaming through Ellis Island, many of whom could not speak enough English to name the town but carried with them the trademark landscape postcard of Butte that included the seven slender smokestacks of the Neversweat Mine. Government officials unfailingly recognized the view and dispatched the would-be mining millionaires on the right train west.

The destination became even more popular after 1909 when railroad owners and promoters pushed Congress to pass its last homestead act, offering 320 acres of public domain land on the Great Plains to anyone who would farm them. This was twice the acreage that had previously been offered, causing a dramatic increase in Montana's eastern rural population, with a noticeable spin-off in Butte.

By 1910, Butte and Silver Bow County had about sixty thousand residents. One-third of them were immigrants, and an additional third were first-generation Americans. The majority still came from Ireland or were of

Irish descent, but representatives of almost every nationality could be found there.

———◦◦◦———

Among the most ambitious were Mary Healy Bottego and her husband, John, who had surprisingly little in common except tough childhoods, a shared drive to get ahead, and their Catholic beliefs.

Mary, born in 1855 in Ohio of Irish parents, had lost her mother as a toddler. Her austere stepmother soon employed the child to help raise her two younger stepbrothers. Her older siblings ran away, the younger to lose his life at fourteen fighting for the Union in the Civil War while brother James, just a few years older than Mary, went off to the California Gold Rush.

Freed by the death of her stepmother in 1873, Mary moved East to work for a wealthy family and later traveled with friends to California, visiting the mining camps where her restless father had gone to join her brother. Settling somewhere in northern California about 1890, she found work, probably once again as a domestic, while acquiring additional education at a Catholic mission. In the process she also met John Bottego, three years her junior, who had considerable experience in the mining industry.

Bottego's father, a wealthy landowner in northern Italy, had actually paid his son to leave home when he grew angry with the lad for ignoring school. Defiant, John had immigrated to Pennsylvania, where he became a metalworker, and then gradually worked his way west. At the time, many mining men were abandoning California for Butte, where it was rumored you could earn $50,000 in just two years. Determined not to miss such an opportunity, Bottego may well have asked Mary to go with him. He was clearly attracted to the pert colleen and she to him. But although she was well past the age when most women married, Mary elected to preserve her independence.

It turned out that Butte did not provide $50,000 payoffs to most hardrock miners, but Bottego easily earned fifteen dollars a day contracting crews to William Clark and F. Augustus Heinze, who became a personal friend. There was also money in the population explosion. Lodging was so tight that newcomers were sometimes forced to share sleeping accommodations in shifts, and families increasingly sought houses. Land was expensive around the city center, but expanded streetcar service made less expensive property easily accessible on the outskirts of town. Bottego got in on the beginning of the boom, buying inexpensive lots, building single-family homes for sale or rent, and then reinvesting the profits.

Knowing Mary Healy had been saving up for a business, and proud of the money he was making, John undoubtedly wrote her of this opportunity, for he continued to lobby her on the matter of matrimony. Finally he got her attention. Following a visit to friends in Salt Lake City, Mary journeyed to Butte to become his wife in 1892. Their first daughter, Marie, was born there the following year. Celestine arrived in 1895, shortly after Mary buried her father in Ohio, and a son, Vittorio, followed in 1897.

The Bottegos' net worth grew at an even better rate than their family. They had just settled for the long haul in a small but pleasant house on South Montana Street when John's only brother, Vittorio, died on a geographical expedition in East Africa. A military man turned explorer, Vittorio had become an Italian hero, adding honor to the family name. The large Bottego estate was at stake, with only John's aging parents to oversee it. In 1899 it was decided that John would return to make peace with his father, taking young Vittorio and Marie with him. Mary and Celestine would remain in Butte until the girl finished school.

To make the trip, John raised $6,000 by selling all the property he could. He left Mary to deal with the rest, hoping she and Celestine could survive on rental income until sales could be made. They couldn't. Some of it was repossessed because John had failed earlier to pay interest on a loan. Mary sued the loan sharks, counting on the family friendship with F. Augustus Heinze to help sway the court in her favor. But Heinze's henchmen refused to deal with a woman, demanding that John return to Butte to handle the matter personally. When he refused, and there was no money forthcoming from Italy, Mary took in boarders to make ends meet. There were more court cases, and never-ending problems with renters. Only Mary's stubborn independence and the engaging company of her daughter saved her.

Celestine Bottego had turned into a tall, beautiful child—surprisingly sophisticated for her years. She delighted, as did her mother, in their Irish heritage and the world of poetry and literature. She loved to have fun. But although she attended strict Catholic schools, she had gotten a good look at Butte's seamy side, which gave her keen understanding of real-life suffering, and she did her best to help her embattled mother.

During Mary's eight years as a Butte resident, she'd watched the increasingly crowded town go from bad to worse with its corrupt court system, out-and-out graft, gin mills, and blatant moral laxity. True, the red-light district had been consolidated, but the women were still all over town in their off hours, and, with an overabundance of young men, it was a tough place to raise a nubile daughter, no matter how worldly.

Finally, her health worn down by the brutal winters and the air pollution, Mary wrote to her husband that she didn't care to remain in Butte. Since no money was forthcoming from him for the trip to Italy, she managed to buy back the property that loan sharks had taken from them and resell it at a profit. Then she arranged for another loan, which would be paid off by their rentals, to purchase steamship tickets following Celestine's graduation in 1910.

Bright and a born overachiever, the girl was named the best grammar school student in the state of Montana that year, and her confessor pressured her to become a nun. Mary, to her credit, allowed the fifteen-year-old to make up her own mind, knowing the girl would be diplomatic.

"I told him that I had to leave for Italy, but confessed that the thought of a religious vocation was 'ever present,'" Celestine reported after carefully weighing the thought of life in a convent against the whole new world that lay outside Butte, Montana. Nor would this free spirit consider a religious vocation again for another forty years.

———◦———

By the end of 1908, Warren Davenport had run out of cash to fund his *X-Ray* newspaper, but at least he had managed to stir up the town. So much so, in fact, that he had narrowly escaped going to jail and still faced a lawsuit or two. His father, a lawyer back in Mt. Pleasant, Iowa, had suggested the writer put his assets in his mother's name because, knowing Warren, that wouldn't be the end of it. And it wasn't because Davenport still had enough in his trust fund to turn the best of his material into a book. What he needed was a good, strong piece to sum it all up. He found it, he decided, in a poem he had written about Butte:

Vulgar manner, overfed
Overdressed and underbred.
Heathen godless—hell's delight.
Rude by day and lewd by night.
Dwarfed the man, enlarged the brute.
Ruled by roué and prostitute.
Purple robed and pauper clad.
Raving, rotting, money mad,
Squirming herd in Mammon's mesh.
Wilderness of human flesh.
Crazed by Avarice. Lust and Rum.
Butte, thy name is Delirium.

One hundred new residences had been built on the flat south of the city, and that was just the beginning. Butte claimed the largest payroll in the world—$1.5 million, with twelve thousand men working the mines and mills, and at least several thousand domestic workers to support the miners. Bank deposits exceeded $15 million. There were twenty-five public and seven parochial schools and forty-two churches. Meanwhile, the red-light district had expanded to become the second largest in the United States, topped only by New Orleans' infamous Corduroy Road. It was estimated that one thousand women worked the district in never-ending shifts.

Tier upon tier of tiny cribs had been built to meet the demand. The high-class houses—suddenly bereft of millionaire clients to pick up the thousand-dollar tabs it took to support an evening of bacchanalian bonding—partitioned their spacious ballrooms, parlors, and bedrooms into smaller units to be worked in shifts by nonresident lovelies who commuted.

On the day before New Year's Eve 1903, police raided Lou Harpell's Victoria, still the grandest of Butte's bordellos. Realizing how exclusive the pleasure palace was and appreciating Lou's long-established connection with men in high places, they didn't march her and her four resident whores off to jail but let them post bail at the house. But the invasion of privacy unnerved Lou, as did the district's new dependence on fast turnover, no doubt hastening her retirement.

Ruth Clifford's hallowed Irish World was not just partitioned; the owners opened one corner of the formerly exclusive establishment to the public as a bar and dance hall. Clifford quit, securing Lou Harpell's old job at the Victoria. When that, too, succumbed to running in shifts, Clifford departed with the rest of her class, seeking more civilized realms.

In contrast, Parisian sisters Camille and Marie Paumie, who established a dry cleaning and dye house in the district in 1888, soon built on a handsome two-story brick addition offering decent little apartments heated by steam from their pressing operations. Its cleaning services were so respected that for the next decade customers mailed in dirty clothes from as far as Idaho and the Dakotas, and the illicit side of the business had an equally good name.

Famed comedian Charlie Chaplin, who explored the Butte tenderloin in 1910 at age sixteen while on a vaudeville tour, rated it well.

"The red light district consisted of a long street and several side streets containing a hundred cribs, in which young girls were installed ranging from age 16 up—for one dollar," he recalled in his autobiography years later. "Butte boasted having the prettiest women of any red-light district in the West, and it was true. If one saw a pretty girl smartly dressed, one could rest assured she was from the red-light quarter, doing her shopping. Off duty, they looked neither right nor left and were most respectable. Years later I argued with Somerset Maugham about his Sadie Thompson character in the play *Rain*. Jeanne Engles dressed her rather grotesquely, as I remember, with spring-side boots. I told him no harlot in Butte, Montana, could make money if she dressed like that."

But as the district continued to grow with the town's increasingly transient population, complaints about muggings and robberies began to roll in. Then there was the problem of the Cabbage Patch, a sprawling shantytown just east of the district that was populated by prostitutes past their prime, outlaws, chronic drunks, hobos, and hopheads. The latter were of particular concern.

Several of the dope fiends, as they were commonly called, were former society women whose families had abandoned them because they had grown
dependent on the local opium dens or patent medicines, which packed about
the same wallop. Occasionally other society women, members of girl clubs,
and the Salvation Army practiced virtue by taking food to the unfortunates.
Police judge Alex McGowan had gone so far as to lock up all the hopheads in
the basement of the jail for a few weeks in the mistaken belief that he could
cure them via depravation. But the problems only got worse.

In 1905, Reverend William Biederwolf, a charismatic preacher who had
been raised in Indiana before studying at Princeton and the Sorbonne, came
to Butte's rescue. He had chosen the town because it was the "lowest sinkhole
of vice in the west," the famed revivalist told a crowd of about one thousand
at the Casino.

"The pit was jammed with . . . rounders, gamblers and habitués of the red-
light district," the *Butte Miner* reported. "The boxes filled with women of the
lower world attired in their gaudy dresses of flimsy materials, accompanied by
their secretaries and paramours."

They listened under duress, for no drinks were served during the service,
yet Biederwolf's talk proved so inspiring that later seven hundred of his audi-
ence marched with him into the tenderloin, bellowing hymns. Well pleased,
Biederwolf hosted a second show at the New Opera House. Again results
were impressive, but there were no noticeable long-term improvements in
the "sinkhole."

Change was in the wind nationally, however. In 1901, Chicago had
hosted a group called the Purity Congress, which met there again in 1906 to
lay groundwork for legislating morality. Four years later the U.S. Congress
passed the Mann Act to protect American daughters from white slavers, and
the Women's Christian Temperance Union developed a national reach that
included Montana.

"Petitions of 5,000 names in Butte and 2,000 in Helena were presented to
city councils of these cities asking to close the saloons at midnight," Warren
Davenport reported in 1908. "Helena succumbed to the assassins of personal liberty, but Butte, the greatest mining camp on earth, still possesses her
24-hour saloon." That was enough for Carrie Nation, American's most visible

Prohibitionist, who declared Butte "America's cesspool of alcohol, tobacco, and sinful women."

"I have never seen a town as wide open as Butte!" she announced on landing in January 25, 1910. "I have never seen so many homes consumed to keep up the saloon! . . . I'm talking to the bosses of this town, the rulers of this town, now. I'm talking to the voters. I have brought you a remedy—God's remedy!"

Nation's remedy, for which she was famous, was to invade bars with a hatchet, causing thousands of dollars' worth of damage. Although the sixty-four-year-old crusader looked like someone's sweet grandmother, she was five-foot-ten and weighed 175 pounds. Members of the Butte Bartenders Union, who greeted her citywide with signs that read "All Nations are welcome except Carrie!" flat-out refused to meet with her, so she busied herself with other agendas.

Considering she also crusaded against prostitution, some found it ironic that Nation gave her first press interview from bed, clad only in her plain gold-rimmed spectacles, a plain cotton dressing gown, and a gray shawl, in the guestroom of earnest WCTU president Mrs. W. E. Currah. Still, Nation impressed the young male reporter in such a grandmotherly fashion that he was moved to warn her that visiting the tenderloin might be a waste.

"No! I must go to see the harlots too!" she insisted. "They are poor, miserable creatures. Their lot only shows what vice mixed with drink will do. They live daily with the thought, the hope, of suicide. That is their only release."

Nation's first official talk, before a packed house at the Mountain View Methodist Church, was a rambling condemnation of everything from gin to predation, including tight-laced corsets, stuffed birds on "Merry Widow hats," President William Howard Taft, Democrats, and Republicans in general. Well received, she grew bolder following a second address at the Grace Methodist Episcopal Church, invading the red-light district with five hundred supporters, many wearing the white ribbons of the WCTU and the black armbands of the Salvation Army, loudly belting out temperance hymns. By the time they reached the A.B.C. Dance Hall on South Wyoming, the crowd had grown to about a thousand, including jeering critics and curious bystanders. Boldly Nation invaded the gin mill, taking the floor to lecture the revelers on the evils of drinking and consorting with lewd, wild women, many of whom stopped dancing long enough to listen.

"Honor your mother, my good man!" Nation yelled at the unnerved bartender. "Shut this place down."

"For God's sake, woman, get out of here," he stuttered.

"I will not!" she challenged. "It is precisely for God's sake that I came in here!" But, sensing unrest, she did turn and push her way to the door as the A.B.C. band struck up "What the Hell Do We Care?" apparently on its own volition.

On the street again, backed by fans, she visited a couple of cribs to encourage the stunned occupants to consider a new way of life.

"Leave this hell hole, this life of shame," she urged. "You have a mother? What would she say if she knew you were here? This life leads but to one thing –an early unwept grave—for the wages of sin are death. Leave it! Leave it! For you are still young, and not beyond redemption."

Later Nation attempted a sidewalk lecture amid an increasingly unruly crowd.

"It was an odd spectacle. Prostitutes with painted cheeks, heavy red lips, and leering eyes that betokened too much to drink, and in scant attire, mingled with W.C.T.U. matrons, and rowdies, and the curious. Mrs. Nation was subjected to shouted abuse and insult most vile," the *Butte Miner* reported. "And the French and colored women cursed her and jostled her. Bare heads, shoulders, and arms were thrust out of half closed doors. Women in attire which was sans skirts and most everything else flocked to the scene and shivering, they leered, jeered, and hooted at Mrs. Nation. The din soon became deafening."

The reformer, at the height of her international fame, was not used to losing, so she stomped down Galena Street and on to Mercury with the curious mob at her heels, entering the saloon attached to the Irish World brothel. Here, while pushing her way to the dance floor, she was stopped short by the paintings of naked women decorating the walls.

"See those?" she yelled excitedly. "It's a shame and a disgrace! Those lewd, indecent pictures are there to abuse the lust in men!"

Nation had yet to use her famous hatchet in Butte. What better target could there be? But May Malloy, a forty-three-year-old who had recently moved from working a crib on Galena to replacing Ruth Clifford as madam of the Irish World, did not take threats lightly. Headed to fetch the cops, she ran smack into the righteous reformer, and took her on.

"Get out of my place, get out of my place," she ordered. "Here, you policeman, put this woman out of here. I want these females who are raising a disturbance arrested and taken out of my house.

"You get out of my house!"

"You just hear what I have to say," Nation demanded. But, almost crazed with anger according to reports, Malloy tried to push the reformer out the door, ripping off the old gal's prim bonnet and wrenching her shoulder. Finally delivering a well-placed kick at her stern, Malloy propelled her aged adversary into the street before the now hushed crowd, and everybody decided to call it a night.

Nation remained in town for several more days, lecturing before sympathetic audiences including the Butte Newsboys Association and visiting judge Alex McGowan, perhaps to trade information on how to cure "dope fiends." She predicted that national Prohibition would eventually come to America. She issued an open letter to the bartenders who refused to meet with her, warning them that she planned to return for another round that April. But she would never again employ her famous hatchet for bar smashing. Biographers have speculated that the injuries inflicted by May Malloy may have hastened her death, which followed eighteen months after her Butte visit.

"I—I have done what I could," were her final words and valediction.

In January 1911, one hundred businessmen petitioned Mayor Charles Nevin to move Butte's tenderloin east of Arizona Street, two blocks from its current western limit. A counterpetition signed by fifty upstanding community members including a preacher was submitted immediately, arguing that red-light district buildings would not recycle well. Considering the numbers and interested in reform, Nevin closed the district January 31, surprised no doubt when the whores left "on vacation" with barely a murmur. They had, however, done their math. Based on the monthly fines collected from every working woman in the district, the city averaged at least $2,000 a month and probably considerably more. Two weeks later, sobered by visions of that funding shortfall, the city council considered another petition for reopening. Mayor Nevin held fast on his order that the houses remain shut, only to be ignored by his own police force and citizens alike.

Business had never been better. On Saturday nights and pay nights it was not unusual for as many as three or four thousand men to be crowded along the Board Walk, Pleasant Alley, or the many "terraces" that made up the district.

There was no end of good times in sight.

9

---※---

NEW OPTIONS

～֍ 1916 ֍～

Simply but elegantly dressed, Jeannette Rankin, with her lithe figure, luxuriant dark brown hair, and large hazel eyes, was a striking woman and well spoken in her 1916 congressional campaign. She had gathered a crowd in front of a Butte saloon, but she spoke as easily and simply as if she were in her own kitchen. She didn't sound like the suffragist she was. She talked of home values, of how women needed to be a part of the government that dictated how they would raise their children. How the gentle influence of women in government could make government better. And she made sense.

"There's no threat for men to allow a single camel into the tent, *if* there are no other noses poking under it," one of the mostly male crowd observed drily to a companion.

"Just like Ella Knowles," his friend replied. "A dangerous woman."

---※---

Knowles, also charming, had been the first woman admitted to the Montana bar, having successfully lobbied the legislature to allow women to practice. She had moved to Helena in 1888 from the East, supposedly because of ill health, although the climate was even harsher than that of her native New Hampshire. The daughter of a well-heeled farmer, she began supporting herself at fifteen, the year she graduated from Northwood Seminary to attend teacher's college following the death of her mother. Teaching to pay her tuition, she enrolled at Bates, a near–Ivy League college in Maine, where she had been the first female to edit the college magazine and also the first to engage in public debate, taking top honors for composition and oratory. Graduating magna cum laude in 1884, she studied law with a Manchester firm whose senior member was a U.S. senator but failed to finish her training. Whether because of ill health or because her father remarried, Knowles headed west, landing a job at Helena's Central School.

Offered an appointment as principal a year later, Ella shocked friends by turning down the job to study law with Helena attorney Joseph W. Kinsley, a fellow New Englander. Considering there were only a few women attorneys in all of the United States, and that Montana law forbade their practice, Knowles's decision seemed odd. Most women in that field were relegated to office work rather than to court, and those in independent practice had a hard time making a living. Yet Knowles knew she had a gift for the calling and, having earlier worked with a firm whose senior member was a polished politician, she also understood that field far better than most. Her immediate problem was how to support her studies, something most poor law students did by becoming bill collectors. Knowles's solicitation for work in this field, however, was not well received in Helena.

"They didn't take kindly to a 'woman doing a man's work,'" she later recalled of her second try on a stormy day. Finally noting the rain, one gruff store owner who had already turned her down harshly jokingly suggested she collect three umbrellas customers had borrowed from him, so he could go to lunch without being soaked. It was no easy assignment, but Knowles tracked down two of the offenders. The first complied with her request only after a nasty verbal exchange. The second, Ella recalled, finally handed over her umbrella "accompanied by a look that haunted me in my sleep that night."

Soggy and bedraggled, Knowles returned to the store to present her "collection" to the owner with notice that her fee was fifty cents. Shocked, he refused to pay until Knowles appealed to customers waiting out the storm in his store, explaining her case to their general amusement. Eventually the store owner joined in the laughter, paid, and later became a faithful client. Knowles kept the two quarters he gave her as a hard-won symbol of her new career.

With similar dispatch, Ella lobbied the legislature and then passed the Montana bar with the highest score examiners had ever seen. After practicing with Kinsley for a year, she hung out her own shingle, establishing a practice buoyed by an unusual number of women clients.

It was through no fault of her own that Ella Knowles became known as a dangerous woman. She had aligned herself with the Populist Party because of its declared interest in women's rights, but she was as surprised as anyone when in 1892 she was nominated as its candidate for attorney general during a statewide convention she did not attend. Finally convinced it was not a joke, she telegraphed her acceptance and began boning up on the issues.

The first female ever nominated for a statewide office by a major party, she traveled the territory attracting large crowds and campaigning vigorously. If nothing else, the exposure would benefit her practice, she admitted.

One editor suggested some "good man" ought to protect the blue-eyed, curly-haired little blond from the shocks of political life by marrying her. Another, noting her youthful appearance, wondered if she satisfied the age requirement, which was thirty. Dubbed the "Portia of the People's Party," Knowles lost to the Republican incumbent, Henri Haskell, but garnered 3,671 more votes than the second most popular candidate in her own organization. And she captured Haskell's attention. Less than a year in office, slammed by the growing issues of statehood, Henri asked Governor Joseph K. Toole to appoint Knowles his assistant attorney general, an assignment she accepted happily.

During this period Knowles became the first woman to plead a case in the U.S. district and circuit courts. She had sole charge of a case involving school lands in which she won a favorable decision from the U.S. secretary of interior. Her skillful collaboration with Haskell provided Montana with a formidable legal team, and the couple also connected on a personal level. On May 23, 1895, Knowles, thirty-five, married the fifty-two-year-old widower Haskell, moving with him to Glendive when his term expired a year later.

The marriage did not survive the move, perhaps because Glendive was a small town, off the beaten path except to oil prospectors who would ultimately establish its economic base. However, it is more likely that Ella's ambitions exceeded those of her retirement-aged husband, and she was not content to remain in the backwater that he called home. Despite her fling,

Knowles would ultimately become a superstar, but matrimony was a setback
to her career.

———◆———

Jeannette Rankin did not make that same mistake. Marriage meant a "para-
sitic life," she insisted. It was the "male-dominated . . . family that restricted
women's full development." And, although Rankin was far slower than
Knowles to figure out what she wanted, nothing would get in her way once
she set her course.

Jeannette's mother, Olive Pickering, had traveled to Missoula from New
Hampshire in 1878 at age twenty-four, encouraged by her uncle, William
Berry, who served as sheriff there. Olive's forty-year-old sister, Mandanna, who
joined her and Berry for the excursion, was not impressed. The town had a
population of fewer than three hundred, just two stores, and one bank. The
owner of the house where the sisters boarded had a scar on his head from an
old Indian attack when he was scalped and left for dead. The half-naked Indians who occasionally wandered by to peek in their windows quite unnerved
Mandanna. Declaring Montana "no fit place to raise children," she returned to
New England, while Olive took up teaching in the one-room Missoula school.

A large, good-looking woman with a flair for fashion, domineering but
bright, Olive soon captured the attention of John Rankin, thirty-five, who
owned the local sawmill. Canadian, born of Scots parents, the fourth of
nine children, he had worked his way west as a carpenter, traveling with his
brother. After their boat bottomed out in the Missouri River, John lugged his
tools to Helena looking for a new start, then moved to Missoula, which was
still being built.

The tall, red-bearded, long-haired bachelor had only three years of formal
schooling and a volatile temper and was quick to get in fistfights. Yet he studied on his own to a point that he had engineered a 250-foot bridge across the
Missoula River for the town and built its Methodist church. He was active
in Missoula politics and well respected. Olive wed him in August 1879 and
never looked back.

Their first child, Jeannette, born about ten months later, delighted her
father, who named her after his mother. When two more daughters followed,

he may have given up his dreams of having a son. He treated his eldest as a boy, favoring her with his attention, passing on to her not only his carpentry skills but also his philosophy. Their joined-at-the-hip relationship was so set that the eventual birth of a son, Wellington, in 1884 did little to alter it. This obvious favoritism caused Olive to focus her approval on the boy, dividing the growing family into two camps.

By 1893 the Rankins had produced seven children, one of whom died young. The rest, aged one to thirteen, were living well; John had become one of the wealthiest men in the region. Their three-story Madison Street house topped by a glass-enclosed Burmese-style cupola and surrounding walkway was the first in Missoula to have forced-air heat and modern plumbing. The ranch where they summered six miles out of town lacked few amenities.

Their life was pretty much a circus, however. Olive was bent on broadening their education. Books filled the house, and a large map of the United States had a place of honor in their dining room. Community leaders in unending variety were invited to dine. Their varied viewpoints fostered debate, as did the diversity in the beliefs of family members. John Rankin had been raised a Presbyterian. His wife was a Congregationalist who turned to Christian Science. Uncle John Berry, an ardent atheist, didn't care who knew it. Seldom did any of them attend church.

The children, not surprisingly, were as boisterous as they were bright. Olive, who declared the quick-tempered Jeannette an "unresponsive problem child," finally gave up on her entirely.

"If you can take care of Jeannette, I can take care of the rest of the children," she promised her husband. But even that became too much. Sick with some undefined malady and overcome by the numbers, Olive developed a laissez-faire attitude toward child care. Nor did John Rankin concern himself with discipline.

"He loved children," Jeannette was later quoted as saying. As a result the siblings argued, and when words failed they "threw things at one another—a glass of water if nothing else was handy."

Biographer Norma Smith, who became a close personal friend of Jeannette's, observed that what probably saved them from becoming outright savages is the fact that their father expected them to work like adults, so they had little time to get into real trouble. When Olive became strangely passive and grew increasingly obese, Jeannette took on the job of raising her siblings and running the household. She was by all accounts domineering to the point of being harsh. At one point she arranged for the family doctor to take out the healthy tonsils of her younger sisters with an eye to preventing future medical emergencies. But she was still in school herself, "restless and unhappy," and the responsibility of raising five unruly youngsters weighed heavily on her.

Wellington, who showed signs of besting his father at making money, was handed heavy business responsibilities in his early teens. Harriet, the second oldest, did the family books. Jeannette served as cook for Rankin's lumber camp. And every Rankin child who could walk worked at the family's three-story, sixty-five-room Rankin Hotel in any needed capacity. When Jeannette learned her father had refused to sell it because the prospective buyer demanded he build a boardwalk around it before purchase, she bought lumber and hammered the required walkway in place herself, effectively closing the deal and eliminating that strain on the family, although they still had plenty of work.

Meanwhile, Jeannette finished high school and signed on at Montana State University (later the University of Montana), which had recently been established in Missoula largely through her father's efforts. Though a poor student, she managed to scrape by academically while excelling in organizing picnics and parties. Most memorable, classmates recalled, was the dance she threw on her eighteenth birthday at the Rankin ranch for which her father built a dance floor in the yard, lighted with Chinese lanterns. Wellington and some friends greased a pig for the event, letting it loose among the dancers, and then exchanged all the horses hitched to surreys rented by guests from the local livery stables, causing no end of embarrassment. Jeannette was livid, but Wellington, the family pet who was at least as clever as his older sister, escaped unscathed.

Jeannette celebrated that summer by making a daring unchaperoned trip with two other young women to the West Coast to visit relatives, briefly postponing the awful letdown that would follow. Suddenly, there was nothing on her agenda but to continue filling in for her mother.

Marriage was not an option. She wasn't in love, and she had already turned down a couple of excellent offers from men she enjoyed. The idea of becoming nothing more than a baby factory—something that had dulled her bright mother's enthusiasm—held no appeal for her. Nor did her college major, biology, where her chief work had been cataloging freshwater snails. There were new options for women, of course. Jeannette considered nursing until her father talked her out of it on the grounds it might be hard on her health. Women photographers ran studios in several towns, including Missoula, and one in Miles City—a member of the British royal family named Evelyn Cameron—traveled widely with her heavy equipment to photograph ranchers and sheep herders, actually riding astride wearing a split skirt. Dr. Maria Dean not only practiced medicine in Helena but chaired the county Board of Health. Ella Knowles Haskell was doing even better as a lawyer in private practice than she had as assistant attorney general. But Jeannette's talents all seemed to be domestic, which was not the way she wanted to go.

She considered the odd case of a young man named Charlie Miller, arrested in Helena for a daring series of midnight robberies, who turned out to be a girl. Bertha "Bertie" Helen Forslund had started her cross-dressing career in Missoula as a room clerk at the Grand Hotel and later worked as a bartender without raising any suspicions. Her boyfriend, Henry Clark, had suggested the disguise after he persuaded her to run away from her home near Spokane, noting it would be easier to live together and that men's jobs paid better.

When captured, Bertie was packing two revolvers, garbed in a well-tailored three-piece suit, highly polished boots, and a smart derby hat. She had turned to a life of crime, she confessed, for the money and excitement. Although she had dressed as a man for more than a year and enjoyed it, Bertie agreed to take up female attire again if she could escape going to jail.

With the help of the Helena Temperance League and the Salvation Army, lawyer Joseph Kinsley presented her to the court in a modest dress with tasteful accessories as the good-looking, well-spoken young woman she was. Bertie's lover took full responsibility for the crimes they had committed. Friends in Missoula reported that Bertie had since joined the Salvation Army and was working hard to get a pardon for Clark, who was sentenced to forty years in Deer Lodge Prison.

The idea of cross-dressing was unsettling to Jeannette, who loved feminine attire and had been brought up riding sidesaddle because that's what ladies did. However, low wages for women were an issue with her, and her life as a single girl slipping past marriageable age was deadly dull. Bertie Forslund had at least been creative about exploring new options. Unfortunately, Montana State University had failed to teach Jeannette to think, she complained.

"Go! Go! Go!" she wrote in her journal at age twenty-two. "It makes no difference where you go! just go! go!" But failing to find any meaningful destination, she remained in Missoula, where she got a job teaching second grade at the one-room school at Grant Creek near the ranch, and hated it.

The next year she accepted a similar job at Whitehall, a small town founded just fourteen years earlier as a base for crews and extra railroad engines assigned the task of getting trains over the Great Divide into Butte. Every other building in the business district housed a saloon. There was no central lighting or water system. The population was dominated by multinational railroad workers plus cattle ranchers and cowboys, but to Jeannette's relief there was also a college-educated crowd of young, professional go-getters who were unusually social. The parties, concerts, and dances they organized were a delight, as were their theatricals and literary presentations.

Most popular among them were Dr. Lawrence Packard, just two years older than Jeannette, and his eighteen-year-old wife of one year, Nellie, who became Jeannette's closest friends. The couple owned the town's only bathtub, with running water powered by a windmill in their backyard. The joke was that Jeannette chummed them so she won't have to make the seven-mile trip out to Pipestone Hot Springs where most of her fellow schoolteachers journeyed for their weekly baths, but after the dull life in Missoula, Rankin relished the Packards' lively company.

"Doc," as everybody called him, was a gregarious and well-liked ex–football hero from the University of Nebraska, who played with the town team and knew everybody on a first-name basis. He had just purchased the town's first automobile, a rakish one-cylinder Oldsmobile that was thoroughly hated by fellow citizens because their horses bolted at its approach. Outings in the vehicle at its top speed of thirty miles per hour left passengers windblown, sunburned, and often covered with grime, but Jeannette decided to buy her own as soon as she could afford one.

The year passed pleasantly. Jeannette enjoyed teaching fifth- and sixth-graders far more than her younger students at the Grant Creek School. And, at age twenty-four, she had apparently found romance. Then lightning struck. The official explanation for the fact that Whitehall supervisors did not renew Rankin's teaching contract was that she had been hired under temporary certification and failed to pass the exam required for a license. Years later, when a biographer questioned Rankin about her "embarrassment" in Whitehall, Jeannette turned ashen.

"How did you find out about *that?*" she asked angrily, and walked out on the interview.

Shortly after Jeannette left Whitehall, her brother Wellington began less-than-subtle public criticism regarding his sister's morals, and historians interviewed on the subject form two opposing camps. Some insist Jeannette Rankin was a lesbian, while others claim they can prove that she had an abortion, perhaps through the aid of friends like the Packards. Jeannette, who never married but had a number of close male friends, skirted the issue. It should be noted that Rankin remained friends with Dr. Packard long after she left Whitehall and that, following his divorce and subsequent remarriage, she also befriended his second wife, Fannie Graves.

Whatever the cause, Jeannette's return to Missoula proved timely. In late April 1904 her father came in from working the fields and announced he had been bitten by a tick. Jeannette quit the job she had taken as a hat trimmer at the Golden Rule Department Store to nurse him, but one week later he died of Rocky Mountain spotted (tick) fever. Wellington, who was nineteen at the time and an undergraduate at Harvard, took full control of the family estate, which by today's accounting would have equaled about $3 million. Jeannette became his Montana arm in running it and added her father's family responsibilities to that of her mother's. Well trained for their assignments, they seem never to have missed a beat, although the additional burden must have raised hell with their personal lives.

The strain apparently caught up with Wellington during his senior year at Harvard, when he became so ill that Jeannette traveled to Massachusetts with a woman friend from Missoula to be with him. Happily, he soon recovered to give them such a grand tour they decided to stay on for six months.

Dating Harvard men and enjoying the social whirl, the young women grew so enchanted with Boston they considered enrolling at Massachusetts Institute of Technology until they discovered engineering degrees were reserved for men. In addition, Jeannette got her first mind-jarring exposure to big-city slums and the social problems that they spawned.

Then, in March 1905, a family friend invited them to attend Theodore Roosevelt's second inauguration, which was the most elaborate and diverse of any similar celebration in memory. Among the guests were a number of Roosevelt's Montana cowboy friends, students, miners, soldiers from the Battle of San Juan Hill, and Apache chief Geronimo.

Jeannette's return to Missoula must have been unsettling; although the family employed household help, it became obvious her siblings needed her, as did her mother. In fact, overseeing the Rankin family would keep Jeannette at home for the next three years, while Wellington sailed off to England as a Rhodes scholar, then returned to Harvard for his law degree.

Restless, Jeannette apprenticed as a dressmaker and enrolled in a correspondence course in furniture making. Finally in 1907, badly depressed and battling inflammatory rheumatism from too many harsh Montana winters, she escaped to visit an uncle in San Francisco and see the city, which was in the process of recovering from its devastating earthquake.

Caring little for San Francisco social life, she chanced to tour a settlement house on Telegraph Hill sheltering needy women and children. The social worker in charge explained that the mothers—mostly Italian immigrants who were scrambling to learn English along with some useful trade—were the victims of bigoted and antiquated laws and a total lack of legal protection, and she talked Rankin into volunteering with them as a child-care worker for four months. Under the social worker's tutorship, the sheltered Missoula woman began attending hearings on child labor laws, factory working conditions, and wage legislation.

The next fall Rankin enrolled in the New York School of Philanthropy. One of the finest schools of its kind, the college offered a graphic look at some of the most pathetic social problems of the era, providing brilliant teachers to study and debate them. Never a strong student, Jeannette was challenged, but, unlike at Montana State University, much of the training was hands-on. Students worked on dozens of slum projects including visiting homes and schools to recruit deaf children for special training. Jeannette served two months at night court, working with girls—usually prostitutes—who were first offenders. Since there were no public rehabilitation programs, she became adept at buttonholing charitable institutions and private individuals, but solutions seldom came easy.

She would remember forever a prostitute for whom she secured a factory job, who subsequently lost her fingers in the machinery and had to return to her old profession. The children she placed in foster homes were often returned, like puppies to a pound. Meanwhile she lied to her mother that her work wasn't dangerous while prodding her sisters to consider Wellesley. With her poor education from their tiny frontier college, up against "such well-trained college girls," Jeannette told them she expected to fail her classes. Yet by studying social theory and policy, Jeannette tapped into the school's national network of activists, who spurred her on. To her own astonishment, she graduated in the spring of 1909 with decent grades and headed back to Missoula in search of a mission.

There was none. For a while she focused on the overcrowded Missoula jail, shocked to find that prostitutes were often housed with lumberjacks and burglars in a common bullpen. There were other social problems, but most were so minor that officials did not take her seriously. She also made the mistake of talking down to local prostitutes, who didn't think that any woman backed by the Rankin fortune could grasp the problems they faced. "They laughed at me," she would recall with chagrin. Finally, she took a job with the Washington Children's Home Society in Seattle.

The facility was considered state of the art. Jeannette had expected to be assigned to the field. Instead she found herself working as a babysitter. Casework was left to male employees, and she grew increasingly frustrated with management. Of 286 youngsters placed that year, all but 113 were returned and thirteen died at the facility.

Disillusioned and finding it difficult to keep her temper in check, Jeannette quit to take courses in economics, political science, and public speaking

at the University of Washington, supporting herself by working as a seamstress to supplement the seventy-five dollars per month allowance she drew
from her father's estate. Although long aware that women who ventured into
politics were considered fanatics, she had ceased to care. She had successfully
raised her five siblings and, as a thirty-year-old spinster with no particular
calling, she had nothing to lose.

In the spring of 1910, Rankin spotted an advertisement recruiting volunteers to help plaster the town with posters promoting equal suffrage. The
women of Washington State had gained the vote in 1883 only to see the law
declared invalid because of a defective title. After the legislature corrected
this oversight, the court ruled that Congress had really meant only men
when it allowed states to control suffrage. Finally Washington's legislature
had agreed to put the issue before the voters, and Rankin joined the National
American Woman Suffrage Association, which was leading the campaign for
passage.

The Washington organization was rife with bickering. Abigail Duniway,
who had led the initial fight in the Pacific Northwest, had angered East Coast
suffragists by maintaining that temperance workers were killing the movement because otherwise sympathetic male voters rightly feared women would
back Prohibition. Carrie Hill, a thirty-year veteran of suffrage campaigns,
was also a leading member of the Women's Christian Temperance League.
May Arkwright Hutton was the uneducated but outspoken wife of a rich
miner whose heavy makeup and flamboyant lifestyle fostered rumors that she
was a prostitute. Emma Smith DeVoe was dismissed as an "eastern import,"
although she and her husband became Washington residents before she was
hired by NAWSA to run the campaign. Yet peace was somehow maintained.
Jeannette, a brave and charming sidewalk campaigner and a powerful speaker,
found her niche recruiting votes where others feared to tread.

Washington women won their franchise 56,000 to 29,676, and Rankin
was awarded a job with the New York Woman Suffrage Party as a street campaigner and a lobbyist. Based in New York City, she got to know and work
with leaders of the national suffrage movement, which was gaining strength.
Women had been voting in Wyoming since 1869. After a false start, Utah
granted the women's vote in 1895. Colorado and Idaho joined the group.

California followed Washington State by a year, and Oregon, Kansas, and Arizona were slated for voting rights in 1912.

Back in Missoula for Christmas following her Washington victory, Jeannette learned that a suffrage bill had been introduced into the Montana legislature and that one of its chief sponsors was looking for a speaker to promote it. Wellington, now a successful lawyer in Helena, helped negotiate her legislative invitation, brought Jeannette up to speed on local politics, and rehearsed her unmercifully for the event. Generally recognized as a pinchpenny, he also saw to it that she had an expensive designer dress for the occasion—form-fitting green velvet, elegantly accessorized—that highlighted her striking good looks while making her appear much younger than her thirty years.

There was some grousing. Representative James Lissner of Helena referred to Jeannette publicly as "One lone woman, who, unluckily, has not been able to ensnare a man," and he was not alone in his disgust. But the lawmakers greeted her graciously with flowers and ample applause. She, in return, began in a gentle and ladylike manner, although the intensity of her convictions proved forceful enough to provoke heated debate.

"It is not for myself that I am making this appeal, but for the six million women who are suffering for better conditions, women who should be working amid more sanitary conditions, under better moral conditions, at equal wages for equal work performed," she pleaded.

While calmly maintaining taxation without representation was tyranny, she also noted that Montana women had no wish to step down from the high pedestal on which Montana men placed them. She asked the lawmakers to put the suffrage question before the voters in the next election.

"Men want women in the home and they want them to make the home perfect, yet how can they make it so if they have no control over the influences of the home?" she asked. "It is beautiful and right that a mother should nurse her child through typhoid fever, but it is also beautiful and right that she should have a voice in regulating the milk supply from which the typhoid resulted."

The legislation she requested was defeated by a surprisingly narrow margin. The press gave the event broad coverage after generally ignoring the subject of equal rights for years. Women from all over the state began writing Rankin, asking why no one had mentioned the issue before. Encouraged, Jeannette left Montana to work on campaigns in New York, Florida, and Ohio, gaining additional experience and making valuable contacts that would prove useful on her return.

It was tough, grueling work with a travel schedule so heavy Rankin seldom managed to sleep in the same bed twice. Losing her voice in shouting matches with political opponents, wobbling through bouts of depression, weathering attacks from suffrage leaders with opposing views, she responded simply by working harder. In 1913 she was made field secretary for the NAWSA and directed a staggering victory in North Dakota. Then she came home for a well-planned attack.

Jeannette Rankin was by no means the first to promote suffrage in Montana. A small group of Helena women had organized in 1890, going statewide in 1895. The Populist Party had introduced an equal rights amendment at their behest, which failed on three separate occasions. So the idea had languished, soundly opposed by the liquor lobby. A Butte newspaperwoman had been fighting for the issue since 1903. A few Helena women including Dr. Maria Dean, with Ida Auerbach and Freida Fligelman, the daughters of prosperous merchants, were anxious to try again, but there was more to winning than defeating the booze sellers.

A second barrier to passage was Montana's diversity. Out of a population of 376,000, more than 100,000 were foreigners from dozens of widely differing cultures. Mining communities tended to have different political values from those of ranchers, farmers, homesteaders, and tradesmen, who also played a large part in the economy. Then there was the uncertainty of backing by Anaconda, which now controlled almost all of Montana's newspapers as well as its government and would not be anxious to contend with voting women who might encourage humanitarian and safety legislation, back Prohibition, or raise taxes on the mining industry. But these were issues Jeannette had faced again and again in other states where she had learned to soft-pedal sticky issues. With her prodding, the Montana legislature eventually put equal rights before the voters. And it was no surprise when the *Anaconda Standard* devoted more than half a page to an interview with Rankin on the eve of her departure to march with suffrage leaders in Washington, D.C., the day before Woodrow Wilson's inauguration.

Wilson would be the first Democratic president since Benjamin Harris had left office in 1893, and, for the first time since the fight for suffrage began, the senator who chaired the committee on the issue was not only a member of the dominant party but favored giving women the vote. So did Montana's entire congressional delegation, Rankin told the Anaconda reporter, while noting that women in nine states were already enfranchised.

Jeannette traveled to Washington with Mary Land, a Missoula friend her own age who had married an army man five years their junior and recently moved to Whitehall. The women made the trip east via automobile, considered a daring venture even for men in an era when ignition required a hand crank and tires needed frequent changing. However, the journey proved no more dangerous than marching on the capital with five thousand like-minded women who were cheered and insulted—spat on and pelted with lighted cigar stubs—by half a million spectators.

Sadly, this confrontation would foreshadow suffragists' dealings with the new president, who ignored police brutality toward women picketing the White House to protest his boycott. But the time was right for Montana, and Rankin was right for the job. As a native daughter, she was a grassroots organizer who knew her roots. She represented a large group of Montana women who, like herself, were frontier-bred, unwed, employed, and willing to volunteer. Not the least of them was a prostitute from Glendive whose well-thought-out letters on politics were published by the *New Republic*. Homemakers and men also joined the ranks.

Because Rankin understood the opposition, her first move was to narrow the issue, quelling warfare within her own ranks.

"Women in our organization are from all walks of life, every political party, and every region and faith," she wrote in a letter she sent to every registered voter in the state. "We unite on one point: we want to vote." Her stance disappointed a number of Prohibitionists who had also been soldiering for years for equal rights. But the fact that they had been unsuccessful was not lost on them, so they, too, centered their arguments on the old-fashioned view of women's place in society and the Victorian belief that females were morally superior.

"Votes for women bring happiness into the home," they maintained. "Ask your fathers why they won't let your mothers vote."

Attractive, modestly dressed, and reasonable, Jeannette found herself generally received with courtesy and had learned to control her temper if she was not. When an angry political boss threw a glass of water in her face, she had satisfied her rage by telling him that the woman's vote would eventually mean his destruction. She reacted with similar cool when she was booed off the stage at a Helena debate organized by the National Anti-Suffrage Association.

In addition to constant train travel, Jeannette clocked more than nine thousand Montana miles on her Model T Ford, occasionally miring it to the hubs on muddy roads and sometimes sleeping in it in rural areas, where she sought out women in their kitchens, ranchers, and farmers wherever she could find them. Equally persistent in cities, she managed to give twenty-five speeches during one twenty-five-day period, comfortable in buttonholing voters on sidewalks, in bars, barbershops, pool palaces, union halls and red-light districts.

The vote was close—41,302 for and 37,558 against—but it stood. Triumphant but exhausted, Rankin discovered that her hair had become streaked with gray during the grueling campaign and realized she had come to a crossroads. Though still attractive, she was middle-aged and still hadn't settled on a career. After summering with her family, lecturing on economics at the university, and chairing a statewide convention of the Good Government League, she sailed to New Zealand, where women had been voting since 1893. Again supporting herself as a dressmaker, she studied child welfare laws, pensions for mothers and the aged, health care, and social conditions. But the question that had her stymied was whether she could wage a successful congressional campaign the following spring.

The timing was as good as it could ever be. Not only could Jeannette count on women's votes, the statewide suffrage organization she had established was still in place. Because of her campaigning a year earlier, her name recognition was higher than any candidate except Democratic incumbent John Evans, who was trying for a third term. Evans would be hard to beat, but the homesteading boom had increased Montana's population to a point where the state suddenly qualified for *two* representatives, with candidates for both seats to run at large. All Jeannette had to do was come in second. Her brother, Wellington, would throw his fortune and political savvy behind her.

Briefly the siblings wondered if her personal life might prove a problem. While Jeannette served as field director for the NAWSA—by its very nature a woman-centered organization—rumors that she was a lesbian saw print. Angered, she was planning a libel suit when Wellington convinced her it would only make matters worse, and the rumors seemed not to have followed her home. Nor was there any mention of her youthful indiscretion at Whitehall, where, fortuitously, school records had been destroyed in a tornado.

The press instead took note of her good looks, high energy, and luminous charm. One editor described Rankin as looking like "a young panther ready to spring." Another reported she had "a rare combination of femininity and force." She had learned to talk with men as equals, yet she was still fielding plenty of marriage proposals and shamelessly traded on her reputation for making the state's finest lemon meringue pies.

Still, friends, leading suffragists, and seasoned politicians in her Republican party all predicted she could not win. And, considering that most of her press coverage was relegated to the society page, it is a wonder that she did. Her victory certainly came as a major shock to the *New York Times*, which assured readers that her candidacy was plainly illegal because the Constitution used the word "he" in outlining the qualifications for congressmen.

As Wellington had predicted, Jeannette came in second with 76,932 votes to Evans's 84,499. Her plurality of 22,549 over one of the other four candidates so disgraced him that he committed suicide rather than face the taunt that he had been bested by a woman. Yet voters had wanted a change. With the considerable help of the women of Montana, Jeannette Rankin had just became the first woman elected to the U.S. Congress—indeed the first woman in the world to be elected to a national legislative body—and she was beholden to no man.

EPILOGUE

―◦―

THE WAGES OF SIN

On January 6, 1917, county attorneys throughout Montana received a letter from Sam Ford, the state's newly elected attorney general, ordering them to enforce a law that had long gone unheeded prohibiting houses of ill fame. Ford, who had served as assistant district attorney from 1908 to 1914, had been elected to his new position on a promise to eradicate prostitution, and no one doubted that he was serious. Smaller towns with restricted districts—Dillon, Kalispell, Glasgow, Hamilton, Deer Lodge, even Bozeman and Helena—moved to comply. The Miles City attorney, realizing that license fees from its red-light operations made up at least $9,000 of the council's budget, defied the state's lawman, while Butte—suddenly overrun by working girls displaced from smaller settlements—waited to see what would happen.

Ford immediately filed ouster proceedings against the Miles City attorney who ignored him, resulting in a trial that became a farce. Residents swore they had no idea what went on in the Miles City so-called red-light district, although five of the town's policemen conceded they'd never encountered a "respectable" person there. Hoping to avoid something similar, and realizing how easy it had been to circumvent prohibition, Butte's mayor brutally ordered its district and twelve outlying roadhouses to close immediately.

"Butte's restricted district, supporting the biggest open line in the west and the most up-to-date houses known west of the Mississippi river, is officially closed," the *Butte Miner* reported the next day. "More than 500 women in this county are vitally concerned in the edict announced last night after the conference in County Attorney Jackson's office."

Shortly thereafter, Geneva Gibson, proprietress of the Irish World, was hauled into court with Pansy Brasher, former madam of the Royal, and Edna Long of the Windsor, for allowing girls to reside at their houses. The landladies declared that all their girls had reformed and had no other homes to go to. Brasher told the sad tale of one young woman who, through the efforts of the Good Government Club, had found employment in a cigar store only to be fired when a customer recognized her as a former whore and complained.

"If it is a crime to give food and shelter to women who can't get work, then I want to plead guilty," she told the judge. "Send me to jail for 1,000 years and throw away the keys, because I'm going to give them shelter."

The city attorney said no laws had been violated if former scarlet women were merely residing in a house, and charges against the women were dismissed. So zealous were police, however, that they even arrested Delia Nadeau, who despite her social prominence was apparently lending a hand during the shutdown that jeopardized the better half of Joseph Nadeau's income. According to a brief newspaper report, "Mrs. Nadeau, in charge of the Henderson-Bielenberg block on West Broadway, was accused of failing to keep a register at the rooming house." She escaped conviction, perhaps with the help of her son, Albert, who had recently graduated from Harvard Law School.

Even publicity-shy Harry Adams made news. The longtime manager of the Copper King Hotel and Nadeau's other red-light enterprises, Adams spoke angrily on behalf of some of their inmates who, given no time to prepare for a move, had been caught without funds.

"The five I refer to were tired of living in the underworld and wished to return to the life of purity and to follow the straight path from now on if there was a possible chance to do so," he told a local reporter. "Each of the five girls, and all are nothing but women young in years and in worldly experience, walked up to five days in quest of respectable labor among respectable people. Wherever they went they were referred to with sneers and the general rebuff, 'The public sure would laugh at you, a public prostitute, if you were seen in honorable employment here,' they were told."

Perhaps shamed by Adams's concern, the Florence Crittenden League, Butte's Ministerial Association, the Women's Christian Temperance League, and the Moral Betterment Committee joined forces with the Good Government Club to address the sticky problem. All found rescue work tough going, though. Not only was it hard to place those who wished to be redeemed, but it was even harder to find those seeking redemption. Two women who canvassed the entire Copper King block on behalf of Morals Betterment reported that not one of the many girls to whom they offered assistance was disposed to accept it.

"Get me a job where I can earn $50 a week and I will go with you," one responded. Others made it clear they were asking favors from no one, the good women reported. But disappointment was in store for good-time girls who were waiting for the coast to clear as it had after the 1911 shut-down, when they were soon allowed to return to business as usual.

On America's entry into World War I, shortly after this forced closure, the federal government gained the power to put prostitutes out of business in the name of venereal disease control, reinforcing Attorney General Ford's edict. While Butte would remain a town where "anyone could get anything they wanted" until the late 1960s, it would do so only on clandestine terms, as predicted by a young prostitute in a letter to the editor just before the district closure.

"Go as far as you like with the liquor question, but this vice [prostitution] is something you can never stamp out, even if you close the lines," she warned. "For we live on just the same. We will move into some hotel or apartment house. Your wives and daughters will live next to us. You can choose for yourself."

The closing proved so unpopular that Mayor Lane was not reelected and Ford, who ran for governor following his term as attorney general, was also defeated. But there would be no reprieve for the restricted area. The colorful sexual circus it had hosted with unprecedented success had pulled up stakes and decamped forever.

———⬥———

As for the sinful survivors, they quite literally went subterranean in Butte, abetted by its huge network of underground tunnels, while, as in several other cities, their illegal operations were also favored by the benign neglect of law enforcement. From this point, of course, it is difficult to follow Montana's working girls, although there are occasional glimpses of their fate.

It seems fitting that the death of Lizzie Hall, "the darkest black woman in Butte," followed almost immediately the district closure in 1917. She had called Butte's red-light area home since its founding and had pioneered her profession in Montana long before that. Although Hall somehow managed to convince a Butte census taker that she was only forty in 1900, pioneering miners were enjoying her services in Bannack as early as 1863 when, according to that record, she was only two years old.

"If the wages of sin are death, Nigger Liz sure took a long time to qualify," one of her customers concluded.

Butte's top-grossing madams, Lou Harpell, Grace McGinnis, Ruth Clifford, and May Malloy, all vanished well before the district's final days, as did most of the popular inmates of their high-class resorts. Much has been made of the appalling suicide rates and short life spans of early prostitutes, even those who worked at the high end. Bestselling historian Anne Butler declared in *Daughters of Joy, Sisters of Mercy* that frontier prostitutes were poor, wretched, with no chance to escape the life once they were in it, but there are no figures to bear this out, even for the lowest crib workers.

"If in fact, many prostitutes killed themselves, we would find evidence for their suicides in the coroner's reports and in the vital statistics register mortality rates," argued Paula Petrik, who did an amazingly thorough demographic analysis of the working girls in early Helena. "To be sure, there are suicides in the tenderloin (two over a thirty-five-year period in Helena), but there are far more suicides among men. We should also find in the vital stats, women perishing from drug overdoses, venereal disease, and so on. We don't. Western cemeteries are not filled with poor prostitutes who took their own lives nor were victims of occupational hazards. We can, then, ask ourselves: What happened to them? This is a far more interesting question."

The likes of Liz Hall excepted, the working life of the average prostitute during this period appears to have been five to ten years, and longer if she moved up into management. More than a few appear to have quit early because the trade offered opportunities for marriage not available to single women in other fields. Since most did not market themselves under their real names, it was simple to vanish by returning to the use of the name on their birth certificate.

———◆———

A case in point is that of Madeleine Blair, who wrote a controversial autobiography following her long career as a prostitute and madam yet remains anonymous to this day. According to her account, she kicked the gambling addiction she had acquired in Butte and returned briefly to her lover there before moving over the border to Malta, Canada (also an alias), where she opened a very successful whorehouse on the prairies with the blessings of the Canadian Mounted Police. Here things went well until Blair nearly ruined herself with alcohol addiction. Saved by a priest from a church of which she was not a member, she gave her business operation to her housekeeper and returned to the States in search of a new life. It is clear from her last chapter that Madeleine again became a respected citizen, but she provided no details about how she made the transition or where she ended up.

Her book, *Madeleine: An Autobiography*, was published in 1919 by Harper & Brothers of New York with a sympathetic introduction by Judge Benjamin Barr Lindsey, an eminent social reformer. Immediately thereafter, however, the Society for the Prevention of Vice complained to the district attorney that *Madeleine* constituted "objectionable reading material" under New York's Penal code. Clinton Tyler Brainard, president and treasurer of Harper & Brothers, was arrested.

It wasn't that the book was graphic in sexual details, the prosecution conceded, but that its author was critical of Christian reformers and showed absolutely no remorse for her life of sin. Finding herself unwed and pregnant in her mid-teens, she had chosen independence instead of a morally approved course like incarceration in a Magdalene home for fallen women or suicide.

"I, an attractive, young girl, homeless, defenseless, hungry and in a few months to become a mother, had no choice between the course I took and the Mississippi River," she brazenly insisted, adding that government propaganda about the white slave trade was nothing but myth. Women became prostitutes because they wanted to, and they had reason to be proud of their work. Prostitutes did not cheat in the delivery of merchandise for which they were paid. On the contrary, the women who sold themselves into "loathsome" marriages were as guilty of sin as any scarlet woman, she wrote.

The bail for Harper's president was set at $500, and he faced a fine of $1,000 or a year in jail or both. He could have escaped trial by divulging the real name of the author, but he stoutly refused. Found guilty, Brainard shelled out the $1,000 fine and appealed. On July 10, 1920, a higher court reversed his conviction by a vote of four to one.

As for Madeleine, her fate remained as much in question as her identity, even after republication of her biography sparked new interest. A turning point may have come in May 2006 when Dr. Lindsey McMaster of Nipissing University, Ontario, crafted a paper on Blair claiming that the Canadian prairies and the free-spirited men who settled them had the power to revitalize the lives of women oppressed by urban dens of iniquity and a hard life on the streets.

"For Madeleine, free to walk the prairie at dawn following a night of unusually pleasant encounters with Canadian men, the spiritual and even sexual suggestions of nature give us a prairie replete with unexpected associations—far from a space of exile, imprisonment, and self-denial, it becomes a source of welcome renewal and self assertion," McMaster wrote. "As she walks the prairie at daybreak, Madeleine says, 'in my dawning womanhood I felt that somewhere and somehow I should demand from life the things that had been denied me.'"

McMaster did not divulge the real name of Madeleine Blair, nor did she seek it, but her paper elicited an interesting response from Bill Hillen, who mans the Lethbridge railroad station in Alberta. Restoration of the landmark drew heavily from details Madeleine had provided in her autobiography from her stops there, and Hillen, with help from fellow members of the Great Canadian Plains Railroad Society, has been gathering information on her ever since. Hillen's suspect as author of the book matches Blair's description in almost every detail. Positive proof has yet to be established and may never be, but if Hillen is correct, Blair married happily, returning to Canada where she and her wealthy husband became such an integral part of the Lethbridge community that they are still well remembered there today.

Unlike Madeleine, Dolores Jarra of Helena appeared often on public records, both as a prostitute and later as a respectable citizen. The problem is that she was too much on the record with too many names. She also did business as Delors Hara, Laura Jarra, Laura Washburn, Delorus Washburn, and later as Laura Stanchfield and Mrs. Charles Stanchfield. And there is dazzling variation in the spelling of her various monikers by public officials because Dolores, who could not write, had no way to correct them.

It is certain that after Dolores and her husband, Charlie, made a small fortune in their red-light operations and Butte real estate transactions, they returned to Helena planning to enjoy well-financed respectability and hope for even greater wealth. Instead, they went broke following the Panic of 1893, after Charlie mortgaged everything to start an ice business. Dolores's youngest daughter, Louisa, had married a Butte drugstore clerk just three years earlier, but the rest of the family left the state, apparently in the hopes of starting over.

At that point, even enthusiastic Stanchfield genealogy experts give up. Charlie's branch of the family disappears, and Dolores apparently never had one. There is some evidence they may have divorced and that Charlie moved to California, where he became a farmer and wed a younger woman, while Dolores returned to Montana under her original work name of Hars. But no matter where they ended their days, it is safe to say that their decision to abandon the red lights of Butte for respectability in Helena did not serve them nearly as well financially as that of their old neighbors, the Nadeaus, who elected to pioneer Butte's fledgling underworld and make crime pay.

According to the paid-for, two-page bio in *A History of Montana*, published in 1913, Joseph Nadeau had "made a considerable amount of money" in his French restaurant, which he then parlayed into an international corporation with his brother, Arthur, who had returned to Quebec. Joseph and Delia now resided in a beautiful suite of rooms in the Napton block, "the most elegant and fashionable apartment house in Butte," they informed the writer. And their large family had turned out well.

The couple's first son, Adelord, became a druggist in Los Angeles. Daughters Rosella and Phedora married Canadian brothers who became physicians.

Rosella's husband, F. L. St. John, practiced in Anaconda, while Joseph St. John, who wed Phedora, ran a hospital in Wallace, Idaho. Ovila, the Nadeau's second son, was secretary and treasurer of the Nadeau Investment Company (which the glowing write-up failed to mention included the red-light empire). Albert, the youngest, made it through Harvard Law School in 1911 and later practiced in Lewistown.

That the Nadeaus survived the district's official closure is borne out by the census three years later, which shows Joe and Ovila holding down quarters next to Harry Adams, still managing the fully occupied Copper King Hotel, while Delia resided in splendor at the Napton apartment. One might suspect, however, that family relationships were crumbling: Joseph's obituary five years later noted he was living at the West Park Street home of his daughter Rosella in Butte, and there was no mention of her husband. Daughter Phedora's husband was mentioned with "Dr." no longer appended to his name, perhaps substantiating a rumor that he lost his license to practice because of some scandal at Wallace. Nor was there any mention of the rest of the family, including Delia, who, like the Stanchfields, disappeared from record.

———◦———

Stanley Ketchel, wrongly targeted as a pimp and forced to leave Butte by the local police, is the easiest resident of the restricted district to track because he soon became its most famous. Banishment from Montana propelled him to the big leagues of boxing, although he was so angry at his eviction he refused to allow mention of the state in his press releases and never returned to it. In 1908 in California, Ketchel flattened Montana Jack Sullivan to win the vacant world middleweight championship. Jack was the twin brother of Ketchel's old nemesis, Montana Mike, with whom he'd tangled unsuccessfully in Butte.

Still growing, Ketchel wrested the world's light heavyweight title from "Philadelphia Jack" O'Brien in March 1909 and then challenged his friend Jack Johnson, reigning world heavyweight champ. The black boxer, who outweighed Ketchel by twenty-five pounds and towered over him by nearly half a foot, proved the lightweight's undoing. Although Ketchel floored the big man in the twelfth round, Johnson rose from the mat to knock out Ketchel (along with all his teeth).

Ever optimistic, Ketchel was planning his comeback when he was murdered at age twenty-four by a farmhand who was jealous of the attention his girlfriend was paying to the handsome contender. Almost universally recognized as the greatest boxer of his time and class, Ketchel was mourned not only by sports fans but by dozens and dozens of young women who appreciated his energy in other fields. For twenty-two years after his death, a small notice appeared in the classifieds of a San Francisco paper that read "Ketchell, Stanley—In loving memory of Stanley Ketchell, Died October 15, 1910. Olga." The sponsor turned out to be a Ziegfeld Follies star who apparently had no romantic relationship with the handsome boxer but was indulging a girlhood crush quite fittingly shared by many other young girls of Ketchel's era.

***

Charlie Russell, the cowboy best known in his early years for his enthusiastic patronage of whorehouses in Helena, also went on to fame as the country's best-loved Western artist. A seemingly hopeless alcoholic, at thirty-two Russell fell in love with a pretty eighteen-year-old named Nancy Cooper and took the pledge to marry her. Although she had little education and her early background is a bit murky, the ambitious young woman promoted Russell's painting career, providing the means for his talent to flower. The match produced no children, perhaps explained by the fact that on autopsy Nancy was discovered to have syphilis. How she contracted it and whether she brought about Russell's total reform is questionable, but the artist was still writing her misspelled but wonderful love letters a decade after they wed in 1909.

***

The "royalty" of Miles City is also easy to trace. Sydney Paget, son of Lord Alfred Paget, recovered from the bleak winter of 1886–1887 with the help of his trust fund. Connie Hoffman remained his mistress, traveling to England to be with him after he went there to visit his family for the hunting season of 1888. That fall the "Cowboy Queen" returned in the company of Lady Minnie Lindsey, close to her own age, who was a relative of Walter Lindsey, a boyhood friend of Paget's who was building his Cross S into the state's largest horse ranch. Hoffman also appears to have traveled to England in the summer of 1889, returning to New York on September 13 listed as Lady Hoffman, in the company of Miss M. Hoffman, J. O. Hoffman, a maid, and a one-year-old child. That may have been the end of the relationship. Back in Miles City later that year Sydney posed alone for a photographer wearing the gold braid–embellished uniform of a British Army officer, complete with sword, and marched off to achieve the rank of lieutenant as a machine gunner during the Second Boer War.

By the time Paget returned to raise polo ponies for multimillionaire W. C. Whitney on his Big Horn Ranch, Connie Hoffman was no longer with him. For company, Sydney found solace with Walter Lindsay, one of England's best-known steeplechase riders, and his young bride, Lady Kathleen Lindsay, who were encamped in comfort (complete with a grand piano) at the neighboring Cross S Ranch.

Paget also began to spend time on the East Coast and traveling the international racing circuit, where his mounts won the Belmont Stakes, the Kentucky Derby, and the Preakness. Finally at age forty-nine he astonished fellow members of the New York Bachelors' Club by marrying a beautiful actress named Marie Miller and returning to the family fold in England.

Of Miles City American pioneers, William Bullard and his mistress, Maggie Burns, seem to have fared the best. After a major fire swept the town in 1886, with losses totaling more than $60,000, Maggie backed her lover in establishing a brick factory, which proved as profitable as it was timely. The entrepreneur also added wholesale liquor distribution to his beer dealership and celebrated his tenth year on the city council.

Maggie seems to have abandoned her career as a madam for finance after she sold her famous whorehouse, but she waited another decade before marrying her lover, apparently wanting to make certain it was a good match. Following William's sale of his Bullard block in 1907, the couple moved with two of Bullard's nephews to a farm near Corpus Christi, Texas. Ten years later, they were still together in that state.

In contrast, it was waning luck that caused Miles City's most prominent black madams to pull up stakes. Uninsured when her mansion of joy burned for a second time, Annie Turner managed to get by with income from her California Restaurant and rentals on some of the small shacks in her backyard that had escaped the blaze. But it was nowhere near the money she had been earning with her well-furnished bordello and the weekly dances she had sponsored in its "ballroom." The last mention of her for the record was in April 1887 in connection with a celebration she threw for her son Eugene Miles Turner's tenth birthday, a landmark occasion perhaps because that "first child born in Miles City" had recently survived a citizen's arrest for stealing some moccasins from the Smith and Haynes department store.

Fannie French seems to have made her last stand shortly after the local paper reported that a patron visiting her new location in the Steamboat Building fell through the ceiling of W. B. Skinner's grocery store below. The client sustained no apparent injury except to his reputation, but French's profile had become too high. Singled out and convicted of running a house of ill repute while dozens of Miles City women who engaged in the same trade went unmolested, she was also sandbagged in the appeal she had made to the Montana Supreme Court in 1886—perhaps because she was the first black woman to take on the system.

Finally, in January 1895, following the election of Henri Haskell as attorney general with Ella Knowles as his assistant, French got her day in court. Her attorney, Charles Middleton, had served in the 1889 legislature that allowed Ella Knowles to take the bar exam, and he voted in her favor under protest. A woman's place was in the home, Middleton maintained, free from the "sights and scenes of court rooms, where the demoralizing and degrading trials and tribulations of mankind were ever in progress." But since Fannie French had not wanted to be there in the first place, Middleton went to bat for her. The justices waived French's jail time but insisted on payment of the fine. In the aftermath, French moved to Billings, where no questions were asked when she established a whorehouse. In fact she openly declared its operation as such in the 1900 census.

———— ✦ ————

Also due for a change of venue was Martha Jane Cannary, whose honest try at rebuilding her troubled life in Miles City would be her last. Back on the bottle and restless, she wandered the railroad circuit—working in dance halls and whorehouses, bumming drinks from aging pioneers who knew her when, and peddling her autobiography, a highly fictionalized account of her life as a scout for Custer and her romance with Wild Bill Hickok.

In 1893 she appeared in Buffalo Bill Cody's Wild West Show as a rider and marksman, and she also participated in the Pan-American Exposition in 1901. But at forty-one she was less than dependable, which numbered her days as a performer. In 1903 she returned to Madam Dora DuFran's whorehouse in the Black Hills, where she earned her keep by cooking and doing laundry when there wasn't much call for her usual services. Then, restless, she moved on to Terry, South Dakota, where she died of pneumonia at age fifty-one. According to her wishes, friends buried her alongside Wild Bill Hickok in the Deadwood cemetery, a move her Wikipedia page creator observed was a "posthumous joke" on Hickok, who had vehemently insisted he had absolutely no use for the woman who claimed him as the love of her life.

———— ✦ ————

As for the "respectable" women who took life into their own hands at a time when women were not expected to do so, Mary Healy Bottego, Ella Knowles, and Jeannette Rankin all paid a stiff price for checkered success.

Bottego, who had narrowly staved off financial disaster in Butte after her husband returned to his family estate in Italy with their two oldest children, stubbornly supported herself and their youngest daughter, Celestine, by any means at hand when no help came from abroad. Finally she managed to settle their Montana business affairs and reunite the family in Italy, where she had every reason to be miserable. Irish to the core, Mary spoke good English but no Italian, and her two oldest, Marie and Vittorio, had forgotten much of the English they had learned. Her husband, John, had developed a life of his own focused on his Italian family. Ill much of the time, probably suffering from a lung disease like so many Butte miners, Mary depended on the daughter she had raised in the States to bridge the gap between their two worlds. Quick to learn the language, gregarious and outgoing, Celestine immersed herself in the new culture while quietly retaining her Montana roots and her mother's fiercely independent spirit. When her older sister joined a convent, Celestine did not follow suit. Nor was she drawn to traditional family life.

Celestine Bottego became a professor, teaching ably in schools where women were seldom hired, and devoting the rest of her time to helping her family, community service, and travel among the poor in India and China. During World War II she worked with the underground against Mussolini's Fascists. But, although she had become a Benedictine oblate, a religious commitment lay people are allowed to make to a particular monastery, Celestine flatly turned down an appeal of her church to found a female order of Xaverian missionaries in 1943.

"I am more capable to destroy God's work than to make it happen," she insisted. Yet at the war's bloody end, she would take on the assignment, fielding it so well that following her death in 1980 she was nominated for Catholic sainthood, with her beatification now in progress.

———※———

Ella Haskell Knowles, who had challenged the rules to become a lawyer and served well as Montana's assistant district attorney, also prospered in private practice as one of the state's leading experts in mining law. She was so well regarded, in fact, that she was accorded a three-page spread in the 1902 edition of *Progressive Men of Montana*.

Although Ella had left her husband, popular attorney general Henri Knowles of Glendive, in an era when divorced women were considered disgraced, she resettled in Butte with community approval as a member of the Women's Relief Corps, the Order of the Eastern Star, the Women's Club, and Daughters of Rebecca. A popular speaker, she had just presented an illustrated lecture on her recent globe-encircling tour to a full house in the Butte Auditorium in January 1911 when she died unexpectedly of a lung infection. She had never remarried, was fifty-one at the time, and apparently had invested well in mining ventures.

More precarious was Jeannette Rankin's career following her election to Congress in 1917. She had been up-front during her campaign about the fact she was a pacifist, and the majority of Montana voters seemed to be with her on the issue, but her stance became less popular as World War I escalated. President Woodrow Wilson, who had won his second term with the campaign slogan "He kept us out of war," asked Congress for a declaration of war on April 2, 1917, and Rankin voted no.

Although forty-nine of her fellows also voted against entering the conflict, the Montana representative was the first woman ever to be elected to Congress. Because this was her first vote in that capacity, she was singled out by critics. Knowing she could not possibly win (373 voted with the president with nine abstaining), she had placed her personal ethics over the needs of her constituents against the advice of her most trusted political advisors.

Then, following Butte's Speculator Mine fire, which killed at least 162 workers that June and ignited a series of strikes over Anaconda's frightful working conditions and disregard for worker safety, Rankin sided with the miners, including a new union formed through the Communist-backed International Workers of the World. When Frank Little, a national IWW leader, was hung from a Butte railroad trestle, supposedly at the urging of the mine-owing monopoly, Rankin succeeded in getting the U.S. Army to guard the mines and roundly criticized Anaconda in a speech before the House and the press.

Although every piece of legislation Rankin introduced to better the lives of women and children passed within her lifetime, and universal suffrage became an American reality in 1920, the legislation wasn't passed during her watch. The press—and historians, too—showed less interest in her legislative accomplishments than in whether she was having an affair with Fiorello LaGuardia, eventual mayor of New York, who served with her as a freshman representative. And Anaconda saw to it she was defeated for reelection.

Rankin would have a second chance when Montana sent her to Congress again in 1940, but, as fate would have it, the beginning of her term coincided with the Japanese bombing of Pearl Harbor, and this time she was the only congressional member to vote no on entering a world war. Her political career stymied, Rankin devoted herself to lobbying and travel, living long enough to march with protesters of the Vietnam War and feminist activists who gave her the status of a hero.

———◦———

No similar honors can be accorded the Copper Kings and their heirs, who took their multimillions and vanished from Montana with nary a trace. Despite the vast fortunes they had made, they left it to the Work Project Administration during the Great Depression to pave hundreds of miles of streets, install sanitary sewers, develop parks and playgrounds, and provide an art center for Butte, while they endowed symphony orchestras, libraries, and art galleries in the big cities to which they moved. Worse, all sold out to the Anaconda monopoly, which released its stranglehold on the state only after copper resources neared exhaustion, leaving behind a history of strikes, violence, and martial law, plus toxic waste, poison in the water table, and soil that experts agree it will take centuries to clean up.

Add to Montana's woes the fact that, through a miscalculation in the draft formula and the vigorous volunteering of patriots, that state contributed 40 percent more men than any other to the armed forces during the World War I, with 26 percent more dead and wounded. No longer a young man's country, Montana's depopulation continued in the 1920s when a change in the weather patterns and poor advice originally given to homesteaders made Montanans the first to feel the effects of the Dust Bowl and the Great Depression that followed. Meanwhile, as mineral and timber resources gave out, jobs vanished on all fronts. Counties that had been subdivided by greedy politicians, increasing in number from nine to fifty-six, had trouble supporting themselves on a drastically shrinking tax base, and once-viable settlements statewide became ghost towns.

The most spectacular was (and remains) Butte. Abandoning underground mining for an open pit very close to the heart of town, Anaconda reduced its workforce from seventy-eight hundred miners to eight hundred before moving operations to Chile. Butte's population had dropped from a high of nearly fifty thousand to its all-time low of about twenty-three thousand by 1968, leaving hundreds of empty buildings rattling in the winds.

Beverly Snodgrass, then the town's most prominent madam who had been operating the old Irish World and Victoria brothels at much diminished capacity, threw in the towel when the Internal Revenue Service moved to investigate her. She and her seven poodles disappeared from the scene in her pickup camper after she told her story to the *Great Falls Tribune*, claiming she wanted to "boost the crusade to shoot down prostitution, gambling and corruption in Butte being waged by the Civic Action Committee and backed by prominent citizens." But the truth of it was that sin in Butte just didn't pay very well any more.

———⊙———

Today both the Victoria and the Irish World have fallen to the wrecker's ball, and the old red-light district is mostly a parking lot. Except for a modest historical plaque and a wall painting of female silhouettes, only the once-grand Dumas and the Blue Range cribs remain as reminders of Butte's sinful past, and neither is open to the public.

"The bad woman had both glamour and power, but her career was so brief—she always comes rapidly to a bad end—that she had no lasting impact," academic Sue Armitage noted in a study of female stereotypes in the American West.

"Best forgotten," locals echo. But in 1992 the *Montana Standard* broke the story that an abortionist who had practiced in Butte from about 1920 through the 1950s had made big money selling babies born of prostitutes and other morally compromised young women to respectable Montana families.

———⊙———

Gertrude Pitkanen was very careful and very clever. She was never caught. She had moved to Montana from Illinois at age twenty-six in 1907 as one of the first surgical nurses at St. James Community Hospital. There she worked with Dr. Gustavus Pitkanen, forty, born in Finland, who was also new to town and a kindred spirit. Later Gertrude earned a degree from the Palmer School of Chiropractic in Iowa and then returned to Montana to wed Gustavus, whose private practice included performing abortions.

During World War I, Gustavus was jailed under Montana's sedition act after he commented, "This is a rich man's war brought about by the politicians and the munitions makers and the capitalists for the purpose of making money profits." With friends in high places, he managed to escape conviction, but apparently Gertrude took over the illegal side of his practice while he was fighting for his freedom and continued to assist until his death in 1930, when she assumed it full-time.

Charged with manslaughter or homicide in three abortion deaths during her long career, Gertie always beat the rap. Those who followed her career recalled that she carried a little black book and all she had to do was open it for the judge to dismiss her case. Also in her favor was the fact that her second husband was a detective with the police department.

Virtually nothing was known about Pitkanen's baby sales, though, until long after her death when her "merchandise" began to seek their roots and medical histories. They learned instead that they had forged birth certificates saying they were the natural offspring of their parents and that the doctor who had delivered them was a chiropractor whose patients included a disproportionate number of prostitutes.

The few adoptive parents who were forthcoming explained they had purchased their newborns on short notice, wet from delivery, for $500 each. Subsequent investigation showed that Gertrude had sold at least twenty-eight of them, and probably many more, with slightly over a dozen located at this writing. Yet despite the fact that they joined forces more than fifteen years ago, with national publicity, not one birth mother has come forward to claim any of them, which is not the case with similar groups in other states.

The problem is that if their Montana mothers came from prominent families, they are ill positioned to reach out, while Butte's prostitutes usually traveled a circuit from as far away as California. Few in later years spent more than a month or so in any location, which makes them especially difficult to trace.

So—like it or not—the independent spirit of Madeleine and her sisters in sin lives on in Montana's gene pool. It could be just about anywhere.

MAJOR PLAYERS

—=•«◉»•=—

THE WOMEN AND MEN WHO MADE
THE MOST OF A WILD FRONTIER

❧ THE WOMEN ❧

LIZZIE ABASCAL—The sister of William A. Clark accompanied Anna LaChapelle on her first trip to Paris under Clark's sponsorship in 1895. Lizzie's husband, Joaquin Abascal, was apparently too busy with politics to be very attentive, and she welcomed the chance to travel on her own.

MARY STUART ABBOTT—The daughter of an Indian mother and Granville Stuart, she married cowboy E. C. "Teddy Blue" Abbott with her father's blessing in 1888.

LOTTIE ABLES (A.K.A. SORREL MIKE)—Well known in Helena for her suicide attempts, the prostitute wed bartender James C. Pickett and moved with him to Butte for a new start in 1879. After the marriage failed, the census reported her living alone, although it appears she may have teamed with another woman to help pay her rent.

AH-CHOI—The legendary Chinese prostitute is given credit for pioneering the female slave trade between China and the American West. Finding herself on her own in San Francisco at the height of the California Gold Rush, she sold herself with enough success to open a brothel stocked with Chinese women she had recruited, often under misleading circumstances. The venture and subsequent spinoffs made her wealthy, but by 1854 the slave trade she established had been taken over by Chinese secret societies.

NANNIE ALDERSON—The wife of a cattleman with a remote spread, the young housewife sometimes sought medical attention in Miles City and moved there briefly after marauders burned their ranch. Her autobiography, *The Bride Goes West*, inadvertently provides us with some startling insights into the life of prostitute Connie Hoffman, although Alderson was shocked to discover the girl's trade after befriending her.

MADELEINE BLAIR—According to her autobiography, *Madeleine*, this upscale prostitute came to Montana in about 1894 in search of her lover, Paul Martin, while recovering from a nervous and physical breakdown. Her book, published in 1919, offers what is believed to be an authentic picture of Butte's demimonde although her actual identity has never been revealed.

ELLA DRIGGS BORDEAUX—Born to a pioneering family of good repute in Butte, Bordeaux had the courage to sue her wealthy husband, John, for a large settlement after he filed for divorce and charged her wrongly with desertion and adultery in 1899.

CELESTINE BOTTEGO—Named the best grammar school student in Montana in 1910, the girl resisted the urging of her Catholic teacher to become a nun and went on to teach in an Italian college that seldom hired women. Only late in life did she answer the calling of her church, doing so with such intensity that she is currently being considered for sainthood.

MARY HEALY BOTTEGO—A young woman of unusual independence who came to Butte in 1892 where she married John Bottego, a builder and developer who had long been courting her. Seven years later John left her in Butte with their oldest daughter, Celestine, taking a younger daughter, Marie, and their young son, Vittorio, back to his home in Italy to care for his wealthy mother. Finding herself without resources to settle their business affairs, Mary struggled to support herself until 1910, when she finally managed to sell enough property to reunite the family overseas.

MAGGIE BURNS—The most successful madam in Miles City, the fiery-tempered, red-haired madam insured her business by romancing William Bullard, who began his career as the town's deputy sheriff and worked his way up to city council. With Maggie's financial backing, Bullard also became a highly successful businessman.

MARTHA JANE CANNARY (A.K.A. CALAMITY JANE)—Orphaned young, Jane established herself early as a teamster and prostitute. Later she made an attempt at respectability, sobering up and settling near Miles City about 1880 as the wife of Frank King, a well-liked rancher from the Judith Basin. The reformation didn't last, but Jane would remember her stay there as one of the happiest periods of her life.

CARMEN—reputed to be of "Spanish" descent and dishonest, she was one of the first prostitutes on the scene for the Bannack gold rush. She moved on to Virginia City and Helena before disappearing from the record.

ANNA LACHAPELLE CLARK—Her heart set on a theatrical career, the Butte girl decided to find a wealthy patron to help overcome her family's failing finances. Her first choice, James Murray, a wealthy mining man who owned the local opera house, suggested she look to William Clark, who was even wealthier than he. Mustering her considerable acting skills and abetted by considerable personal charm, she snared Clark. Although it took Anna more than a decade to be recognized as his wife, and she was forced into a restrictive prenuptial agreement, Clark became one of the ten richest men in the United States and she outlived him, making even a limited share in his fortune a stunning inheritance.

HUGUETTE MARCELLE CLARK—Born in 1906 following the death of a brother, Huguette became the favorite of her mother, Anna LaChapelle, but failed to bond with her father, William Clark. Although she married a Wall

Street banker in 1928, she refused to consummate the union and lived with her mother for the rest of Anna's life.

WILHELMINA LOUISE AMELIA "ANDREE" CLARK—This daughter of Anna LaChapelle and William Clark, born in 1902, became her father's favorite child and a genuine charmer. Her death in 1919 left both her parents devastated.

RUTH CLIFFORD—The young Butte prostitute took over the management of the Windsor in 1907, presiding over its reopening as the Irish World.

FANNIE CORBIN—The gifted Butte High School teacher captured the mind and heart of Mary MacLane, who was her English student in 1899 and would later become a famous writer. Corbin and her younger sister, Clara, also a teacher at the school, had labored long there in an attempt to support their widowed mother, but it would be Corbin's last year in the city. Following study at Harvard she became a full professor at the University of Montana.

"BIG LOU" COURSELLE—An early Helena prostitute from California, she worked Last Change Gulch when gold was discovered there in 1866. She later moved on to become a prominent madam in Bozeman after fire destroyed her Helena property in 1874.

BELLE CRAFTON (A.K.A. MOLLY BYRNES)—In 1887 the pioneering Helena prostitute built a lavish bordello she aptly named the Castle; she profited handsomely at her trade for nearly a decade.

MARGARET CARTER CRUSE—One of the few Helena residents who believed in Tom Cruse, Margaret helped him during his early years and later married him although she was half his age. She died just after giving birth to their daughter, Mary, in 1887.

MARY "MAMIE" CRUSE—Motherless, she was raised by her superwealthy father, Tom Cruse, a senior citizen who did his best to keep her from the outside world. A control freak, Cruse countered Mamie's eventual rebellion

by foiling her elopement with her first love and destroying both of her marriages. Cruse quite literally (though inadvertently) drove Mamie to drink
and drugs and then institutionalized her "for her own good" in the name of
the church.

Madam de Cervellon—William Clark hired the Parisian to chaperone
Anna LaChapelle during her student days in Europe. She traveled with
LaChapelle from 1895 through at least 1902, when the Montana girl gave
birth to a child fathered by her benefactor.

Eleanor Alphonsine Dumont (a.k.a. Madame Mustache)—Foot-
loose, Dumont occasionally worked as a prostitute or madam as she successfully gambled her way through many of the Western boomtowns. She set
up shop in Helena about 1867, shortly after gold and silver were discovered
there, but soon moved on. A beautiful French Creole, she picked up her nickname after menopause provided her with a striking crop of facial hair.

Dutch Leina—The Helena prostitute was a special friend of cowboy artist
Charlie Russell. When she committed suicide in 1884 he was devastated.

Laura Edgar—Charlie Russell's first love apparently reciprocated his affec-
tions, but when her family objected to him she married into New Orleans
society.

Bertha "Bertie" Helen Forslund (a.k.a. Charlie Miller)—The
cross-dressing young woman successfully passed herself off as male to work as
a Missoula hotel clerk and later as a bartender. In 1891 she was charged with
a series of armed robberies in Helena. After promising to reform and to return
to wearing dresses, she escaped going to prison when her boyfriend, Henry
Clark, took the rap.

Fannie French (a.k.a. Fannie Hendricks)—The handsome Creole
helped establish the black section of Miles City's red-light district and also
owned her own livery stable with a string of horses. When city police singled

her out for arrest for lewd behavior while running a house of ill fame in 1894, she sued, taking her case to Montana's highest court.

CHOY GAY (A.K.A. LENA QUONG)—Although well aware that her husband, Quong Tuck Wing, had another wife in China, Gay made no protest until 1902, when she discovered he planned to make their thirteen-year-old servant girl wife number three. Then she sought help from the Butte Chinese Baptist Mission to rescue them both.

GENEVA GIBSON—The madam of the Irish World in 1917 when Montana's red-light districts were officially shut down, Gibson was hauled into court with two other madams, Pansy Basher of the Royal and Edna Long of the Windsor, for letting their girls remain in residence. After Basher told the judge that if it was a crime to give out-of-work girls food and shelter, he could lock her up, all three women were released on the order of the city attorney.

LIZZIE HALL (A.K.A. NIGGER LIZ)—A black prostitute from Maryland who pioneered the gold camps at Bannack and Virginia City in the early 1860s. She moved on to Helena and was working her trade in a Butte alley at the turn of the century. She died in that city in 1917, still a favorite with old customers.

LOU HARPELL—Once a famous madam in Chicago, the German-born Harpell arrived in Montana around 1885 at age forty-seven. About 1900 she opened the Victoria, Butte's most pretentious whorehouse, billing her four employees as "the Most Beautiful Girls in the World." She may have had the backing of Copper King Marcus Daly, whose colors she and her girls always wore to the local racetrack. By 1905 she disappeared from record.

KITTY HARDIMAN—The young entrepreneur owned a large dance hall in Miles City that featured, among other wonders, a grand piano.

ELLA KNOWLES HASKELL—Born in New Hampshire and a graduate of Bates College in Maine, Ella became the first woman allowed to practice law in Montana and the first in the United States to run for a statewide office.

Although she lost her bid for attorney general by a narrow margin to incumbent Henri Haskell, she was soon appointed assistant attorney general by her opponent and later married him.

JOSEPHINE HENSLEY (A.K.A. CHICAGO JOE, MARY WELCH, JOSEPHINE AIREY, AND JOSEPHINE HAWKINS)—Joe emigrated from Ireland in 1858 at age fifteen to succeed as a prostitute in Chicago. In 1867 she opened a dance hall in Helena, established herself as a capable madam, and became one of the largest property owners in town. Later she launched legitimate theater and invested widely in reputable businesses. All but wiped out in the Panic of '93, Joe survived on a shoestring until her death made front-page news in 1899.

CONNIE HOFFMAN—One of the most popular prostitutes in Deadwood, Hoffman was even more sought after following her move to Miles City, where she won the devotion and support of not only leading ranch owners but also English nobility who invested in Montana lands.

DOLORES JARRA (A.K.A. LAURA JARA, DELORS HARS, MRS. LEWIS WASHBURN, AND LAURA STANCHFIELD)—The Illinois native became a dance hall girl in Helena and invested well in the red-light district there. Later, with Helena bartender Charlie Stanchfield, she pioneered the demimonde of Butte before returning to Helena as a wealthy woman. Jarra was devoted to her two daughters, Louisa and Minnie Washburn, and managed to raise them as respectable citizens despite her early callings and the fact they were born out of wedlock.

WILLIE JOHNSON—This very young madam managed a Miles City brothel that was patronized by cowboys in the late 1800s.

MARY KELLY—Chicago Joe Hensley and accomplices unsuccessfully tried to commit this Helena prostitute to a mental hospital in 1874, apparently so they could take her property.

YOW KUM—Brutally stabbed by her Butte owner, Gong Sing, in 1881, the young girl was quickly resold to Ah Kum, another resident of the local Chinatown. Kum, in turn, sold her to be Jim Hong's bride. Her initial owner was arrested but never tried.

AMELIA LACHAPELLE—Born in 1878, the lovely girl was wafted to good fortune via the efforts of her younger sister, Anna, who snared William Clark, one of Butte's richest citizens, as a patron.

BERTIE LESLIE—The thirty-nine-year-old charmer ran Butte's Richelieu brothel in 1900, successfully changing its name to the Windsor for a new start.

DOROTHY MACLANE (A.K.A. DOLLY)—The older sister of writer Mary MacLane found work in the Butte library after graduating from high school and later went on to marry happily and become a successful newspaper reporter. Mary objected to Dolly because she always seemed to do everything right.

MARY MACLANE—Unhappy with her mother's second marriage, she moved with her family to Butte. When she could not find a meaningful job after graduating from high school, the teenager wrote a shocking book about her attraction to the devil, which became a national bestseller in 1902. It was a triumph she would never top, although she continued to write both for print and later for movies. Conflicted sexually, addicted to gambling, and humbled by having to return to her Butte family when her financial resources played out, Mary found life increasingly rough going.

MARGARET MACLANE—Following the death of her wealthy husband, James, the Canadian-born widow wed American Henry Klenze, the executor of James's estate. A mining man, Klenze moved Margaret with her three young children—-Mary, Dorothy, and James—-to Minnesota and then Butte, Montana, where he proceeded to run through their money at a rapid pace.

INEZ MAYBERTON—The Butte prostitute killed herself with an overdose of morphine when her lover deserted her in 1881.

ANNIE MCDOUGAL (A.K.A. COWBOY ANNIE)—This open-handed Miles City prostitute rode with the cowboys on roundups for the fun of it. An excellent horsewoman, she was much loved beyond the usual expectations of her profession.

GRACE McGINNIS—Manager of the Dumas in Butte at the turn of the century, the German-born madam made good money for Joseph Nadeau and the brothel's official owner, his wife, Delia.

LILLIE McGRAW (A.K.A. BRIDGET RYAN)—An Oregon girl, McGraw opened several houses of ill repute in Helena in the late 1870s and became a wealthy woman. She survived the Panic of '93 with the backing of banker Tom Cruse only to die in 1898 of cirrhosis at age sixty-one.

ANNIE McGREGOR (A.K.A. FRANKIE BLAIR)—The Oregon girl became a noted prostitute in Miles City just before the turn of the century.

MATTIE MEMS—An unusually popular Butte prostitute who worked at Lou Harpell's Victoria brothel in her prime, she had been reduced to working as a chambermaid at the time of her death in 1911.

HARRIET MONROE—Born to a prominent Chicago family, the beautiful poet became one of the most respected writers and editors of her day. Writer Mary MacLane, whose editor was Harriet's sister, Lucy, promptly fell in love with her, as did many others, male and female. Monroe was best known for founding *Poetry: A Magazine of Verse* in October 1912 and editing the monthly for twenty-four years. She never married.

LUCY MONROE (A.K.A. LUCY CALHOUN)—As acquisitions editor for publisher Herbert Stone in Chicago, Monroe discovered writer May MacLane in 1901 and helped the teenager at the beginning of her career. Monroe, well known in the literary world herself, married William James Calhoun and went with him when he served as the American ambassador to China.

CARRIE NATION (A.K.A. CARRY NATION)—The Prohibitionist descended on Butte in 1910, declaring it the most wide-open town she'd ever seen.

Hundreds turned out for her fiery lectures, but her attempt to march on the red-light district was aborted when May Malloy, madam of the Irish World, expelled her in an assault that may have hastened the reformer's death.

NORMA—The fictitious name for a friend of Madeleine Blair's, with whom she had worked at Lizzie Allen's brothel in Chicago. Norma's move to Butte with a gambler addicted to horse racing proved so unsuccessful that Madeleine had to give up on her.

KATHERINE O'SHEA—Billed as a nurse and companion for Tom Cruse's rebellious daughter, Mary, O'Shea was actually hired as her jailer. She testified on Tom's behalf in 1915 in a suit brought by Mary's widower, Harry Cotter.

AH OIE (A.K.A. ALICE LAMB)—Orphaned early, the pretty Chinese child with a fine singing voice was sold in 1884 to a cruel woman who in turn sold her to a San Francisco whorehouse. Rescued by workers from the Occidental Board Presbyterian Mission Home, Ah Oie went on to embrace the faith and marry Dr. Wah Jean Lamb, a Butte physician.

ANNA PARKER—The Butte prostitute tried unsuccessfully to commit suicide after being arrested for stealing from a customer in 1880. Somehow she mustered $700 bail and disappeared from the record.

CAMILLE AND MARIE PAUMIE—The Parisian sisters started a dry cleaning establishment in Butte in 1888, eventually expanding it to include small apartments (heated by the cleaning steam) that they rented to prostitutes. Their operation was so successful on all fronts that it remained a gold mine for the next decade.

GERTRUDE PITKANEN—Trained as a surgical nurse, in 1907 she found work at St. James Community Hospital, where she met her future husband, Dr. Gustavus Pitanen. After earning a degree at the Palmer School of Chiropractic in Iowa she returned to Butte, where she helped Gustavus with his practice, which included abortion. When he was jailed for sedition during World

War I, she carried on alone. Although she never qualified as a medical doctor, she wielded enormous power over Butte's movers, shakers, and lawmen, practicing illegally with little interruption. After her death it was discovered that she had also been in the business of selling babies.

MARY CRUSE RAE—The daughter of Tom Cruse's brother, William, was given a job as Tom's hostess as well as overseeing the care of his daughter, Mary, shortly after Tom's wife died. Apparently well paid, Rae stuck with the assignment until her charge's mysterious death at age twenty-six.

LADY ISABEL RANDALL—Although her father was a baronet and her husband was a well-heeled Oxford graduate, the English socialite spent her early married years trying to keep up appearances on a rough-hewn ranch near Three Forks, Montana. Her resulting book, *A Lady's Ranche Life in Montana*, did not speak well of the locals, but it did interest many fellow Europeans in investing in Western ranchlands.

JEANNETTE RANKIN—Born into a wealthy family in 1879, the Missoula girl managed to graduate from Montana State University before the death of her father in 1904 and her mother's illness left her with the job of raising her three younger sisters with the help of her nineteen-year-old-brother, Wellington. She eventually found success campaigning for women's suffrage. Then, with the help of her brother, she became the first woman to win a seat in the U.S. Congress. Defeated for reelection after she cast a vote against America's entry into World War I, she won again in 1940 to find herself similarly compromised, yet she survived to march with feminists in the 1970s.

NANCY COOPER RUSSELL—The independent woman was eighteen when she fell in love with what many assumed was a "wasted" cowboy, Charlie Russell, but she promoted his artistic talents so well that he became Montana's most famous painter.

MOLLIE FORREST SCOTT (A.K.A. HIGHKICKER)—A prostitute who married her pimp, Joe Scott, during the Black Hills gold rush in 1875, Mollie was engaged as a dance hall girl in Butte five years later when Scott shot her dead following an argument. Amazingly, he not only beat the rap but also declined to pay for her funeral.

INEZ SEXTON—A legitimate performer billed as the "Queen of Operatic and Ballad Song," the singer quit Deadwood's Gem Theater when she learned from owner Al Swearengen that she was also expected to entertain customers on a highly personal basis. Stranded, without resources, she was rescued by "respectable people" in town who held a benefit to send her off on the straight and narrow.

ROSE SHEEHEY—Hired as a governess for Tom Cruse's daughter, Mary, Sheehey served as Mary's jailer as well, helping her father maintain control over his daughter's life until the girl's suspicious death at age twenty-six.

BEVERLY SNODGRASS—Butte's last prominent madam resigned after the Internal Revenue Service moved to investigate her in 1968. She had been quietly running the old Victoria and the Irish World, but after the Butte Civic Action Committee launched a campaign to shut down prostitution, gambling, and corruption, the business apparently didn't pay as well as it had in the past.

DU TOY—Listed in the Helena census of 1880 as living with a household of Chinese pimps, she may have managed to purchase her freedom—she is listed in the Butte census of 1900 as a prostitute working on her own. She appears to be one of very few Chinese women who survived the trade in Montana.

HARRIET TRUETT—Daughter of a U.S. congressman, the society matron was the mother of a respected Helena judge. During the early 1870s she loaned money to Chicago Joe Hensley for red-light investment.

ANNIE TURNER—After serving as a laundress at Fort Keogh, the black prostitute established a successful brothel and restaurant in Miles City. Her main claim to fame, however, was that she sued the solder who fathered her first son in 1878. The lad had the distinction of being the first baby born in that town that was not Indian.

MARY FERRIS WEINARD—The Irish-born niece of Chicago Joe Hensley moved to Helena to work for her aunt in 1880 and fell in love with Phil Weinard, a fellow employee. Despite Joe's stout opposition, she eloped with the talented cowboy.

KATHLYN WILLIAMS—This extremely beautiful and talented Butte girl won William Clark's support to pursue an acting career in 1901. Her relationship with Clark may have pushed Anna LaChapelle into succumbing to the multimillionaire's romantic overtures after half a decade of saying no. Williams went on to become a famous movie star.

LON YING (A.K.A. LOWYEN QUON)—The Occidental Board Presbyterian Mission home rescued the thirteen-year-old girl from the clutches of Butte merchant Quong Tuck Wing, who wanted to make her his third wife without benefit of divorce in 1902. She later married well.

ℳ THE MEN ℳ.

E. C. "TEDDY BLUE" ABBOTT—A cowboy who made Miles City and its bordellos his base of operations during the 1880s. His autobiography, *We Pointed Them North: Recollections of a Cowpuncher*, provides a great picture of the region for the twenty years that followed.

JIM BARNES—A night sergeant on the Helena police department in 1912, the lawman was hired by Tom Cruse to kidnap Cruse's daughter, Mary, and take her to a Catholic home for wayward girls where she was imprisoned.

DR. GEORGE BEAL—The medical man's preference for alternative medicine made him suspect by fellow Montana physicians, but Beal, who made big money through his mining ventures, could not have cared less. He employed nearly a hundred Chinese in his search for gold and carried so much clout in Butte that he was elected mayor in 1880.

WILLIAM BERRY—The Missoula sheriff interested his sisters, Olive and Mandanna Pickering, in visiting Montana from their home in New Hampshire in 1878. Olive stayed to marry John Rankin, soon to become one of the wealthiest men in the state. Mandanna left, declaring the Montana wilderness was no place to raise children, but Olive and John went on to have seven of them, most of whom did very well in life.

REVEREND WILLIAM BIEDERWOLF—In 1905, the internationally renowned revivalist unsuccessfully attempted to rescue Butte from sin.

JOHN BORDEAUX—A newcomer to Butte from Mississippi, the wealthy mining man made the mistake of marrying into one of the town's first families. He would have cause to regret the match during his long, drawn-out divorce.

TOM BORDEAUX—Brother of John, the Butte man lied brazenly on behalf of his sibling during John's 1899 divorce hearing.

CLINTON TYLER BRAINARD—Because he was president and treasurer of Harper & Brothers publishing company, he was arrested for printing *Madeleine*, the autobiography of a prostitute, in 1919, not because of graphic sexual details in the book but because its writer showed no remorse for her life of sin. Brainard, who could have saved himself the trouble by giving the courts Madeleine's real name, refused but won on appeal.

GENERAL JAMES BRISBIN—Although he knew next to nothing about ranching, the Indian fighter wrote and published *The Beef Bonanza: Or, How to Get Rich on the Plains: A Description of Cattle Growing, Sheep Farming, Horse Raising and Dairying in the West* while stationed at Fort Keogh near Miles City. When the book became a bestseller in Europe, he made even more money brokering ranching real estate sales to restless royals but never gave up his military career.

CHARLIE BROWN—The owner of one of the most popular saloons and livery stables in Miles City, Brown was a solid citizen and a popular pioneer.

WILLIAM BULLARD—Paramour of Maggie Burns, Miles City's most successful madam, Bullard pioneered building of the town near the Fort Keogh military instillation beginning in the mid-1870s and grew rich by backing it.

JOHNNY BURNS—As manager of Deadwood's Gem Theater for Al Swearengen, Johnny was essentially running a whorehouse, which he did with brutal efficiency. He may or may not have been the husband of Maggie Burns, who later succeeded in the same business in Miles City.

ROBERT E. CAMPBELL—Enjoying breakfast in his home, the Miles City resident, with his wife, daughter, and a boarder, were subjected to a home invasion 1880s style when a drunken bartender barged in to make obscene remarks about the women of the family. The intruder was dispatched by saloon owner Charlie Brown, although a vigilante committee got credit for the drunk's demise.

TOM CARTER—The older brother of Mary Carter Cruse and a lawyer, Carter represented Montana Territory in the U.S. House of Representatives in 1889 and stayed on for a second term when Montana became a state. Later he served two terms in the U.S. Senate.

CHARLIE CHAPLIN—The famed movie actor began his career in vaudeville, playing Butte at age sixteen. Years later, he would praise the town as having the prettiest women of any red-light district in the West.

JOHN CHINNICK—Owner of the Cosmopolitan Theater and one of the first members of the Miles City council, Chinnick also had connections with the underworld that ultimately led to his undoing.

WILLIAM A. CLARK—A Pennsylvania schoolteacher who came west as a teamster at twenty-three to seek his fortune in 1862, Clark ended up as a miner in Bannack a year later. Investing his first gold in trade goods, he became so successful that he opened an even more lucrative bank to back future mining investments. His early success in Butte made him the most prominent of the Copper Kings and also helped him buy a seat in the U.S. Senate.

HARRY C. COTTER—A Butte miner from a wealthy family, he married Mary Cruse in 1911 but lived to regret it when her father interfered.

GOVERNOR JOHN CROSBY—During his tenure in 1883, Crosby killed every bill passed by the legislature to help stock growers, perhaps because he bowed to the will of the powerful mining interests who refused to support them.

TOM CRUSE—The Irish immigrant was regarded as a crazy old duff by Helena residents until his Drumlummon Mine became one of Montana's biggest silver producers and the bank in which he subsequently invested made him one of the wealthiest men in America.

WILLIAM CRUSE—After his brother, Tom Cruse, became one of the wealthiest men in America, William and his children played an important role in Tom's life. William's daughter, Mary, and two of his sons were employed in the Cruse household to help raise Tom's daughter.

LIEUTENANT COLONEL GEORGE CUSTER—In the summer of 1874 led the Seventh Cavalry to the Black Hills, ostensibly in search of a site for a military post. His report of finding gold led to a considerable increase in the number of illegal prospectors in the area. The Indian massacre of the arrogant military leader with his troops two years later gave expansionists an excuse to ignore already-violated treaties and push the Indians out. Fort Keogh, near modern-day Miles City, Montana, was the major staging area for the assault.

MARCUS DALY—Born in 1842 to a poor family in Ireland, he braved immigration and the Wild West to become one of America's wealthiest mining men. In Montana he was hailed as a Copper King after establishing Butte's Anaconda mine, plus a smelter and a town to go with it. Internationally he became famous for raising winning racehorses.

WARREN DAVENPORT—The well-educated son of an Iowa lawyer, he founded a Butte newspaper called the *X-Ray* in 1907, devoting it to exposés on graft and corruption and sarcastic coverage of red-light districts. A year later he underwrote a book of excerpts from his paper, which apparently broke him. He is listed as a miner in a subsequent census and his letters home indicate the exhaustion of his trust fund or savings.

MARQUIS DE MORÈS ET DE MONTEMAGGIORE (A.K.A. ANTOINE-AMEDEE-MARIE-VINCENT MANCA DE VILLOMBROSA)—The French nobleman tried to revolutionize the American meat-packing business in the early 1880s by boycotting the Chicago stockyards and shipping beef directly to market from his ranch in the Dakota badlands. He counted on Miles City as a supply center for his operations.

A. E. DRIGGS—A farmer who established himself early in Butte, Driggs married a sister of William Farlin's, who put the town on the map as a silver producer.

WILLIAM EDGAR—A neighbor of Charlie Russell's wealthy family in New Orleans, Edgar and his family opened their home to the artist after they moved to the Judith Basin in the early 1880s to try ranching. When Charlie fell in love with Edgar's daughter, Laura, however, they discouraged the match.

WILLIAM FARLIN—A determined miner who prospected Butte early without much success, Farlin returned in the mid-1870s to develop the Travona-Dexter mine and stamp mill, showing that silver could be processed profitably. While his efforts made others, most notably William Clark, wealthy, Farlin lost control of his venture and did not end up a rich man.

AH FOK—Living with six women in 1882, the suspected drug lord triggered an unwelcome investigation by Butte police when neighbors heard him cry out that one of his women had been kidnapped. While Fok claimed that only one of the women was his wife, lawmen concluded that Lucy, the "kidnap" victim, had actually fled on her own because she was tired of being number six in line for attention. None of the other women dared make a bigamy complaint.

WAY CHING FOO—In 1892 the businessman complained to the Butte city marshal that the wife he had recently purchased from Lung Sing, also a Butte merchant, had run off with her former husband. Since requests for help from Chinese were rare, the marshal attempted to come to Foo's aid with discouraging results.

SAM FORD—As the newly elected attorney general of Montana in 1917, he made good his promise to enforce antiprostitution laws, shutting down red-light districts statewide and prosecuting any city attorney who bucked him.

PRINCE ALBERT HANKINS—The Chicago gambler, who came to Montana during the Bannack gold rush with brothers Jeff and George in 1867, went on to make a fortune in Blackfoot and Virginia City. He married Josephine "Chicago Joe" Airey on February 14, 1869, but returned to Chicago about 1870. Both soon remarried, although no record of their divorce was ever found.

PETE HANSON—The owner of one of Butte's dens of iniquity, Clipper Shades, the underworld king had a reputation for drugging and robbing patrons. His death from natural causes in 1901 shocked residents, who had expected he would be murdered.

RUSSELL HARRISON—After running the Helena, Montana, assay office from 1878 to 1885, the son of future president Benjamin Harrison married the daughter of the Nebraska governor and returned to the East Coast, where he acquired an interest in *Lesley's Illustrated Newspaper*. By the 1890s he was back in Montana, where he purchased the *Helena Daily Journal* and a local ranch. Harrison was the first to publish the work of Montana artist Charlie Russell nationally.

FRANK HARSTEL—A cowboy and drinking buddy of artist Charlie Russell, he was bushwacked while peeling potatoes on his Judith Basin ranch.

HENRI HASKELL—An able lawyer, born in Maine, who served two terms as Montana attorney general before retiring to Glendive, Montana. He married Ella Knowles, a fellow New Englander, in 1895. They divorced in 1902, probably because he was ready to retire and she was not.

ALPHONSE HASSELMANS—The most famous harpist of his era and also a noted composer, Hasselmans had his pick of students. For this reason Anna LaChapelle was thrilled when the famous musician said he would teach her in Paris, where William Clark sponsored the education of the ambitious Montana girl beginning in 1895.

SAMUEL T. HAUSER—A Helena resident and civil engineer, he became one of Montana's most powerful capitalists by pioneering early mining ventures and perhaps by quietly investing in Butte's red-light district.

FRITZ AUGUSTUS HEINZE—Born in 1869 in New York City, Heinze was the youngest of the Copper Kings and the only one from a well-heeled family. A maverick, he lived an apparently charmed life filled with women of all classes, song, and enough wine to cause his death of cirrhosis of the liver at a young age. He was, however, a gifted mining man and the only one of the Copper Kings to take on the Anaconda mining monopoly, which controlled not only Butte but the state of Montana and its legislature at the beginning of the last century.

JAMES T. "BLACK HAWK" HENSLEY—The teamster moved to Helena after a failed mining venture at Lincoln City, Montana. Finding work as a bartender and bouncer for Chicago Joe Airey, he perfected his gambling skills and eventually helped bankroll her real estate ventures. They wed in 1878 and stayed married until her death.

CAPTAIN CHARLES S. HEINTZELMAN—An army quartermaster, Heintzelman was put in charge of building Fort Keogh. Later he partnered with William Bullard in building a sawmill to furnish lumber for the venture and for the building of Miles City nearby.

JOSEPH E. HENDRY—The young editor of the *Helena Daily Independent* launched his career by publishing exposés on Helena's opium houses and red-light district in 1886, forcing police to make arrests for prostitution for the first time in that city's history. Hendry's death at age twenty-seven the following year ended his crusade.

ANTON HOLTER—An early settler in Helena, Holter grew rich through the building trades and later invested well throughout the state, especially in Butte, where he is reputed to have backed the building of the Blue Range Cribs in the red-light district. Among other honors, he was knighted by the king of Norway.

JAKE HOOVER (A.K.A. LUCKY BOY)—A major gold discovery early in his career should have set Hoover up for life. Instead, he sold out too early to William Clark, later hailed as one of the Copper Kings, to make his living as a trapper and professional game hunter. In the early 1880s, he befriended a budding artist named Charlie Russell when the lad was down and out in the Judith Basin. Without Hoover's help, the city-bred Russell probably would never have made it in the rugged Montana rangeland.

RICHARD HOWEY—When Helena's fair-minded superintendent of schools became mayor in 1887, he insisted the town could not use earnings from prostitutes (collected as fines), so the city attorney refused to prosecute any wayward women who were arrested.

WILLIAM H. HUNT—The righteous Republican district attorney in Helena moved to shut down Chicago Joe Hensley's dance hall in 1886 after the legislature passed a law making "pernicious hurdy-gurdy houses" illegal. Fortunately for Joe, Hunt failed to do his homework.

TOM IRVINE—One of General Nelson Miles's scouts, Irvine built Miles City's first jail and became its first sheriff. He partnered with William Bullard in enforcing local law, just as they had teamed earlier as army recruits.

JACK JOHNSON—In 1909 the reigning world heavyweight champ was knocked down by Stanley Ketchel, many pounds lighter and considerably shorter, in a match that (rumor has it) Ketchel promised to throw. Johnson, who was a close friend, badly injured the lightweight while hanging onto his title.

JOHN HENRY "HARRY" KEENAN—Son of a respected Fort Keogh military man, Harry started his career as a cowboy, turned to gambling, and finally ended up as a lawman. His marriage to a Miles City prostitute apparently did little to cloud his return to polite society because locals were pleased that the couple had reformed themselves.

STAN KETCHEL—Born on a farm in Grand Rapids of Polish immigrants, the short, stocky fighter fled to Butte at age fourteen after a fight with his father and settled into the underworld as a bellman for a hotel in the red-light district. With the help of Charlie O'Conner, who became his manager, Ketchel began to win boxing matches with unusual skills that would eventually make him an international champion.

JOSEPH W. KINSLEY—The Helena attorney took on Ella Knowles as a law intern and practiced with her after she passed the Montana bar in 1898.

WILLIAM KNIGHT—The outspoken editor of the *Yellowstone Journal* provided lively reading for early residents of Miles City. His feud with Annie Turner, which began in 1882, ended with a fire that burned her bordello.

PETER LACHAPELLE—A French Canadian from a farm family of nineteen children, LaChapelle somehow managed to study medicine in Montreal before immigrating to Michigan, where he worked as a tailor. Weary of the job, he decided to reinvent himself in 1889, moving to Butte with his wife, Philomene, and their five children to establish himself as a doctor but was stopped for practicing without a license. Not until his youngest daughter caught the attention of a millionaire, William Clark, did family fortunes turn around.

WILLIAM LaCHAPELLE—The oldest son of Peter and Philomene went to work for William Clark after the multimillionaire took a fancy to his sister. In addition, Clark helped put her younger brother, Arthur, through business school. Another brother had died earlier.

CHARLES H. LANE—After cooperating with the Montana attorney general to shut down the Butte red-light district, the mayor failed to get elected for a second term.

SELIG LAVENBERG—The Helena dry goods merchant, with his brother, Alex, backed Chicago Joe Hensley on several business ventures.

HING LEE—The businessman was well respected by both Chinese and white residents of German Gulch mining camp, where he often served as an interpreter. Yet authorities never solved his murder, even though the culprit made off with $7,000 in gold dust and thirty cases of opium.

YUNG LEE—The upscale opium dealer was arrested during a crusade to clean up Butte in 1896. His testimony was as glowing as any drug company ad, which may have kept him out of jail.

TOM LIN—The mysterious real estate owner long held a large piece of Butte property near the red-light district between Galena and Mercury. When the city razed it in 1936 it was discovered to include a warren of secret tunnels with a mysterious underground chamber, the uses for which have never come to light.

JUDGE BENJAMIN BARR LINDSEY—In 1919 the nationally known social reformer wrote a positive introduction to the autobiography of Madeleine Blair, a prostitute who refused to apologize for her choice of profession. Lindsey's claim to fame today is that he was the brains behind establishing the juvenile court, and Madeleine may well have deserved his protection.

WALTER LINDSEY—A boyhood friend of Sydney Paget's, the Montana rancher was one of England's best-known steeplechasers. He wed Lady Kathleen Lindsey, also of the royal family. Paget was at home on their ranch, which was near his own.

FRANK LITTLE—A national leader in the Communist-backed International Workers of the World, the union man traveled to Butte following a 1917 mining accident that killed at least 162 workers. The morning after his arrival he was found hanging from a railroad trestle, supposedly at the behest of the mine-owning monopoly. No one was ever tried for the lynching.

LESTER LOBLE—As a boy, the Helena judge had grown up next door to Mary Cruse and was one of very few youngsters who was allowed to play with her. His recollection of her affluence and her unhappiness provides most of the insight we have into the heiress's strange childhood.

FRED LOEBER—The Helena miner turned cowboy invested in Loeber's Opera House in 1877. It appears to have been a bar and dance hall, which disappeared from record within the year.

HARVEY LOGAN (A.K.A. KID CURRY)—Before he became a member of the Hole-in-the-Wall Gang and the subject of numerous "Wanted" posters, Logan worked as a cowboy at the Circle Bar ranch near Miles City.

ISAAC D. McCUTCHEON—The gifted lawyer was delighted to defend Chicago Joe Hensley when Helena district attorney William Hunt attempted to shut down her dance hall in 1886. McCutcheon, who had formerly served as Montana's secretary of state, made short work of Hunt.

MAJOR WILLIAM MACQUEEN—Originally in Miles City to do business with Fort Keogh as a trader, the major later built the town's leading accommodation, which he called the Inter Ocean Hotel. Ignoring the pretention, it was usually referred to as the MacQueen Hotel.

JOHN MAGUIRE—The well-known Montana theater man ably managed Ming's Opera House in Helena during the 1880s. Later he moved his base to Butte, where he was one of very few critics to acknowledge the genius of teenage author Mary MacLane.

PAUL MARTIN—Madeleine Blair's fictitious name for her lover, a wealthy, Butte-based businessman who invested in Bannack mining projects.

JUDGE ALEX McGOWAN—A Butte police court judge who locked up all the town's drug users together in 1910 in an unsuccessful attempt to rehabilitate them.

COLONEL HUGH McQUAID—Editor of the *Helena Independent*, the newspaperman became a close friend of prospector Tom Cruse's when virtually no one else in town would support him. Although neither had business training and Cruse could not read or write, they managed to negotiate the sale of Cruse's mining property for a sum that made them both wealthy men.

CHARLES MIDDLETON—The lawyer, who served in the Montana legislature in 1889 and voted under protest in favor of women being allowed to practice law, represented Fannie French when she sued the state for arresting her on prostitution charges. Middleton managed to get her jail time waived, but French was still stuck with a heavy fine.

JUDGE GEORGE ROSZELLE MILBURN—Well connected in Washington, D.C., and a former Indian agent, Milburn was appointed a judge for Montana's seventh judicial district in 1889 and reelected in 1892 with the help of the Republican Party despite the fact he was a Democrat.

GEORGE MILES—The nephew of Fort Keogh commander Nelson Miles and a member of his 5th Infantry, Miles helped establish the town of Miles City adjacent to the base in 1876.

NELSON MILES—The commander of Fort Keogh, established to protect U.S. citizens from hostile tribes, became the most successful Indian fighter of his day, clearing Montana's eastern prairies and the Dakotas for white settlement. Miles City was named in his honor.

JOHN MING—The wealthy Helena rancher built a fine opera house in Helena during the 1880s.

JAMES MURRAY—As lucky as he was handsome and charming, the gambling mining man grew rich by investing in Butte property and also built a successful opera house in the town. Considered one of Montana's most eligible bachelors, he waited to marry until he was sixty-three, choosing Mary Haldron, the former wife of a high-profile New York lawyer who also practiced locally.

JOSEPH NADEAU—This Canadian shoe salesman arrived in Butte in 1878 with his wife, Delia, their growing family, and his brother, Arthur, to start a new life. The establishment of a restaurant and purchase of a modest hotel provided a respectable front for their operations in Butte's red-light district, which Joe and his son Ovila soon controlled under the management of bartender Harry Adams. Meanwhile, Delia found a place in Butte high society.

MAYOR CHARLES NEVIN—His attempt to close the Butte red-light district in 1911 proved short-lived because merchants and city councilmen soon decided the industry of prostitution was vital to the town's well-being.

ALVAR DE COMEAU O'BRIEN—A football quarterback while at Princeton and later a Wall Street broker, O'Brien had the misfortune of falling in love and marrying Mary Cruse in 1909 over the objections of her father, Tom Cruse. Later Cruse threatened to disinherit his daughter if she didn't divorce O'Brien, and she obliged.

CHARLIE O'CONNOR—A photographer by trade, O'Conner became fight manager for Stanley Ketchel, taking him to international championships after his early training in Butte.

WARREN O'MARA—One of Butte's most colorful police court judges, O'Mara reformed and finally married a prostitute known as Lillie the Lush, much to the amusement of the local press.

OOLU JACK—The owner of a Butte opium den was busted in 1879 even though opium itself was still legal nationally and used in many patent medicines. Despite a colorful trial involving Nellie Linwood, a knowledgeable patron, Annie Northcutt, a woman of ill repute from Helena, and Charlie Cummings, a local apparently caught by accident, no one went to jail and Jack stayed in business.

DR. LAWRENCE PACKARD—The popular Whitehall doctor and his new wife, Nellie, became close friends of Jeannette Rankin's when she moved there to teach in 1903. The couple divorced a few years later, but Rankin was also close to Packard's second wife, Fannie, dispelling speculation that Rankin and Nellie might have had a relationship less pure than simple friendship.

SYDNEY PAGET—In the early 1880s, the fifth son and twelfth child of Lord Alfred Paget purchased a herd of Nebraska cattle and pastured them on Montana's upper Tongue River about sixty miles from Miles City. Later he would purchase land in Wyoming, but he continued to work out of Miles City, where he took up with the town's most famous prostitute, Connie Hoffman, and raced his horses at the local track. Although locals considered him nothing but a silly playboy, Paget did well at raising cattle and even better in the horse trade, later winning impressive trophies on a national level.

ROBERT LEROY PARKER (A.K.A. BUTCH CASSIDY)—During a career as a cowboy and rustler before train robbery became his career of choice, Parker often frequented Miles City.

"BIG NOSE" JOHN PARROTT—The murderous road agent made big money in Miles City because he was in league with popular theater owner George Chinnok, but he was later hung by a mob in Wyoming.

JESSE PHELPS—The manager of the OH Ranch near Utica, Montana, who hired Charlie Russell as a hand during the savage winter of 1886–1887, asked the artist to draw something that would make owners of his herd understand why the animals had died off. Russell's small watercolor of a dying steer facing hungry wolves later became a symbol of the tragedy that destroyed the fortunes of many Montana cattlemen.

HENRY PLUMMER—Though elected sheriff of Bannack in 1862, he secretly headed a gang of cutthroat highwaymen. Because he was charming, married to a well-respected local girl, and went through the motions of being a fine lawman, Plummer's duplicity was not discovered until 1864, when vigilantes hung him.

DR. HUIE POCK—The well-respected Chinese doctor had at least as many white patients in Butte as he did fellow countrymen and moved surprising well in the town's elite society. Among those who paid homage to Hum Fay, the bride he won from a rich Spokane family in 1896, were U.S. Senator Tom Carter and mining magnate James Murray. Later, during Butte's flu epidemic in 1918, Pock's herbal medicine saved many lives.

JOHN A. QUIRK—The oddly named Helena policeman was given the thankless assignment of arresting Chicago Joe Hensley and one of her girls during an attempt to shut down her dance hall in 1866.

DR. A. D. RALEIGH—The racist Methodist minister campaigned for Chinese exclusion throughout the state of Montana just after the turn of the century.

WILLIAM RIGNEY—The Miles City bartender fell victim to vigilante action in 1883 because he accosted a respectable family while drunk.

PAT RILEY—A friend of artist Charlie Russell's, this Judith Basin–based cow puncher was killed while sleeping off a drunk on the open range.

THEODORE ROOSEVELT—Broken over the death of his wife, Alice, and his mother in 1884, the future U.S. president turned to ranching in what became North Dakota near the spread of his friend the Marquis de Morès. Roosevelt also spent time with industry leaders in Montana, where he made many friends.

CHARLIE RUSSELL—Born into a well-to-do New Orleans family where he didn't fit, Russell left home early to become a Montana cowboy and later its most famous artist despite legendary drinking problems. Although he made Helena his base of operations during the 1880s, he relocated to Great Falls when fame finally found him.

JOSEPH SCOTT—The cattleman took over as president of Montana's Board of Stock Commissioners following the resignation of Granville Stuart in 1888.

BERTIE SIMPSON—The fictitious name Madeleine Blair made up for a wealthy Chicago patron she encountered in Butte.

GONG SING—As an employee of Butte mayor Dr. George Beal in 1881, the Chinese man escaped imprisonment for stabbing a woman he had purchased when his deal to resell her went wrong. Beal was not reelected mayor, however.

ONE LUNG SING—Because women were considered chattel by his culture, the Butte merchant apparently did not consult his wife when he sold her to Way Ching Foo, a fellow tradesman, for $750 in 1892. This proved to be a mistake that would return to haunt him.

LYMAN SISLEY—John Bordeaux claimed the Butte mining broker had committed adultery with his wife, Ella Driggs Bordeaux, according to testimony at the Bordeaux divorce hearing in 1899.

CHARLIE STANCHFIELD—Arriving in Montana during the Virginia City rush, Stanchfield learned the bartending trade and moved on to Helena, where he apparently failed as a bar owner. Then, teaming with Dolores Jarra, whom he later married, he moved to Butte for a fresh start. Eventually the couple parlayed dance hall ownership into a real fortune and returned to Helena, where they were accepted as respectable citizens.

THOMAS STEPHENS—The legitimate Butte businessman had invested heavily in the low end of its red-light district before his death in 1891. His son, Thomas, transferred the property to Stephens Investment Company and continued to run the operation, which included a slum full of cribs known as Little Terrace.

B. J. "Long Green" Stillwell—When the would-be professional gambler failed miserably in Helena, he took off for Alberta, Canada, with Charlie Russell and his friend Phil Weinard, but he did not stay for long. In later life he became a lawman in Washington State.

Herbert Stone—The successful Chicago publisher was the first to identify bestselling writers Kate Chopin and Mary MacLane, to the chagrin of the Eastern establishment that refused to give the Windy City much credit for its literary scene.

Pete Stone—The Billings, Montana, boxer undertook Stanley Ketchel's training in Butte, Montana, in around 1902, helping him become an international champion.

Granville Stuart—One of the first prospectors to find gold in Montana, Stuart was also the reputed leader of vigilante operations in the boomtown of Bannack. He later turned to cattle ranching in the eastern part of the state and became an industry leader.

George Stull—Although a citified greenhorn when he arrived, this Methodist minister adjusted quickly to the brutal rowdiness of Miles City, managing to shoot his way to local respect.

Jack Sullivan—Butte's most famous boxer lost his international title to Stanley Ketchel in 1908 after Ketchel had been run out of town by police. Sullivan's brother, Mike, also an international contender, was defeated by Ketchel in that year.

Al Swearengen—The owner of the Gem Theater in Deadwood was famous for recruiting women for prostitution under the pretense of legitimacy. In 1880 his theater burned for a second time, but he remained a moving force in Deadwood as long as it was a boomtown.

JOSEPH SWITZER—The Helena liquor wholesaler backed Chicago Joe Hensley in many of her business ventures because she was one of his best customers.

JOSEPH K. TOOLE—The former governor, still a good-looking bachelor, unblushingly paid homage to Chicago Joe Hensley by riding in an open carriage in her funeral possession in 1899. She had helped him in time of need, as she had so many others, he explained.

EUGENE MILES TURNER (A.K.A. JOHN TURNER)—The son of Annie Turner, a base laundress at Fort Keogh, and Sergeant Eugene Allen was the first child born in Miles City who was not of Indian descent. He was listed under several names while his mother sought to legitimize him. He had acquired an arrest record before his paper trail disappears in Miles City in 1887.

LEWIS WASHBURN—The Helena homesteader worked for a local transfer firm through the mid-1870s. Where he came from and where he went remain a mystery, but Washburn was the acknowledged father of Dolores Jarra's two children, Minnie and Louisa.

ELBERT D. WEED—Helena's assistant district attorney had a flair for lofty oratory, which he demonstrated to the advantage of Chicago Joe Hensley during her trial for running a hurdy-gurdy house in 1886.

PHIL WEINARD—A teenage runaway from a family of German artists living in Minneapolis, Weinard became a skilled cowboy. Also a jack-of-all-trades, he formed a strong friendship with Chicago Joe Hensley and her husband when he worked for them in Helena for a couple of years in the 1870s. On his return in 1881 to help the Hensleys build a new theater, Phil befriended artist Charlie Russell and fell in love with Joe's nice, Mary Ferris, disrupting everyone's life including his own.

FRED WHITE—The pioneer businessman owned the only dance hall in Helena until Chicago Joe Hensley went into competition with him in 1867.

PIERRE WIBAUX—The son of a wealthy French manufacturer, he established a large ranch in Mingusville, Montana, and subsequently got his ranch hands to petition for a name change to Wibaux. Capitalizing on the bad winter of 1886–1887, he purchased the stock of failed ranchers at a discount and prospered.

W. J. WILCOX—The police court judge came to the rescue of Yow Kum, who staggered into his Butte police court one day in 1881 after having been stabbed by her owner. The owner eventually went free, much to the frustration of the court.

TIME LINE

FROM THE BROTHELS TO
THE CONGRESS

1854

* Ah-choi, a beautiful Chinese woman, finds herself on her own in San Francisco after her escort dies. She is so successful at supporting herself by prostitution during the California Gold Rush that she opens her own brothel and begins importing women to run the operation.

1862

* Early travelers to Idaho Territory find gold in the Rockies but keep their discoveries quiet. However, when a small party makes a big strike on Grasshopper Creek while searching for a pass over the Continental Divide, news spreads fast.

1863

* Miners establish the town of Bannack, which soon has more than a thousand inhabitants. It will produce nearly $5 million in gold.

❧ On May 26 a second big find is made on a small creek flowing into Stinking Water River. Christened Alder Gulch, it is eventually renamed Virginia City, Montana.

❧ 1864 ❧

❧ On January 1, Martha Jane Cannary, eleven, faces starvation with her family in Virginia City where she and her younger sister with baby brother in arms beg for food. Shortly thereafter both her parents die and she is left to support her siblings.

❧ Wanting to control their own destiny, Montana miners convince Congress on May 26 to separate their new discoveries from Idaho Territory. Bannack becomes their territorial capital.

❧ A large gold find is made on July 14 at Last Chance Gulch, which soon becomes the city of Helena.

❧ Butte goes on the map as a placer gold producer. The discoverers are Chinese.

❧ The first Montana silver discovery, near Bannack, is christened Argenta.

❧ Chicago gambler Al Hankins sets up shop in Bannack with brothers Jeff and George. Soon they move to Virginia City and then neighboring Nevada City, where they make big money.

❧ 1865 ❧

❧ Northern Pacific becomes the largest landholder in Montana and residents hope a railroad to the outside world will follow. It doesn't.

❧ Black prostitute Fannie Bird on June 14 is the first prostitute to record a land transaction at Last Chance Gulch.

❧ Virginia City wrests the territorial capital from Bannack as the gold reserves of Montana's first town dwindle.

❧ 1867 ❧

- Butte City, which has about five hundred residents, becomes known as the most lawless town in Montana.

- Josephine "Chicago Joe" Airey moves to Helena to open a dance hall and invests heavily in its red-light operations.

❧ 1868 ❧

- America's Burlingame Treaty with China accords visitors all the rights of American citizens except naturalization.

- Treaty be damned! On July 4 a white miner hangs a Chinese rival from a tree at Rocker near Butte for good luck. It is not known if the fortunes of this one-man lynch mob improved.

❧ 1869 ❧

- The Union Pacific Railroad is built across Nebraska and Wyoming to join with the Central Pacific in Utah, becoming the first transcontinental line. However, to reach Montana requires traveling twenty-five hundred miles by steamboat up the Missouri from St. Louis or a week or more travel by wagon along rugged trails from distant rail points.

- Butte fast becomes a ghost town as its gold is worked out.

- Three major fires cause more than $1 million damage in Helena. The town establishes a fire department and rebuilds.

- Chicago Joe Airey weds Albert Hankins on February 14 and they join the gold rush at White Pine, Nevada.

❧ 1870 ❧

- There are forty prostitutes in Helena.

- Chicago Joe Airey returns to Helena and hires James T. "Black Hawk" Hensley as a bartender and bouncer.

ᗷ 1871 ᗷ

❖ On October 1 a fire in Helena levels most of its main street, and a week later the Great Chicago Fire wipes out most of the companies insuring it. Helena rebuilds.

❖ Mrs. Harriet Truett, mother of Helena's judge, on October 11 loans money to Chicago Joe to expand her red-light empire.

ᗷ 1872 ᗷ

❖ The Butte Miners Union is able to establish an eight-hour day for underground work.

ᗷ 1873 ᗷ

❖ The Northern Pacific Railroad, which has promised to connect Montana with the world, falls into bankruptcy. Montana seems destined to remain isolated.

ᗷ 1874 ᗷ

❖ On January 9, fire guts Helena, destroying the town's most prized possession, the library and archives of the ten-year-old Montana Historical Society. It also wipes out the finances of many prostitutes including Big Lou Courselle, who sells out to Chicago Joe. Although her own dance hall has also burned to the ground, Joe rebuilds.

❖ During the summer, Lieutenant Colonel George Custer leads an army expedition to the Black Hills, ostensibly to locate the site for a future military post, but he reports finding gold.

❖ The Montana legislature passes a statute allowing women to own property.

ᗷ 1875 ᗷ

❖ Helena wrests the territorial capital from Virginia City.

❧ William Farlin pioneers mining and reducing silver ore in Butte.

❧ The Page Act allows the commissioner of immigration to prevent certain classes of people including "lewd or debauched" women from entering the United States. Because of this law, bribery becomes an industry in the trafficking of foreign women for prostitution.

❧ 1876 ❧

❧ Gold is discovered about twenty miles from Deadwood, Dakota Territory, by black prospectors. Fearing for their own safety they quietly take out all they can get without filing a claim before word spreads.

❧ William J. Parks, working alone in Butte, hits pure copper at 150 feet. He is regarded by the general public as crazy because the ore can't be processed locally and is too heavy to ship without great expense.

❧ Lieutenant Colonel George Custer and 209 men are killed by the Sioux at Little Big Horn on June 25.

❧ 1877 ❧

❧ Montana volunteers rush to the aid of Colonel John Gibbon to fight against the Nez Perce at the Battle of Big Hole. The army wins before Butte volunteers under William A. Clark can arrive.

❧ Helena red-light operator Dolores Jarra moves to Butte with her two illegitimate daughters, Minnie and Louisa Washburn, and her lover, Charles Stanchfield, hoping to make a fresh start. Jarra backs Stanchfield in leasing a dance hall.

❧ On June 25, five hundred construction workers land on a branch of the Tongue River off the Yellowstone in eastern Montana to begin construction of Fort Keogh under the command of Colonel Nelson Miles. Built to hold fifteen hundred men, the fort becomes a major staging area for army action against the Indians.

≈ 1878 ≈

※ Canadian Joseph Nadeau moves to Butte with his family and his brother, Arthur, to open a restaurant and lease a hotel. They also begin investing heavily in the red-light district.

※ Congress deems laundry service too expensive for military posts and does away with it, forcing many base prostitutes working under cover of that occupation to move to nearby ranches and towns.

※ Thousands rush to take advantage of a silver strike in Leadville, west of Denver. By 1882 it has peaked.

※ Butte incorporates as a city.

※ The Helena Board of Trade funds a road to Butte.

※ Tom Cruse establishes the town of Marysville around his rich Drumlummon Mine near Helena.

※ Miles City is established in March near Fort Keogh, a seeming oasis in the midst of endless prairie, 297 miles from the nearest train station. Among its founders is William Bullard, who has served in the army under Fort Keogh commander Nelson Miles and invests heavily in a hotel and brewery.

※ In April, Butte officials make an attempt to close down dance halls. Charlie Stanchfield is arrested and fined for running one, but he leases a new establishment, which succeeds under another name.

※ Annie Turner, a former laundress at Fort Keogh and the owner of what the local paper calls a "Coon Row" brothel, gives birth in April to John Turner, Miles City's first child not of Indian descent. Later, Turner sues his white father, Sergeant Eugene Allen, for support.

※ On December 17, Chicago Joe Airey weds James "Black Hawk" Hensley in Helena.

≈ 1879 ≈

- The *Butte Miner* launches an unsuccessful crusade against opium. The drug is still legal in the United States and is used as the basis of many patent medicines.

- Fire wipes out Butte's business district in September. Its city council bans wood frame buildings.

- On September 26, fire destroys three hundred Deadwood buildings. The town rebuilds, but many of its citizens including prostitutes Maggie Burns and Connie Hoffman move to Miles City.

≈ 1880 ≈

- Sixteen-year-old Charlie Russell during the summer moves to the Judith Basin, about two hundred miles north of Miles City. There he works for trapper/prospector Jake Hoover until he is hired as a night-riding cowboy.

- Pimp Joe Scott kills his wife, prostitute Mollie Forest Scott, in a Butte dance hall on August 4.

- On September 2, John Ming, a wealthy cattle baron, builds an opulent opera house in Helena.

≈ 1881 ≈

- Helena incorporates.

- Martha Jane Cannary, a.k.a. Calamity Jane, settles down on a homestead near Miles City as the wife of Frank King, a respected rancher from the Judith Basin.

- General James Brisbin, stationed at Fort Keogh, publishes *The Beef Bonanza: Or, How to Get Rich on the Plains: A Description of Cattle*

Growing, Sheep Farming, Horse Raising and Dairying in the West.
Inspired by the bestseller, hundreds of would-be ranchers, including
many members of European royal families, flood eastern Montana.

Sydney Paget, fifth son and twelfth child of a wealthy British lord,
takes up ranching in Montana with Miles City as his base. The town
is scandalized when Paget is less than discreet in making Connie
Hoffman, a popular local whore, his mistress.

Thomas Edison's invention of the electric light and the inauguration
of the first plant for the generation of power in the United States set
in motion a demand for copper, which increases with the growing
popularity of the telephone.

On November 4, Yow Kum is brought to police court by friends after
she is stabbed by her owner. It is the first glimpse Butte residents get
into the lucrative trafficking of Chinese women, for the town's large
Chinese community is secretive and generally avoids the American
court system.

Inez Maybert commits suicide with morphine on November 10.

On December 15, prostitute Lottie "Sorrel Mike" Ables Pickett is
shot in Butte.

By December 26, a rail spur is built to Butte by the Utah Northern
Railroad, finally making it profitable to mine copper.

1882

Copper King William Clark and friends organize Butte's exclusive
Silver Bow Club for the town's wealthiest men.

Maggie Burns builds the fanciest whorehouse in Miles City, allowing
the customer who buys the most drinks on opening night to name it.

In the summer, Texas cattle drivers begin making Miles City their
destination because it is finally connected to the Chicago stockyards
by the Northern Pacific Railroad.

❧ On December 14, Annie Turner's bordello burns to the ground. She had been carrying on a very public spat with the local newspaper owner, which one might suspect was the cause of that blaze.

❧ 1883 ❧

❧ Montana Territory ranks as the nation's second largest producer of silver.

❧ The Northern Pacific Railroad finally completes a line to Helena and extends to Butte.

❧ Martha Jane Cannary, a.k.a. Calamity Jane, is arrested for drunkenness in Miles City, having recently lost an infant son, her husband, and their ranch.

❧ Copper King Marcus Daly builds a huge copper smelter twenty-six miles from Butte and surrounds it with a town called Anaconda.

❧ Montana's Supreme Court denies the right of foreigners to own mining claims.

❧ Miles City vigilantes on July 22 hang William Rigney, a local bartender who offended the wife and daughter of a respectable citizen while drinking.

❧ 1884 ❧

❧ Montana holds a constitutional convention with William Clark presiding.

❧ Butte's first red-light district is established on the south side of East Galena between Main and Wyoming within one hundred yards of its main street.

❧ The open range closes in Texas, so thousands of cattle are moved to government-owned grasslands in Montana and Wyoming.

❧ William Clark builds a thirty-four-room mansion in Butte. It costs more than the local courthouse.

- Helena finally passes a law against soliciting for prostitution.

- James Murray builds a fine opera house in Butte.

- The Casino, a huge dance hall and den of vice, is established at Galena and Main in Butte.

- In March, Teddy Roosevelt buys a ranch just over the Montana border.

- An 8.5-mile spur from Butte to Anaconda is completed on July 15 by the Utah and Northern Railroad. The trip takes one minute, twenty-seven seconds.

- Ranchers in eastern Montana execute dozens of suspected rustlers vigilante-style after the government refuses to assist in arresting the thieves.

1885

- That year's legislature is known as the Cowboy Legislature because the ranchers finally win over the mining interests, which have previously managed to kill just about any bill the ranchers submitted.

- Butte booms, attracting hundreds of miners of every nationality. In addition, hundreds are employed in smelters and for driving the eight- and ten-horse ore teams. The population approaches twenty-two thousand.

- The Montana legislature passes an anti-hurdy-gurdy bill. Legislation against wife beating fails to pass.

- Helena is shocked at its first suicide ever by a prostitute.

- The Montana Club, "for gentlemen only," is established by the elite in Helena. Today it is the oldest private club of its kind in the Northwest.

- On March 12, Helena passes an ordinance prohibiting women from working at any form of employment on its main street.

- In November, Fannie French, a Miles City Creole, is indicted for "lewd and boisterous behavior" while running a house of ill fame. She is fined $300 and sentenced to three months in jail but appeals all the way to the Montana Supreme Court.

⚶ 1886 ⚶

- Helena officials try unsuccessfully to close Chicago Joe's Red Star Saloon.

- Police make the first arrests ever for prostitution in Helena.

- Helena's newly wealthy Tom Cruse, fifty, marries Margaret Carter, twenty-five, sister of soon-to-be U.S. Senator Thomas H. Carter, on March 2.

- Beef prices slump during the summer. Nature produces signs of a bad winter ahead.

- In August, Anaconda doubles the capacity of its smelter, but when copper prices drop the plant is closed temporarily, throwing thousands out of work.

- An early morning fire on August 7 that spread from Miles City's main street causes more than $50,000 in damage, wiping out the bordello that Sydney Paget had recently purchased from Maggie Burns for his mistress, Connie Hoffman. Also lost is a legitimate restaurant owned by black madam Annie Turner.

- On August 30, Chicago Joe Hensley and two of her girls are brought to trial by the district attorney for running a hurdy-gurdy house in Helena. They beat the rap by explaining their house features a real orchestra, not a hurdy-gurdy instrument.

- Temperatures fall below zero on November 16 in the Rockies, beginning the worst winter in their recorded history. The majority of eastern Montana's livestock perishes.

～ 1887 ～

◈ Lady Isabel Randall publishes *A Lady's Ranche Life in Montana*. She does not view locals kindly.

◈ Butte officially becomes a union town when miners organize the first strike in Montana's history.

◈ In late fall, Phil Weinard moves in with Chicago Joe Hensley and her husband, James, to help them build a palatial theater in Helena. There he befriends Charlie Russell, a fledgling artist who makes his living as a night-riding cowboy.

◈ A daughter, Mary, is born to Mr. and Mrs. Tom Cruse on December 15. Her mother, Margaret Carter Cruse, dies mysteriously eleven days later.

～ 1888 ～

◈ Every building along East Galena between Main and Wyoming in Butte houses prostitution, and the district begins expanding.

◈ William Clark runs unsuccessfully for Congress.

◈ In May, Phil Weinard elopes with Mary Ferris, niece of Chicago Joe Hensley, against the wishes of her aunt, sending the girl to live with his parents in Minneapolis until he can make a home for her in Alberta, Canada. Charlie Russell and one of his friends ride north with Weinard, where they spend a lazy summer.

◈ When Chicago Joe Hensley opens her New Coliseum Theater on July 4, critics are skeptical, but the $23,000 vaudeville house enjoys lasting success.

～ 1889 ～

◈ Fritz Augustus Heinze, twenty, a soon-to-be Copper King from a wealthy German family, comes to Montana to work as a mining engineer for Boston and Montana Consolidated Company for one hundred dollars per month.

❖ The Montana legislature makes it legal for women to become lawyers.

❖ The Catholic Sisters of Good Shepherd arrive in Helena to establish a home for wayward women and girls.

❖ Helena is the first town in Montana to build an electric streetcar system. Butte and others follow within months.

❖ On November 8, Montana becomes a state.

1890

❖ The new state disgraces itself by sending four senators to Washington—two Democrats and two Republicans.

❖ Congress passes the Geary Act, which removes most legal protection for Chinese.

❖ Montana is producing 50 percent of the nation's copper and also leads the nation in percentage of men employed.

❖ Three Chinese men are murdered in Butte and another is found hanging from a tree in Anaconda. The murderers are never caught.

❖ The real estate of Helena's eight proprietor prostitutes is assessed at $102,560 and they contribute nearly $1,000 to the city budget in personal property taxes.

1891

❖ The first signs of economic trouble appear in Helena. Many grand hotels close or change hands.

1892

❖ Helena becomes the richest town per capita in the United States.

❖ Populist Ella Knowles loses election for state attorney general by only five votes.

≈ 1893 ≈

✧ Anaconda boycotts Chinese workers and businesses. Butte citizens refuse to join the boycott.

✧ The Sherman Silver Purchase Act is repealed in June, which disrupts silver mining. There follows the Panic of '93, which turns into a brutal depression, leaving about three million unemployed nationwide. Many Montana businesses topple.

✧ Fifteen-year-old Anna LaChapelle catches the eye of William Clark, who becomes her patron.

✧ Marcus Daly successfully prevents William Clark from winning a seat in the U.S. Senate.

≈ 1894 ≈

✧ Helena beats out Anaconda as Montana's seat of government.

✧ Chicago prostitute Madeleine Blair comes to Montana in the spring to vacation with her lover, a wealthy Butte businessman.

≈ 1895 ≈

✧ Montana leads the nation in per capital income.

✧ Marcus Daly's company incorporates as the Anaconda Mining Company with the help of wealthy backers from San Francisco.

✧ Madeleine Blair leaves her lover in Butte to wander the casinos of Europe with a moneyed earl.

✧ Butte produces more than one-fourth of the world's copper. Its sixty-four hundred miners collectively take home $640,000 every month.

✧ In January, Montana's Supreme Court finally decides Fannie French need not serve three months' jail time to which the Miles City court had sentenced her in 1885 for running a house of ill repute. She is, however, required to pay a $300 fine.

1896

- Independent prostitutes lose control of their Helena property.

- Labor union members block doorways and discourage customers from entering Chinese restaurants and laundries in Helena.

- Florence Crittenden Homes are opened in Butte and Helena to rescue fallen women and wayward girls, but Butte's home soon closes for lack of interest.

1897

- The Montana legislature passes an antigambling bill and games go underground.

1898

- Butte's Comique dance hall and theater is closed. Competition from theaters and honky-tonks in the district half a block away proved too much for it.

- On July 3, several hundred Montana volunteers depart in thirty-five railroad cars to fight in the Spanish-American War.

1899

- Crooked Pete Hanson, known as the King of Galena Street and all the rest of Butte's red-light district, dies of natural causes on January 12.

- William Clark bribes the Montana legislature, which elects him to Congress. His enemies get the election thrown out and Clark is forced to resign.

- Butte is wired for electricity from the Big Hole River plant near Divide.

- Standard Oil, led by Henry Rogers and William Rockefeller, buy the Anaconda Company and make it the centerpiece for their Eastern-based monopoly.

- Chicago Joe Hensley, fifty-six, dies of pneumonia on October 23. There is a huge turnout for her lavish Catholic funeral.

ᘓᕘ 1900 ᕙᘐ

- William Clark is appointed to Congress by Governor Robert B. Smith.

- Helena's population drops from 13,840 to 10,770 while Butte's is 30,470 and growing.

- The first factory-made automobile appears in Butte.

- The Montana School of Mines opens in Butte.

- Grace McGinnis becomes madam of the Dumas, a brothel at 45 East Mercury in Butte. Joe Nadeau built the opulent parlor house but recorded it in the name of his wife, Delia.

- Butte's plush Windsor brothel opens at 7 and/or 9 Mercury Street.

- Lou Harpell's exclusive Hotel Victoria at 11 East Mercury in Butte advertises that its whores are among the most beautiful in the world.

- The cheap cribs of Butte prostitutes fill Pleasant Alley behind the Dumas from South Wyoming through most of the block.

- Copper King Marcus Daly dies in his suite at the Hotel Netherlands in New York City on November 12. He leaves no endowments for Montana.

ᘓᕘ 1901 ᕙᘐ

- Mary MacLane starts her diary in Butte on January 13.

- On April 6, the *Butte Miner* begins a successful campaign to get the red-light district moved to the edge of town.

- On May 1, the Montana legislature mandates an eight-hour working day.

❧ Chicago hosts a meeting of the Purity Congress, part of a national moral reform movement.

❧ William Clark claims May 25 as the date of his marriage to Anna Eugenia LaChapelle in France. At the time he was actually making a transatlantic crossing.

❧ On May 28, Kathlyn Williams graduates from boarding school. William Clark sends the girlish beauty to the American Academy of Music and Arts in New York City.

❧ John Bordeaux sues his wife, Ella, on August 16 for divorce on the grounds of adultery and desertion. To his astonishment, she fights him in court, even though the suit ruins her social standing in Butte.

❧ 1902 ❧

❧ Stanley Ketchel, fourteen, arrives in Butte where he falls in with the demimonde and begins to excel at boxing.

❧ On January 20, Butte city fathers institute monthly fines for prostitutes and insist they draw the blinds to street-front cribs during the day.

❧ In August, Wilhelmina Louise Amelia "Andree" Clark is born to William Clark and Anna LaChapelle in Cape Matifou, Algeria.

❧ Also in August, *The Story of Mary MacLane—by Herself* is published by Herbert S. Stone & Co.; it becomes an immediate bestseller.

❧ In November, the carcasses of dead horses and other livestock are found in increasing numbers around Butte and Anaconda because of bad air produced by the mining operations.

❧ During the winter, Chinese slave girl Lon Ying is rescued along with Choy Gay, wife number two of her Butte owner, by Mrs. A. F. Browne from Presbyterian Mission in San Francisco.

❦ 1903 ❦

❖ Sales for Mary MacLane's new book, *My Friend Annabel Lee*, are disappointing.

❖ In January, Butte officials enforce a resolution consigning red-light operations to the alleys between Mercury and Galena. All blacks and Asians are forced to move half a block farther south on the alley. Only bordellos can house prostitutes, and not on the ground floor.

❖ In July, Senator William Clark finally reveals to his grown children and the press that he has a two-year-old child by Anna LaChapelle. He claims to have married her more than a year before the baby was born, but no record can be found.

❖ On July 25, Anaconda builds a three-hundred-foot stack on its smelter that is supposed to eliminate smoke, but livestock still die from polluted air.

❖ Martha Jane Cannary, a.k.a. Calamity Jane, dies in Terry, South Dakota, on August 1.

❦ 1904 ❦

❖ Mary "Mamie" Cruse attempts to elope with the son of a good Helena family but is stopped by her father, Tom Cruse.

❦ 1905 ❦

❖ The Deer Lodge Valley Farmers Association sues the Anaconda Copper Mining Company for smoke damage.

❖ Butte's red-light district is reported to be the second largest in the United States, just behind New Orleans' infamous Corduroy Road.

❖ On April 19, Copper King Fritz Augustus Heinze sells out to Anaconda and Standard Oil, something he said he'd never do. The giant's monopoly in Montana is almost complete.

❖ In May, Reverend William Biederwolf proclaims Butte the "lowest sinkhole of vice in the west." His revival service, held at Casino in Butte, attracts nearly a thousand.

❧ 1906 ❧

❖ The Purity Congress meets again in Chicago to lay the groundwork for legislating morality.

❖ Stanley Ketchel lands in police court. Mistaken for a pimp, the champion boxer is run out of Butte.

❖ Sarah Bernhardt performs *Camille* in French at Butte's Holland Street Roller Rink on May 6.

❧ 1907 ❧

❖ Ruth Clifford hosts a party for the grand opening of her Irish World brothel with enthusiastic coverage from Butte's new weekly paper, the *X-Ray*.

❖ The year is an economic disaster, with strikes in Butte and Anaconda. It is referred to as the Panic of '07.

❧ 1908 ❧

❖ The Prohibition movement that is sweeping the United States hits Montana. Butte ignores it.

❧ 1909 ❧

❖ Although homesteads were traditionally 160 acres, Montana's Enlarged Homestead Act offers 340 acres to those who apply to farm them. As a result there is a dramatic increase in eastern Montana's rural population and a shift in the economy to farming.

❖ In January, Mary "Mamie" Cruse marries broker Alvar O'Brien in a big fancy wedding despite the fact her wealthy father, Tom Cruse, objects.

❧ On April 26, Judge Hunt dismisses the suit of the Deer Lodge Farmers Association against Anaconda Copper.

❧ The Helena city council orders prostitutes out of their district by September. They get to stay till November 1910 before moving farther from the center of town.

❧ In October, Stanley Ketchel is beaten badly by Jack Johnson after flooring the black world champion in a boxing match Ketchel had apparently agreed to throw.

❧ On December 6, James R. Mann of Chicago successfully introduces a Congressional bill titled the White Slave Act. It is prompted by unjustified international hysteria over the kidnapping of white women for purposes of prostitution.

❧ 1910 ❧

❧ On January 25, Prohibitionist Carrie Nation campaigns in Butte where she is spectacularly unsuccessful.

❧ Washington State women win the right to vote. Jeannette Rankin, a Missoula girl, is a key player who goes on to campaign in New York, Florida, and Ohio.

❧ Butte now has seven thousand men working 344 mines.

❧ Mary MacLane is so broke she returns home to take a job writing for the *Butte Evening News.*

❧ Celestine Healy Bottego is named Best Grammar School Student in the state of Montana on July 24.

❧ On October 5, Stan Ketchel dies following an altercation with a jealous farmhand.

❧ 1911 ❧

❧ After Butte businessmen in January petition the mayor to move the red-light district farther out of town, the occupants go on strike. Realizing the city needs their fines to operate, officials allow the district to reopen.

❧ On January 27, Ella Knowles dies unexpectedly of a lung infection.

❧ On February 1, Jeannette Rankin addresses the Montana legislature, urging members to consider allowing women to vote. She is the first woman to address the all-male body.

❧ Mattie Mems, once the leading girl in Lou Harpell's house, dies nearly broke in a shabby rental on August 28.

❧ On October 27, Mary "Mamie" Cruse O'Brien weds Harry C. Cotter, a Butte miner from a well-to-do family. Her father, Tom Cruse, refuses to recognize the match.

❧ 1912 ❧

❧ In the fall, Tom Cruse hires a policeman to kidnap his daughter, Mary, from Butte and incarcerate her against her will in a Helena home for wayward girls from which she cannot escape.

❧ 1913 ❧

❧ The 16th Amendment to the U.S. Constitution establishes the income tax.

❧ In November, Mary "Mamie" Cruse dies at age twenty-six of unknown causes at the home of her father, Tom Cruse, in Helena.

❧ 1914 ❧

❧ The Butte city directory lists sixty-two Chinese businesses, including four physicians who practice herbal medicine. It is the last town in Montana with a sizeable Chinese population.

❧ Women win the right to vote in Montana thanks to Jeannette Rankin and her cohorts.

❧ A total of 20,662 allotments have been claimed under Montana's new homestead law. This is the peak year.

❧ Butte has become one of the most expensive cities in the United States, and wages for unskilled labor have not kept pace.

❧ Martial law is declared in Butte on September 1 due to labor unrest that includes mob rule, the dynamiting of mining offices, and the mayor's killing of a would-be assassin.

❧ On November 4, Copper King Fritz Augustus Heinze, forty-eight, dies of cirrhosis in Sarasota, New York. Nearly broke, he leaves a motherless two-year-old-son in the care of his sister and no legacies in Montana where he made many millions.

❧ 1915 ❧

❧ A drop in the price of grain is followed by a long drought, causing many homesteaders to fail.

❧ 1916 ❧

❧ Butte's population has risen to ninety thousand, making it the largest metropolis in the five-state region of the northern Rockies and plains.

❧ Jeannette Rankin gets elected to the U.S. House of Representatives. She is the first woman in the world elected to a national legislative body.

❧ 1917 ❧

❧ In January, reforming attorney general Sam Ford orders all Montana's red-light districts shut down. Most towns comply, but those in Butte and Miles City simply go underground.

❧ The United States finally declares war on Germany on April 6. Jeannette Rankin votes against entering the war and, although she is one of forty-four representatives to do so, the vote dooms her career.

❧ Because of World War I, copper is even more in demand. Every rifle cartridge contains an ounce of pure copper. Due to the boom, Butte's population rises to ninety-six thousand.

- Mary MacLane writes and stars in a movie titled *Men Who Have Made Love to Me*. Although Mary gets fair reviews, the film does not enjoy financial success.

- "Nigger Liz" Hall, Montana's longest-tenured prostitute, dies in Butte. She had begun her career in Bannack in 1863.

- A fire on June 8 at Butte's Granite Mountain Mine takes the lives of at least 163 men and management is forced to address shoddy safety practices.

- On August 17, masked men in Butte lynch Frank W. Little, an organizer for the Industrial Workers of the World. Jeannette Rankin gets the government to send federal troops to maintain peace.

1918

- Montana passes a Sedition Act, which sends everyone who speaks against the government to jail. Dr. Gustavus Pitkanen, rumored to be Butte's leading abortionist, is among those convicted. Meanwhile, his wife, Gertrude, carries on in his stead even though she is licensed only as a chiropractor.

- The Chamberlain-Kahn Act gives the federal government the power to quarantine any woman suspected of having a sexually transmitted disease. Local reformers find this federal mandate useful in closing red-light districts.

- A long cycle of drought begins in Montana, kicking off the Dust Bowl, which leaves frontier farmers destitute.

- The Armistice of World War I is announced on November 11, and martial law finally ends in Butte.

1919

- Montana's Prohibition law goes into effect on January 1. Fifteen days later a national ban on alcohol is ratified.

❧ Charged with stealing some dresses, Mary MacLane appears in a Chicago court wearing an embroidered Japanese kimono and a feathered hat. She beats the rap but this is her last media event.

❧ *Madeleine*, the autobiography of prostitute Madeleine Blair, is published by Harper & Brothers. The publisher is immediately arrested because the writer of the book shows no remorse for her life of sin.

❧ 1921 ❧

❧ On June 3, federal officials estimate Butte leads the nation in per capita consumption of illicit liquor. A citywide network of underground tunnels makes bootlegging easy there.

❧ 1925 ❧

❧ On March 2, William A. Clark dies at his New York mansion at age eighty-six. Although he is one of the ten richest men in America and gave generously to the arts and charity in New York and California, he leaves no significant endowments for Montana.

❧ 1929 ❧

❧ The price of Anaconda stock rises to $175 a share but plummets after the stock market crash of October 29 that brings on the Great Depression.

❧ On August 1, Mary MacLane dies alone and broke in a cheap Chicago boardinghouse with her press clippings spread out around her.

❧ 1932 ❧

❧ Twenty percent of Silver Bow County's population is on relief.

❧ Anaconda stock drops to from $175 to $3 per share.

1933

- Anaconda stock is worth only six cents a share.

1939

- Butte mine employment drops from seventy-eight hundred to eight hundred. Virtually all the city's fifty thousand people depend on those seven thousand jobless miners, directly or indirectly.

1940

- Jeannette Rankin is again elected to the U.S. House of Representatives from Montana, but casts the only vote against America's entry into World War II, ensuring an end to her political career.

1955

- Anaconda begins open pit mining. Ecological disaster follows.

1963

- On October 12, Anna LaChapelle Clark dies at eighty-five. She leaves generous bequests for the arts in California, New York, and Washington, D.C., but nothing for Montana.

1968

- On January 15, Jeannette Rankin leads five thousand women in a march on Washington to protest the war in Vietnam. She is eighty-seven.

- Butte's last high-profile madam closes shop and moves away on October 13.

NOTES

". . . there is not a respectable woman" Edward Laird Mills, *Plains, Peaks and Pioneers: Eighty Years of Methodism in Montana* (Portland, OR: Binford and Mort, 1947), 28.

INTRODUCTION: SINFUL CITIES, 1863–1919

Almodovar's attempt to turn At this writing Almodovar still runs the International Sex Worker Foundation for Art, Culture and Education out of Los Angeles promoting art and legalized prostitution. For her story read her autobiography, *Cop to Call Girl: Why I Left the LAPD to Make an Honest Living as a Beverly Hills Prostitute* (New York: Simon & Schuster, 1993).

PROLOGUE: MADELEINE: A SELF-MADE WOMAN, 1894

she possessed a stunning figure Anonymous, *Madeleine: An Autobiography* (New York: Harper and Brothers, 1919, new edition New York: Persea Books, 1986). While the author refers to herself as Madeleine Blair in the book, she tells the reader this is the name devised for her by the first madam for whom she worked in Kansas City. She describes herself as not being a beauty but with a lovely mouth, perfect teeth, a dimpled smile, and a fine figure. She is also careful in discussing her hair, saying only that it is curly and a "beautiful color" (68, 97, and 129). Her editors did such a good job of hiding her identity that her real name was never revealed. However, it is believed throughout the industry that this book was written by an experienced prostitute. My description of her as auburn haired is based on accounts of the colors she wrote she preferred to wear.

The red-light district also ran Michael Malone, *The Battle for Butte: Mining and Politics on the Northern Frontier, 1864–1909* (Helena: Montana Historical Society Press, 1981), 73–74.

The Denver Sun had just admitted Writers Project of Montana, *Copper Camp: The Lusty Story of Butte, Montana, the Richest Hill on Earth* (Helena, MT: Riverbend Publishing, 1973, first published by Montana State Department in 1943), 300.

Montana led the nation David Emmons, *The Butte Irish: Class and Ethnicity in an American Mining Town, 1875–1925* (Urbana and Chicago: University of Illinois Press, 1989), 23.

The Comique featured nationally known C. B. Glasscock, *War of the Copper Kings: Builders of Butte and Wolves of Wall Street* (New York: Glasscock, 1935; new edition Helena, MT: Riverbend Publishing, 2002), 78–79.

"Seventeen and a black one" Anonymous, 210.

at Lizzie Allen's palatial brothel One of the few undisguised names the author of *Madeleine* uses is that of Lizzie Allen, one of Chicago's most famous and successful madams, for whom she said she worked off and on for about five years. At the time, Allen's bordello was considered one of Chicago's finest.

Although Butte and the track Patrick F. Morris, *Anaconda Montana: Copper Smelting Boom Town on the Western Frontier* (Bethesda, MD: Swann Publishing, 1997), 85.

a *macque* [pimp] in the house In that era the French word for pimp was common.

'Am I my sister's keeper?' Anonymous, 218.

Bertha, one of Lou's girls "It was not uncommon for groups of the girls from the red-light section to be seen on a summer afternoon cantering though the business district on blooded saddle horses, clad in the latest riding habits." Writers Project of Montana, 8.

she'd soon be able to leave In the 1900 census Lou Harpell is listed with four girls, two Chinese servants, and a cook at 11 East Mercury, which was the most expensive section of Butte's red-light district. Although her age was given as sixty-two, her occupation was recorded as "prostitute" as well as head of the household. Her place of birth and that of her parents was Germany. Roll T623, roll 914, page 133. Also see Curt Johnson, R. Craig Sautter, and Roger Ebert, *The Wicked City: Chicago from Kenna to Capone* (Chicago: December Press, 1998), 74.

Lou, who was seldom wrong Madeleine wrote that she visited one of the town's two first-class parlor houses but did not name them. According to tax records and newspaper accounts, her choices would have been the Dumas, the Windsor, and Lou Harpell's Hotel Victoria. Lou was the most experienced madam and from the same town where Madeleine had previously worked.

She'd enjoyed it and returned Anonymous, Book II, Chapter 1.

"I was an object of much curiosity" John K. Hutchens, *One Man's Montana* (New York: J. B. Lippincott Company, 1946), 30.

Worst of the outlaws, they told her Anonymous, 231–234.

A few days later she won H. Minar Shoebotham, *Anaconda: Life of Marcus Daly the Copper King* (Harrisburg, PA: Stackpole Company, 1956), 149, 152.

Daly's fine racetrack was the place Anonymous, 235.

Old Joe Nadeau and his ridiculous wife Ellen Baumler, "Devil's Perch: Prostitution from Suite to Cellar in Butte, Montana," *Montana Magazine*, vol. 48, no. 3 (Summer 1998): 9.

CHAPTER 1: THE SUMMER WOMEN OF HELENA, 1867

a crude camp they called Bannack According to Rich Aarstad et al., *Montana Place Names: From Alzada to Zortman* (Helena Montana Historical Society, 2009), 12, the name is a corruption of that of the Bannock Indian tribe affiliated with the Shoshones.

they mined out about $5 million worth "The Editors," *Montana: The Magazine of Western History*, vol. 14, no. 3 (Summer 1964): 22.

White's widow and child Louis Schmittroth, "Whatever Happened to John White?" www.yanoun.org/mont_vigi/johnwhite/article.html (accessed August 27, 2009).

Hankins's older brother, Jeff "The Hankins," *Chicago Tribune*, February 14, 1875, 3.

were too busy getting rich to care "The Editors," 23.

the brothers enjoyed even greater success "The Hankins."

"full blossomed Spanish rose" Writers Project of Montana, *Copper Camp: The Lusty Story of Butte, Montana, The Richest Hill on Earth* (Helena, MT: Riverbend Publishing, 1970, first published by Montana State Department of Agriculture), 184.

Actually Martha Jane Cannary James McLaird, *Calamity Jane: The Woman and the Legend* (Norman: University of Oklahoma Press, 2005), 21. The unnamed paper was dated January 31, 1864, when Cannary, whose family was in the area, would have been nine years old according to her biographer.

Her strictly Catholic family Rex Myers, "An Inning for Sin: Chicago Joe and Her Hurdy-Gurdy Girls Girls Girls Girls," *Montana: The Magazine of Western History*, vol. 27, no. 2 (Spring 1977): 27.

joined by a second black woman William C. Campbell, "From the Quarries of Last Change Gulch Helena," Volume 2 (Montana Record Publishing Company, 1951), 1–12.

Last Chance Gulch welcomed her Hubert Howe Bancroft and Frances Fuller Victor, *The Works of Hubert Howe Bancroft: History of Washington, Idaho and Montana 1845–1899*, Volume 31 (San Francisco: History Company Publishing, 1890), 775.

a rude settlement of hastily built John Taliaferro, *Charles M. Russell: The Life and Legend of America's Cowboy Artist* (Boston, New York, Toronto, and London: Little, Brown and Company, 1996), 32–33. Taliaferro's description of the town, taken from Charlie Russell's letters nine years later, is pretty much the same.

a crude, one-story log cabin   Campbell, 55–56.

competition with Fred White   Myers, 27.

the girls ensured their own safety   Paula Petrik, *No Step Backward: Women and Family on the Rocky Mountain Mining Frontier, Helena, Montana 1865–1900* (Helena: Montana Historical Society Press, 1987), 37.

Dumont dabbled in prostitution   Michael Rutter, *Upstairs Girls: Prostitution in the America West* (Helena, MT: Farcountry Press, 2005), 198–200.

they made 119 separate property transactions   Petrik, 26. The author spent an enormous amount of time checking Helena's property deeds and bank records from 1865 through 1870.

The vigilantes, in Blackfoot at least   "The Hankins."

that criminal charges had been filed   Petrik, 180, footnote 20. The author cites Criminal Case no. 30, Office of Clerk of Court, Deer Lodge County Courthouse, Anaconda, Montana.

whose real name was Prince Albert Hankins   Hankins's tombstone in Woodland Cemetery, McHenry, Illinois, reads PRINCE ALBERT HANKINS, FATHER, 2/27/1842 TO 8/25/1897.

who won almost every footrace   "Al Hankins as a Horseman," *Chicago Daily Tribune*, August 30, 1897, 4.

born on a farm in Indiana   Weston A. Goodspeed, editor, "Albert Hankins," *Histories of the Counties of Porter and Lake, Indiana* (Chicago: Culver, Page Foyne Printer, 1882), 383–384.

she wed the frock-coated dandy   Petrik, 180. Footnote 20 cites Criminal Case no. 60, Office of Clerk of Court, Deer Lodge County Courthouse, Anaconda, Montana, and Marriage Record of Lewis and Clark County, Book A, 1865–1907.

a gold rush to White Pine, Nevada   Myers, 27; Petrik, 29.

a surprising number of blacks   "Home of the Cave Bear," *White Pine Public Museum*. www.wpmuseum.org (accessed August 12, 2009); Fred Holabird, "Bousfield, F. H.," *Gold Rush Collectables from Nevada*. www.holabirdamericana.com /HKA-Spring2008-Cat1/NEVADA03.html (accessed August 12, 2009).

she placed the baby   "'Chicago Joe' Dead," *Daily Independent*, Helena, October 26, 1899, 1. Her obituary said her son, who went under the name Joe Eary, was thought to be in St. Joseph, Missouri.

she and Hankins had gotten a divorce   Myers, 27. According to the *Chicago Tribune*, Hankins returned to Chicago from White Pine in 1868, but according to his marriage record in Helena and historians in White Pine, the reporter was off by a year.

Chief Black Hawk's Indian War   K. F. Weinard, "Phil Weinard Remembers Early Helena, 1880," *Montana: The Magazine of Western History*, vol. 43, no. 3 (Summer 1993): 67.

the rest of Lincoln's citizens "James Hensley," 1870 census, Lincoln, Deer Lodge, Montana Territory, roll M593-827, page 80, image 162.

it looked like the pay dirt "Lincoln Mining District," Montana Department of Environmental Quality. http://deq.mt.gov/abandonedmines/linkdocs/99tech.mcpx (accessed December 2, 2010), 1.

dashingly handsome James "The Duke" Hamilton Interview on October 6, 2009, with Missoula collector Timothy Gordon, who found Hamilton's photo in a collection with those of Joe and her girls. Hamilton's former occupation comes from the Helena census of 1870, Lewis and Clark, Montana Territory, roll M593-827, page 203, image 408. No other Hamiltons are listed in town at the time.

fast becoming a ghost town Michael P. Malone and Richard B. Roeder, *Montana: A History of Two Centuries* (Seattle and London: University of Washington Press, 1976), 65.

half of which she had Petrik, 29–30.

estate of her late husband "Col. H. B. Truett," *Daily Gazette*, Helena Extra, April 24, 1869; and *Montana Post*, April 30, 1869. Clippings were included with a typed manuscript titled "The Case That Made Lincoln," draft by Willard I. King, filed under "Henry B. Truett," Montana Archives.

court records make no mention Petrik, 37.

Outside capital dried up Malone and Roeder, 130, 142.

making drink purchase mandatory Myers, 27. Petrik, note 180, is uncertain about how much property Airey actually lost in the fire but estimates the damages at $3,500.

taking advantage of the rail link Petrik, 29.

arrived looking for bargains Petrik, 31, 34. McGraw was also known as Bridget Ryan, which might help explain Joe's association with her.

the doctor who evaluated the girl Petrik, footnote 28, 180. The author quotes Montana Territory, Executive Office, Record Series 40, Montana Historical Society Archives, and notes that insanity petitions seem to have been a device used in the demimonde to control its residents and illegally obtain property through guardianship. Early insanity cases were unnamed.

Black Hills of South Dakota were teeming Deadwood-Lead '76 Centennial Committee, Gold-Gals-Guns-Guts (South Dakota Bicentennial Commission, Deadwood-Lead, 1976), 12.

Helena merchant John How Malone and Roeder, 142–143.

highly relieved to make it official Myers, 29; Petrik, 31.

CHAPTER 2: BUTTE, THE BLACK HEART OF MONTANA, 1877

the Black Heart of Montana Writers Project of Montana, *Copper Camp: The Lusty Story of Butte, Montana, the Richest Hill on Earth* (Helena, MT: Riverbend Publishing, 1973, first published by Montana State Department in 1943), 15.

an odd combination of crumbling shacks Mary Murphy, *Mining Cultures: Men, Women, and Leisure in Butte, 1914–41* (Urbana and Chicago: University of Illinois Press, 1997), 77; George Wesley Davis, *Sketches of Butte: From Vigilante Days to Prohibition* (Boston: Cornhill Company, 1921), 141; and 1884 Sanborn map of Butte.

it cornered China Town Mary Murphy, "Women on the Line: Prostitution in Butte Montana 1878–1917," master's thesis, University of North Carolina (Chapel Hill, 1983), 35; 1884 Sanborn map of Butte.

a growing population of white prostitutes 1800 census, Butte City, Deer Lodge, Montana, roll T9-742, family history film 1254742, page 111.3000, enumeration district 10, image 0228.

majority of prostitutes there Murphy, "Women on the Line," 55.

the ill-reputed "Twin Cottages" Paula Petrik, *No Step Backward: Women and Family on the Rocky Mountain Mining Frontier, Helena, Montana 1865–1900* (Helena: Montana Historical Society, 1987), 35. Petrik did a meticulous study of Jarra's finances, which are footnoted on 180–181.

a German saloon owner 1870 census, Virginia City, Madison, Montana Territory, roll M593-827, page 243, image 489.

a Helena miner turned cowboy Helen Fitzgerald Sanders, *A History of Montana* (Chicago: Lewis Pub. Co., 1913), 1342.

urging Charlie to join them "Lizzie Stanchfield," 1880 census, Butte City, Deer Lodge, Montana, roll T9-742, family history film 1254742, page 114.2000, enumeration district 10, image 0235.

unsuccessful suicide attempts "Attempted Suicide," *Butte Daily Miner*, August 28, 1879.

Liz Hall and Carmen Murphy, "Women on the Line," 62; and Writers Project of Montana, 184.

an amazing discovery of copper Ellen Baumler, "The Devil's Perch: Prostitution from Suite to Cellar in Butte, Montana," *Montana: The Magazine of Western History*, vol. 48, no. 3 (Summer 1998): 8.

he was stuck with court costs *Territory of Montana v. Stanchfield*—Indictment by District Attorney, April 22, 1878; *Territory of Montana v. Stanchfield*—Memorandum of Costs, April 22, 1878, Butte, Deer Lodge County.

families of miners and tradesmen 1880 census.

Dolores as the major attraction Petrik, 35; and "Stanchfield & Co.," Charles E. Proprietor, Variety Hall, *Butte Directory of 1879* (Helena: Fisk Brothers), 117, 119. H. C. Caldwell, formerly a traveling salesman, was a partner in the original venture. Also "Hugh C. Caldwell," 1910 census, Kalispell, Flathead, Montana, roll T624-832, page 4A, enumeration district 31, image 421.

Even more lethal The Montana legislature did not pass a law against wife beating until 1885, and then not everybody took it seriously.

swearing she had committed suicide "A Lively Time in Helena Hotel," *Butte Daily Miner*, July 27, 1880; "A Cold Blooded Tragedy: Mollie Scott Foully Murdered by Her Husband," *Butte Daily Miner*, August 5, 1880; and "A Park Street Killing—Scott's Story," *Butte Daily Miner*, August 7, 1880.

Escorted to her room "One of the Girls, Charged with Grand Larceny, Attempts Suicide," *Butte Daily Miner*, October 6, 1881.

Her suicide note instructed "In the Dark Valley: Suicide by Morphine of Inez Mayberton on Park Street," *Butte Daily Miner*, November 11, 1881.

bartender James C. Pickett County Clerk's office, Anaconda, Montana, County of Deer Lodge. She wed him under the name of Lottie Reamer, with both claiming residency in Helena on August 18, 1879.

only to be rescued *Butte Daily Miner*, August 28, 1879.

insulting her with foul language Jay Moynahan, *Murder in Butte: The 1881 Killing of Prostitute Sorrel Mike* (Spokane, WA: Chickadee Publishing, 2003), 29. The author cites the *Butte Daily Miner*, October 1879, but gives no exact date. The customer was William Maurice.

"Some innocent may suffer" "Who Did It? An Unfortunate Woman on Park Street Fatally Shot," *Butte Daily Miner*, December 16, 1881.

"It seems to be the general impression" "The End: Coroner's Inquest on the Remains of Lottie Pickett," *Butte Daily Miner*, December 17, 1881.

never been a successful suicide Petrik, 38.

not only by outlaws and the homeless Writers Project of Montana, 3, 134.

the daughters of Helena's elite The Sisters of Charity of Leavenworth, Kansas, *Prospectus of St. Vincent Academy and Chronicle of Events, Nineteen Hundred Twenty-Three and Twenty-Four*, St. Vincent's Academy, Z 373.H36710Z, Montana Historical Society Research Center, Helena.

the territory's leading mining town Writers Project of Montana, 14–15; Michael P. Malone, *The Battle for Butte: Mining & Politics on the Northern Frontier, 1864–1906* (Helena: Montana Historical Society, 1981), 15.

City fathers incorporated Murphy, *Mining Cultures*, 3.

the town was quickly rebuilt AOL Hometown. www.AOL.hometownmembers .aol.com/Gibson08127/htm (accessed October 10, 2008). Note: This site was shut down November 6, 2008.

town's future was secured Patrick F. Morris, *Anaconda Montana: Copper Smelting Boom Town on the Western Frontier* (Bethesda, MD: Swann Publishing, 1997), 269.

impressive city hall on Broadway C. B. Glasscock, *War of the Copper Kings* (Helena: Montana Historical Society, 1962, originally published in 1935), 123–124.

Several variety theaters attracted vaudeville 1884 Sanborn map.

sometimes forced to spend the night Murphy, "Women on the Line," 43.

Butte's Silver Bow Club   Writers Project of Montana, 298.

sole tradership declaration   Petrik, 36.

the couple invested so widely   Silver Bow Basin tax records, Butte–Silver Bow
Public Archives.

flimsy one-story shacks   Murphy, "Women on the Line," 36–38.

the largest mining camp in the West   Workers Project of Montana, 299.

where prostitutes were housed   Murphy, "Women on the Line," 40.

"With a few drinks"   Workers Project of Montana, 193.

CHAPTER 3: MILES CITY AND THE WILD WEST, 1880

bought her a ticket back home   "Al Swearengen," Digital Deadwood. www
.digitaldeadwood.com/history link/people/swearengen.html (accessed December
16, 2009); and Kathy Weiser, *Legends of America.* www.legendsofamerica.com
/SD-DeadwoodPaintedLadies2.html (accessed December 26, 2009). Both insist
the women of Deadwood raised money to send Inez home. Barbara Fifer, *Bad Boys
of the Black Hills: And some Wild Women, Too* (Helena, MT: Far Country Press,
2008), 146, wrote that Inez arrived with a variety company where she was billed
the "Queen of Operatic and Ballad Song" and that "no one can sing higher, lower,
softer or sweeter." Respectable women held a benefit for her with Swearengen himself listed as one of the performers, but she stayed in town several years after her
arrival in December 1879.

decided she would do better   Maggie Burns is listed as a dressmaker married to
liquor dealer J. S. Burns in the 1880 Deadwood census, roll T9-113, family history
film 1254113, page 258.300, enumeration district 120, image 0235. Her birthplace
is listed as Ohio, when later Maggie consistently listed it as Iowa, and she appears to
be two years older than the Maggie Burns later recorded with Bullard in Texas.

Swearengen was rebuilding   Kathy Weiser, "Al Swearengen and the Notorious
Gem Theater," *Legends of America.* www.legendsofamerica.com/WE-GemSaloon
.html (accessed November 29, 2009).

a military campaign with Colonel Nelson Miles   The battle of Rosebud took
place in June 1876.

Fort Keogh on the lower Yellowstone   Joseph James Warhank, "Fort Keogh: Cutting Edge of Culture," master's thesis, California State University at Long Beach
(Long Beach, 1983), 70.

one of the country's largest   Warhank, 11; and "W. H. Bullard," *Illustrated and
Historical Edition of the Yellowstone Journal, Supplement* (Miles City, MT: Yellowstone, September 27, 1900), 27.

Captain Heintzelman had just brought   Warhank, 9.

some fifteen hundred soldiers   Warhank, 13. Fort Commander Nelson A. Miles,
now a brevet (acting) general, originally requested fifteen hundred men, which was

due his rank and appropriate because of the threat of numerous hostile tribes. By late 1876 he had assembled a force of 850.

only thirteen dollars a month   Jeremy Agnew, *Life of a Solder on the Western Frontier* (Missoula, MT: Mountain Press, 2008), 95, 114–115. Officers made $115 a month but also had higher expenses.

Citizens named it Miles City   Jean Freese, "A Town Is Born," *Centennial Roundup* (Miles City, MT: *Miles City Star*, 1987), 5. The author notes that the original town site now lies under the city's sewer lagoons, "which from the way the man for whom it is named felt about it, is where it belongs." Also see Lorman L. Hoopes, "George M. Miles," *This Last West* (Helena, MT: Dr. Lorman L. Hoopes, 1990), 245.

"One was a Methodist"   Norman J. Bender, "Presbyterians and Higher Education in Montana—1869–1900," *Montana: The Magazine of Western History*, vol. 28, no. 2 (Spring 1978): 18, cites J. H. Hewett to Sheldon Jackson, January 28, 1878, Jackson correspondence, vol. VII, 254, Presbyterian Historical Society, Philadelphia.

"about 350 residents"   Hoopes, "Thomas Howard Irvine," 174.

There was no hotel   Clyde A. Milner and Carol A. O'Connor, *As Big as the West: The Pioneer Life of Granville Stuart* (Oxford and New York: Oxford University Press, 2009), 174. Stuart arrived in April 1880.

the two successfully pursued   Hoopes, "William H. Bullard," 41; and "Thomas Howard Irvine," 174.

a horrific fire   Weiser.

Indians killed the U.S. mail carrier.   Warhank, 23. The unfortunate express rider was Henry Friese.

ably put down the Cheyenne   John Halbert, "The General," *Centennial Roundup* (Miles City, MT: *Miles City Star*, 1987), 9–10.

done away with laundry service   Michael Rutter, *Upstairs Girls: Prostitution in the American West* (Helena, MT: Far Country Press, 2005), 40.

Many now operated   Milton F. Ayers, "Cowtowns," Montana Writers Project papers, Miles City Public Library.

all of whom were white   According to Warhank, black Buffalo soldiers were not stationed at Fort Keogh until 1890. Photos taken by Miles City photographer Miles R. C. Morrison, whose studio was on Pleasant Street near a cluster of bordellos before that era, show five white customers with four very good-looking mulatto women wearing lavish nightgowns. Morrison collection, Box 11, #18, Montana State Archives, Helena.

he officially lived alone   "W. H. Bullard," 1880 census, Miles City, Custer, Montana, roll T9-742, family history film 1254742, page 91.3000, enumeration district 6, image 0186; "Wm H. Bullard," 1900 census, Miles City, Custer, Montana, roll T623-910, page 10 B, enumeration district 202; and Sue Connors, "The Parlor Houses," *Roundup* (Miles City: *Miles City Star*, 1987), 21.

"Lively little town" *Yellowstone Journal*, November 5, 1881. The visitor was D. S. Wade, judge of Montana's first judicial district.

a brewery and bottling plant "W. H. Bullard," *Yellowstone Journal*.

a thousand bottles of beer Mark H. Brown, *The Plainsmen of Yellowstone Basin: A History of the Yellowstone Basin* (Lincoln: University of Nebraska Press, first printing Putnam and Sons, 1961), 246.

cattle drivers from the Lone Star State John Halbert, "Classic Cow Country," *Centennial Roundup* (Miles City, MT: *Miles City Star*, 1987), 77; and Mills, 59.

Nor were ordinary cowboys Harry Sinclair Drago, *Notorious Ladies of the Frontier*, Volume 1 (New York: Ballantine Books, 1969), 10.

new business buildings Jean Freese, "Main (Trail) Street," *Centennial Roundup* (Miles City, MT: *Miles City Star*, 1987), 41.

110-room MacQueen Hotel Freese; "Inter Ocean Hotel," Hoopes, 173; and "William Macqueen," Hoopes, 211. MacQueen first named this business the Inter Ocean Hotel, but locals ignored the name to honor the owner.

To celebrate its opening Hoopes, "Maggie Burns," 45, and "Forty-Four Parlor House," 124. Eri Coggshall was the lucky winner.

would hire a horse from the livery stable "Wild West Women, as told by Frank Murphy," *Miles City Star*, January 10, 1932. Murphy was a longtime cowboy on the Mizpah River.

they rallied as a group E. C. "Teddy Blue" Abbott with Helena Huntington Smith, *We Pointed Them North: Recollections of a Cowpuncher* (Norman: University of Oklahoma, 1984), 105–108.

A singularly beautiful brunette "Connie Hoffman," 1880 census, Deadwood, Lawrence, Dakota Territory, roll T9-113, family history film 1254113, page 265.1000, enumeration district 120, images 0248 and 0249; "Charles Hoffman," same census, image 1254114, page 119:3000, enumeration district 115, image 0253; and "Deadwood Girls, Frail & Fallen Sisters, Fair Amazons, Soiled Doves, Madam and Demi Monde." http://deadwoodgirls18001880s.blogspot.com (accessed August 24, 2009). The madam who hired Connie was New England–born Ida Clark.

embroidered with local cattle and brands "Connie Hoffman," Hoopes, 161–162. The rancher was Henry G. Ware, who owned the Cross Arrow Ranch in Wyoming, just across the Montana border.

frequently sat upon *Yellowstone Journal*, December 16, 1882.

an Oregon girl "Frank Blair," 1900 census, Miles City, Custer, Montana, roll T623-910, page 12B, enumeration district 202.

so into management Abbott, 109; and Lee Murrah, "The First Honky Tonks." www.murrah.com/essay/honkey_tonk (accessed December 2, 2009).

were also doing well Robin Gerber, "Early Brothels a Part of Area's History," *Miles City Star*, December 8, 1998.

nearly one-third of the cowboys Sara R. Massey, ed., *Black Cowboys of Texas* (College Station: Texas A & M University Press, 2000), introduction by Alwyn Barr, xii–xiii.

Most successful was Fannie French "Fannie French," 1900 census, Billings, Yellowstone, Montana, roll T623-915, page 32A, enumeration district 197; and *Pacific Reporter*, vol. 93 (St. Paul, MN: West Publishing Co., 1885): 93.

nearly unheatable, vermin-infested shack Gerber; Alice Blackwood Baldwin, *Memories of the Late Frank D. Baldwin, Major General* (Los Angeles: Wetzel Printing Co. 1929), 14–18. Baldwin complained of vermin in the base's early housing and that wood provided for fireplaces "emitted little other than a shower of inefficient sparks," and she was an officer's wife. One can hardly imagine what an unmarried black woman might expect for government housing on Suds Row. French was also known as Fannie Hendricks.

boasted a ballroom complete with piano Montana Writers Project, "Cowtowns" and "Prostitution"; and Hoopes, "Fannie French, Fanny Hendricks," 127.

Miles City's most notorious madam Census records and Mark H. Brown, *The Plainsmen of the Yellowstone Basin*, 349.

a respected Miles City merchant Hoopes, "Eugene Allen" and "Sgt. E. H. Allen," 4. In 1880 Allen became clerk for John J. Graham.

the notice she had published On April 10, 1880.

a string of bedroom-sized shacks Hoopes, "Annie Turner," 351.

"girls were hot and sweet" *Yellowstone Journal*, November 4, 1882.

According to the opening notice "New Restaurant," *Miles City Daily Press*, November 20, 1882, 4.

whose coverage had grown increasingly hostile Gerber.

"Annie Turner's house" *Yellowstone Journal*, July 15, 1882, 7.

after Knight referred to her *Yellowstone Journal*, November 19, 1882, 4.

"I pay my debts" *Daily Press*, November 20, 1882, 4.

more were moving in Montanas Writers Project.

the largest he'd ever handled Tricia Paterson, "Banking on Progress," *Centennial Roundup* (Miles City, MT: *Miles City Star*, 1987), 53; and Connors, 21.

the respectable citizens of Miles City Interview with Bob Barthelmess, Range Riders Museum, October 12, 2009; "Nancey H. Keenan," 1880 census, Miles City, Custer, Montana, roll T9-742, family history film 1254742, page 92.100, enumeration district 6, image 0188; "Nancy H. Keenan," 1900 census, Miles City, Custer, Montana, roll T623-910, page 12A, enumeration district 202; and "Death Overtakes Mrs. Keenan After Lingering Illness," *Miles City Star*, February 5, 1926, 5.

picked this time to marry James D. McLaird, *Calamity Jane: The Woman and the Legend* (Norman: University of Oklahoma Press), 24–25, 56–59.

added to their income "Wild West Women, as told by Frank Murphy."

"queer freak of nature" *Yellowstone Journal*, July 8, 1882.

any odd jobs she could get McLaird, 21–23.

"a heart as large as a wagon box" Elmer Crawford interview by the Montana Writers Project, November 19, 1940, Miles City Public Library.

quite fashionably dressed Brown and Felton, 147. The photo was taken in 1880.

a son who died in infancy McLaird, 20; *Custer City Chronicle*, November 18, 1882; and Elsie P. Johnson, *Laurel's Story: A Montana Heritage* (Laurel, MT: Laurel Historical Research Committee, 1979), 44.

King died shortly thereafter "Wild West Women, as told by Frank Murphy."

arrested with a partner Mark H. Brown, *The Plainsmen of the Yellowstone Basin*, 351.

like train robber Butch Cassidy Gail Drago, *Etta Place: Her Life and Times with Butch Cassidy and the Sundance Kid* (Plano: Republic of Texas Press, 1996), 38. Drago says Cassidy worked the area in 1886.

a number of personable outlaws Hoopes, "Kid Curry, Harvey Logan," 82. According to Hoopes, Harvey was there with his brother Harry in 1884.

not only from hostile Indians Dan Morrison, "The Right Gear," *Texas Highways*, vol. 41, no. 9 (September 1994): 8.

usually former slaves Massey, xii–xiii.

less prone to carry social diseases Phone interview with Professor Eric Thomas, Colby College, Waterville, Maine, December 2, 2009. Thomas, whose father was born in Miles City, was also raised there.

that very night her bordello Hoopes, "Annie Turner," 351.

"by a lamp being upset" "Last Night's Blaze," *Yellowstone Journal*, December 15, 1882, 4.

she estimated losses "Annie Turner," 1880 census, Miles City.

failed to attack her as vehemently Hoopes, "Fannie French, Fannie Hendricks," 127.

joined forces in a rare alliance *Yellowstone Journal* and *Live Stock Reporter*, September 6.

"lewd and boisterous behavior" *Yellowstone Journal*, November 29, 1884.

sentenced to county jail "The State vs. Hendricks," January 21, 1895, *Pacific Reporter*, vol. 39 (St. Paul, MN: West Publishing Co., 1895): 93–95.

moving to several new locations Hoopes, "Fannie French, Fannie Hendricks," 127.

"Someone's been killed, sure," Abbott, 109.

a patron got his throat slit   Brown and Felton, 139.

which took place on the faro table   Freese, "Fifth and Main," 49.

No one was ever convicted   Freese, "Main (Trail) Street," 44.

swinging from a bridge trestle   Mills, 36–38.

a posse of forty men   Brown and Felton, 159; and Conners, "'Wide Open Berg,'" *Centennial Roundup* (Miles City, MT: *Miles City Star*, 1987), 14.

burned the Cosmopolitan   Loomes, "William (Bill) Rigney," 298.

highwayman was subsequently hung   Brown and Felder, 157–158.

trying to disarm him   *Illustrated and Historical Edition of the Yellowstone Journal,* September 27, 1900, 6.

"accustomed peaceful flow"   Sam Gordon, *Recollections of Old Milestown* (Miles City, MT: Independent Printing Co., 1926), 41–42.

pitched his tent in the area   Ted Binnema, "The North American Journals of Prince Maximilian of Wied, Volume 1," book review, *Montana: The Magazine of Western History,* vol. 50, no. 1 (Spring 2009): 72.

camped near the site   Donna M. Lucey, *Photographing Montana, 1894–1928: The Life and Work of Evelyn Cameron* (Missoula, MT: Mountain Press, 2001), 199.

Great Britain alone   John Halbert, 78.

established the town of Medora   Brown and Felder, 183.

which he ultimately paid   Pierre Wibaux file, Glendive Public Library, Glendive, Montana. Clipping titled "Ranger Review," July 14, 1889, and others.

General James Brisbin   Philadelphia: J. B. Lippincott & Company, 1881.

His tome's favorite phrase Review, *Dumont Maps & Books of the West.* www .dumontbooks.com/cgi-bin/dumont/20564.html (accessed December 6, 2009).

the sons of earls, barons, and other nobility   Michael A. Amundson, "'These Men Play Real Polo: An Elite Sport in the 'Cowboy State,' 1890–1930," *Montana: The Magazine of Western History,* vol. 51, no. 1, (Spring 2009): 18.

championed the lifestyle of a rancher   Republished by the University of Oklahoma Press, 2002. Original version 1887, 85–86, 115.

pasturing them first   *Yellowstone Journal,* October 1, 1881; and Hoopes, "Sidney Paget," 277.

"but we never spoke"   Nannie T. Alderson and Helena Huntington Smith, *A Bride Goes West* (Lincoln and London: University of Nebraska Press, 1961, first printing Farrar & Rinehart, 1942), 114–117.

until it burned to the ground   *Yellowstone Journal,* August 14, 1886.

money was not too difficult to secure   Brown and Felton, 150–151.

established a polo circuit   Amundson, 9.

negotiating ranch sales   William S. Reese, "Granville Stuart of the DHS Ranch, 1879–1887," *Montana: The Magazine of Western History*, vol. 31, no. 3 (Summer 1981): 24.

cattlemen were concerned about three   Reese, 22–23.

revived the Montana Stockgrowers Association   Miner; and O'Connor, 217.

they accused Granville Stuart   Reese, 22; and Halbert, 79.

missed his chance of becoming president   Morris, 270.

went quietly down in history   Halbert, 79.

cattlemen finally overcame mining interests   Reese, 23.

Kansas entirely outlawed   "Texas Fever," *The Handbook of Texas Online*. www .tshaonline.org/handbook/online/articles/TT/awt1.html (accessed December 5, 2009).

hoping for a Chicago price rise   John Taliaferro, *Charles M. Russell: The Life and Legend of America's Cowboy Artist* (Boston, New York, Toronto, London: Little, Brown and Company), 61.

a blue haze lifted   Dee Brown, *Trail Driving Days* (New York: Ballantine Books, 1974), 149.

the banana crop was a failure   Taliaferro, 62.

a host of well-established cattlemen   Reese says 60 percent, citing the *Report of the Governor of Montana to the Secretary of Interior, 1889* (Washington, DC: Government Printing Office, 1889). Halbert, 79–80, whose focus is on Miles City, estimates 70 percent.

"financially annihilating our solidest men"   Halbert, 80.

listed as owing a moderate amount   "Delinquent Tax List, 1882," *Yellowstone Journal*, June 25, 1883.

the sale of one of her houses   Abstract no. 1667, issued by Custer Abstract Company from official records, March 29, 1886, Book A of Agreements, page 300, March 17, 1868; and Quit Claim Deed, March 26, Book E of Deeds, pages 137–138.

Fannie French was last heard from   Hoopes, "Fanny French, Fanny Hendricks," 127; and "Drovers House (Hotel)," 98.

it took three men to jail her   Corners, 21.

When Blue saw her last   Abbott, 105.

"Had the winter continued"   Halbert, 80.

also owned Montana ranching property   "Russell B. Harrison Collection, 1880–1908, Biographical Sketch," Indiana Historical Society, Manuscripts and Archives. www.indianahistory.org/library/manuscripts/collection_guides/m0387 .html (accessed December 13, 2009).

"**Drought without parallel**"   Montana Stockgrowers Association. www.mtbeef
.org/Public/Contents/3 (accessed December 2, 2010).

CHAPTER 4: THE LAST OF THE SILVER YEARS, 1887

a killing in silver at Philipsburg   Michael P. Malone and Richard B. Roeder,
Montana: A History of Two Centuries (Seattle and London: University of Washington Press, 1976) 144–145.

whose brother would soon be   Ellen Baumler, "The Cruse Tragedy," *Helena Inde-*
pendent Record, November 23, 1995.

There was music in Joe's hurdy-gurdy   John Taliaferro, *Charles M. Russell:*
The Life and Legend of America's Cowboy Artist (Boston, New York, Toronto, and
London: Little, Brown and Company, 1996), 73. Taliaferro cites correspondence
between Phil Weinard and James B. Rankin, October 3, 1938.

ramrodded through the 1885   "John Marion Robinson Family Papers, 1866–
1890." www.lib.montana.edu/collect/spcoll/findaid/0012.php (accessed December
17, 2009). Robinson, a Gallatin County rancher, father of four, part-time preacher,
and board member for the Montana Agricultural College, sponsored the legislation.

Hunt sent officers   Rex Myers, "An Inning for Sin: Chicago Joe and Her Hurdy-
Gurdy Girls Girls Girls Girls," *Montana: The Magazine of Western History*, vol. 27,
no. 2 (Spring 1977): 27–29.

former secretary of state   Hubert Howe Bancroft and Frances Fuller Victor, *His-*
tory of Washington, Idaho, and Montana: 1845–1889, Volume 31 (San Francisco:
The History Company, 1890), 689.

"An Inning for Sin"   Myers, 30.

the frontier code of "live and let live"   Paula Petrik, "Strange Bedfellows: Prostitution, Politicians, and Moral Reform in Helena, 1885–1887," *Montana: The*
Magazine of Western History, vol. 35, no. 3 (Summer 1985): 3.

the governor's Queen Anne–styled mansion   "Helena, Montana," *Helena Cham-*
ber and Visitor Bureau. http://helenacvb.visitmt.com/history.html (accessed September 5, 2009).

exclusive Montana Club   Paula Petrik, *No Step Backward: Women and Family on*
the Rocky Mountain Mining Frontier, Helena, Montana 1865–1900 (Helena: Montana Historical Society Press, 1987), 16.

no room for scarlet women   "Ming Opera House." www.metnet.mt.gov/Special
/Quarries%20From%20The%20Gulch/HTM/ming.shtml (accessed December 18,
2009).

"This insult to a sisterhood"   *Helena Daily Independent*, August 14, 1884.

Wood, Bridge, and Clore streets   The *Helena Daily Independent* reported the creation of Ordinance 7 on June 6, 1885.

undertook an exposé *Helena Daily Independent*, March 3, 1886.

the collection of fines Petrik, "Strange Bedfellows," 6–9.

no woman in Helena Petrik, *No Step Backward*, 37.

sixty-five white and Chinese ladies Ellen Baumler, "Soiled Doves: Life on Helena's Tenderloin." www.metnet.mt.gov/Special/FOV7-001039B2/I0013B383.0 /Soildove.pdf. Baumler, who coordinates Montana's National Register of Historic Places, noted that during this period fifty-two white prostitutes were arrested, which would make the number of Chinese women taken in this bust at thirteen. It is puzzling that no black women were included because according to William Lang, "The Nearly Forgotten Blacks of Last Chance Gulch, 1900–1912," *Pacific Northwest Quarterly* (April 1979), 55–57, there were a considerable number of them working the red-light district on Clore.

business as usual, and better Petrik, "Strange Bedfellows," 11–12.

Sanford-Perris insurance map Petrik, "Prostitution in Helena, Montana, 1865–1900," *Montana: The Magazine of Western History*, vol. 31, no. 2 (Spring 1981): 36.

prohibited the sale of liquor Petrik, "Strange Bedfellows," 8.

also turned to Tom Cruse Petrik, *No Step Backward*, 39, 54.

published legal notices *Helena Daily Independent*, January 7, 10, and 11, 1883.

he was the only man High River Pioneers' and Old Timers Association, "Philip Weinard *Leaves from the Medicine Tree: A History of the Area Influenced by the Tree, and Biographies of Pioneers and Oldtimers Who Came Under Its Spell Prior to 1900* (Lethbridge, Canada: *Lethbridge Herald*, 1960), 44. www.ourroots.ca/e/page .aspx?id=862257 (accessed December 11, 2009).

crewing on riverboats "Phil Weinard Was a Link in the Old West," *Salmon Arm Observer*, September 25, 1943; and "Philip Weinard," 1880 census, Minneapolis, Hennepin, Minnesota, roll T9-621, family history film 1254621, page 53.1000, enumeration district 230, image 0731.

only one year in the territory Ancestry.com: New York Port, Ship Images, 1851–1891, Provo, Utah: MyFamily.com, Inc., 2004. Original data: New York Port, Ships Images, 1851–1891 obtained from and reproduced courtesy of Mystic Seaport, documents her arrival in New York, April 23, 1886, on the Inman Line; According to the 1906 Canadian Census, ancestry.com, Census Place:27, Calgary, Alberta, page 1, family no:1, she was born about 1866.

he had been hired to ride range Taliaferro, 74.

overdose of morphine Ginger K. Renner, "Charlie and the Lades in His Life," *Montana: The Magazine of Western History*, vol. 34, no. 3 (Summer 1984): 53; names "Dutch Lena, Maggie Murphy, Lil and Lou" as Helena women of the evening favored by Russell, cites his friend Judge Bollinger. The suicide of Lena, often referred to as Leina, was covered in the *Helena Daily Independent* on May 9, 1884. Suicides in the red-light district were rare during this period. Leina's appears to be the second on record.

providing the soon-to-be-millionaire Earl L. Jenson, "Russell's First Friend in Montana," *Montana: The Magazine of Western History*, vol. 34, no. 3 (Summer 1984): 27.

"that kid's goin' to be OK" Ramon F. Adams and Homer E. Britzman, *Charles M. Russell: The Cowboy Artist* (Pasadena, CA: Trail's End Publishing Co., 1948), 57.

bushwhacked while peeling potatoes Taliaferro, 47, cites Russell's correspondence with Harry T. Duckett.

outmatched by other suitors Renner, 38–39.

dashed off a watercolor Taliaferro, 65–66.

recognized Charlie's special gift Brian W. Dippie, "Charles M. Russell and the Canadian West," *Alberta History* (Spring 2004). www.thefreelibrary.com/Charles+M .+Russell+and+the+Canadian+West.-a0115843925 (accessed December 11, 2009).

they had their photo taken Richard B. Roeder, "Charles M. Russell and Modern Times," *Montana: The Magazine of Western History*, vol. 34, no. 3 (Summer, 1984): 6; Taliaferro, 73. Roeder says the event took place in 1887 while Taliaferro says it was Washington's Birthday, 1888.

glad for their company Taliaferro, 74, 77.

agreed to manage the spring roundup Hugh A. Dempsey, "Tracking C. M. Russell in Canada: 1888–1889," *Montana: The Magazine of Western History*, vol. 39, no. 3 (Summer 1989): 7–9.

"I had a chance to marry" Taliaferro, 78, quotes Russell's letter to Charles M. Joys, May 10, 1892.

Russell would confess John Taliaferro, "The Curse of the Buffalo Skull: Seventy Years on the Trail of a Charles A. Russell Biography," *Montana: The Magazine of Western History*, vol. 46, no. 2 (Summer 1996): 8.

without notice to the Weinards Taliaferro, *Charles M. Russell*, 81–82.

Chicago Joe struggled Myers, 32, July 4 program.

completely without family "'Chicago Joe' Dead," *Daily Independent*, October 26, 1899.

once-skeptical Independent Petrik, *No Step Backward*, 45; and Myers, 31.

"a picture pleasing to behold" *Helena Daily Record*, February 14, 1889.

She paid taxes Myers, 33.

Charlie was arrested *Helena Independent*, September 9, 1886.

Chicago Joe understood Petrik, *No Step Backward*, 36.

On his return from Canada *Helena Weekly Herald*, September 27, 1888.

a spread of the cowboy's sketches Dempsey, 44. The spread appeared May 18, 1889, with Jerome H. Smith credited with producing the layout.

the first city in Montana Vivian Paladin and Jean Baucus, *Helena: An Illustrated History* (Helena, MT: Bar-Wineglass Pub., 1983), 46.

the first electric streetcar system   Patrick F. Morris, *Anaconda Montana: Copper Smelting Boom Town on the Western Frontier* (Bethesda, MD: Swann Publishing, 1997), 104.

"Our Would Be States."   Vol. XXVII, no. 2, February 1889.

the fifty-room Hotel Broadwater   "The Hotel Broadwater and Natatorium." www.lifelikecharm.com/Broadwater1.htm (accessed December 23, 2009).

Helena's well-equipped fire department   "The Fire Tower," Old South Main. www.helenahistory.org/fire_tower.htm (accessed December 23, 2009).

A group of nuns   www.helenahistory.org/good_shepherd.htm (accessed December 23, 2009).

the property of the town's eight   Petrik, *No Step Backward*, 53.

majority of owners remained local   Malone and Roeder, 85.

33 percent of the state's population   Michael P. Malone, *The Battle for Butte: Mining & Politics on the Northern Frontier, 1864–1906* (Helena: Montana Historical Society, 1981), 85.

Helena had led   William L. Lang, "Montana Communities in Conflict, 1888–1894," *Montana: The Magazine of Western History*, vol. 37, no. 4 (Autumn 1987): 39.

America stopped coining silver   The Bland-Allison Act of 1878.

insisted it would soon reopen   Petrik, *No Step Backward*, 18; and "silver standard," *Encyclopaedia Britannica*. www.britannica.com/EBchecked/topic/544915/silver-standard (accessed December 23, 2009).

took up residence there   Helena, Montana, city directory, 1891.

"Mills, factories, mines"   Joyce Litz, *The Montana Frontier: One Woman's West* (Albuquerque: University of New Mexico Press, 2004), 81.

"the most incongruous procession"   A. C. McMillian, "A Young Clergyman Looks at Granite's Glittering Glory," *Montana: The Magazine of Western History*, vol. 14, no. 3 (Summer 1964): 8.

soon become a moot issue   Petrik, *No Step Backward*, 20.

Cruse curtly turned them down   Ann Conger, "Cruse: Tragedy in Life, Death," *Independent Record*, August 15, 1971.

"ye may all go t'hell"   Paladin and Baucus, 62.

causing her financial collapse   Petrik, *No Step Backward*, 54.

the only capitalist venture   Petrik, "Capitalists with Rooms," 39.

had been strangled to death   "Al Hawkins Killed," *Chicago Daily*, August 26, 1897, 3.

his own remote company town   Malone, *The Battle for Butte*, 104.

former governor Joseph K. Toole   "'Chicago Joe' Dead," *Daily Independent*, October 26, 1899; Myers, 33; and " 'Chicago Joe' Found Dictionary Better Defense than Statues in 'Hurdy Gurdy' House Trial," *Great Falls Tribune*, Sunday, July 10, 1955, 13.

Chapter 5: The Celestial Sex Trade, 1900

the Great Potato Famine   See David Emmonds, *The Butte Irish: Class and Ethnicity in an American Mining Town, 1875–1925* (Urbana and Chicago: University of Illinois Press, 1994), for a good overview.

in their own mysterious ways   "Queer Spots in and About Butte: No 10 Chinatown" *Anaconda Standard*, May 20, 1906, 1.

through her silk cheongsam   The cheongsam, the garb that westerners most commonly associated with Chinese women, was a long, close-fitting dress with short sleeves, a slit up one side, a mandarin collar, and a fastening across the right side of the upper breast. In the late 1800s it was referred to in English simply as a sahm. See *Fashion Encyclopedia*. www.fashionencyclopedia.com/fashion_costume_culture /Early-Cultures-Asia/index.html (accessed January 1, 2010). Unfortunately SAHM today is the popular acronym for "stay-at-home mom."

assault with a deadly weapon   "Bathed in Her Gore, You Kim Hatcheted in the Back," *Butte Daily Miner*, November 4, 1881, 2. The girl's name was spelled Yow Kum in a follow-up article November 10.

Beal's medical specialty   Ancestry.com. Directory of Deceased American Physicians, 1804–1929 (database online), Provo UT: My Family.com, Inc., 2004.

nearly one hundred Chinese   "Montana Abandoned Mines," *Department of Environmental Quality*. http://deq.mt.gov/abandonedmines/linkdocs/99tech.mcpx (accessed December 2, 2010).

tied the knot   Writers Project of Montana, *Copper Camp: The Lusty Story of Butte, Montana, the Richest Hill on Earth* (Helena, MT: Riverbend Publishing, 1973, first published by Montana State Department in 1943), 116–117.

Beal was not reelected   Writers Project of Montana, 48; and "City of Butte Mayors," Elected Officials in Butte, Montana, *History Wiki*. http://montanahistorywiki .pbworks.com/Elected+Officials+-+Butte (accessed January 1, 2010).

august *New York Times*   David Langum, *Crossing over the Line: Legislating Morality and the Mann Act* (Chicago and London: University of Chicago Press, 1994), 23, 28–29.

paid by vengeful masters   "Highbinders," *Desert Weekly*, Volume 46 (Salt Lake City: Church of Jesus Christ of Latter-Day Saints, 1893), 288.

brief and often brutal   Mary Murphy, "Women on the Line: Prostitution in Butte, Montana, 1878–1917," master's thesis, University of North Carolina (Chapel Hill, 1983), 55–58.

the discovery of gold   Carrie Schneider, "Remembering Butte's Chinatown," *Montana: The Magazine of Western History*, vol. 54, no. 2 (Summer 2004): 67.

following the mining strikes Christopher W. Merritt, "The Chinese in Montana," *Drumlummon Views*, vol. 3, no 1 (Spring 2009): 353.

hired out in well-organized gangs George Everett, *The Butte Chinese: A Brief History of Chinese Immigrants in Southwest Montana* (Butte, MT: The Mai Wah Society, Inc., undated), 6.

all the rights of any person Patrick F. Morris, *Anaconda Montana: Copper Smelting Boom Town on the Western Frontier* (Bethesda, MD: Swann Publishing, 1997), 115.

***Butte Miner* concluded** Everett, 11.

one Chinese prospector George Everett, "Butte's Far Flung Eastern Influences," *Butte America.* "http://www.butteamerica.com/fareast.htm"(accessed July 8, 2004).

"not a judicial execution" Writers Project of Montana simply cites a Standard published in 1898; and Morris, 116.

four Chinese women turned out *Helena Weekly*, September 19, 1867, 7.

his 1878 murder *Butte Miner*, October 30, 1877.

argued for their expulsion Michael Rutter, *Upstairs Girls: Prostitution in the American West* (Helena, MT: Far Country Press), 43.

one-third of all placer mines Morris, 115–116.

denied the right of the foreigners Everett, *The Butte Chinese*, 4.

kidnapping was also an option Lucie Cheng Hirata, "Free, Indentured, Enslaved: Chinese Prostitutes in Nineteenth-Century America," *Signs*, vol. 5, no. 1 (Autumn 1979; University of Chicago Press): 4–6.

though heavily weighted Carol Ruth Berkin and Mary Beth Norton, *Women of America: A History* (Boston: Houghton Mifflin Company, 1979), 225–226. There are many other versions of Ah-choi's biography, but in each she ends up a rich and powerful slave trader.

tricking them aboard Rutter, 46. Berkin and Norton call the notorious madam Ah-choi while Rutter's more recent version identifies her as Ah Toy.

the terms of indenture Hirata, 8–10.

contracted venereal disease Martin, 80.

bribe both Chinese and U.S. officials Hirata, 8–11.

One cruel agreement Martin, 81. Given that most of the "stock" was illiterate, a thumbprint was generally required as a signature.

working her way to freedom Murphy, 56.

census takers were as notorious Robert R. Swartout Jr., "Kwangtung to Big Sky: The Chinese in Montana, 1864–1900," *Montana: The Magazine of Western History*, vol. 38, no. 1 (Winter 1988): 67; Michael P. Malone and Richard B. Roeder, *Montana: A History of Two Centuries* (Seattle and London: University of Washington

NOTES

Press, 1976), 75, suggest Chinese made up one-third of the population of Montana at this point.

twenty-one of Butte's thirty-five   Murphy, 57; and Hirata, 13.

50 percent of fifty-three   Paula Petrik, *No Step Backward: Women and Family on the Rocky Mountain Mining Frontier, Helena, Montana, 1865–1900* (Helena: Montana Historical Society Press, 1987), 31.

those who worked as prostitutes   Rutter, 43.

"bleary-eyed males and lewd girls"   Murphy, 39.

"Her testimony was quite interesting"   *Daily Miner*, October 22, 1881, 8.

little more would ever be learned   Murphy, 40.

Ah Fok's remaining wives   "Polygamy Once Existed in Butte—and Kidnapping—With Nothing Done About Either," *Butte Standard*, August 18, 1935.

no follow-up to report   "For Ways That Are Dark," *Northwest Magazine*, vol. 10 (December 1892): 12, with credit to the *Moscow (Idaho) Star.*

Chinese eventually took over   Malone, *Battle for Butte*, 67. According to the Writers Project of Montana, 114, the new residents failed to notify the post office of the name change and remained mystified as to why all mail addressed to Foochow ended up in the dead letter office.

the great Helena fire of 1869   Vivian Paladin and Jean Baucus, *Helena: An Illustrated History* (Helena, MT: Bar-Wineglass Pub., 1983), 29.

"the carelessness of"   Morris, 197.

only six Chinese residents   Swartout, 50–52.

pushed from the job market   George Everett, "Butte's Far Eastern Influences. www.butteamerica.com/fareast.htm (accessed January 3, 2010).

a public meeting was held   Paladin and Baucus, 108.

from $38,900 in 1870   Swartout, 48.

foreigners feared violence   Everett, "Butte's Far Eastern Influences."

three Chinese were beaten   Morris, 118.

decaying corpse of a Chinese   *Anaconda Standard*, February 17, 1893.

Citizens Anti-Chinese Committee   *Anaconda Standard*, February 13 and 14.

astonished members left in haste   *Anaconda Standard*, February 27, 1893.

trusted and efficient Chinese cooks   Baumler, "End of the Line," 285.

Butte Labor and Trades Assembly   *Anaconda Standard*, March 2, 1892.

filed suit against the organizers   Everett, *The Butte Chinese*, 13. Hum Fay, Dr. Huie Pock, Dear Yick, and Hum Tong won their case in court and succeeded in getting an injunction against the boycotts. They were unable to collect damages for the harm done to their businesses, which they estimated at about $500,000, but they did receive $1,750.05 for their legal fees. According to Everett, about 350 Chinese were driven from Butte by the boycott.

"Yung Lee sell dleams"   *Butte Daily Miner*, July 9, 1896; and Writers Project of Montana, 118, 279.

Dr. Huie Pock had introduced his bride   *Butte Daily Miner*, February 14, 1896.

passed every English course   *Anaconda Standard*, January 17, 1909.

advocating the exclusion of Celestials   Morris, 119.

Their price on delivery   Hirata, 12.

immigration agents refused   *Occidental Board Annual Report*, April 1884, 48–49.

headed the rescue mission   Martin, 58.

joined the other girls   Material copied from the *Occidental Board Bulletin*, July 23, 1884, in the Chinese file under "Lon Ying," Butte–Silver Bow Archives.

Lamb was older   "Wah Jean Lamb," 1910 census, Butte Ward 6, Silver Bow, Montana, roll T624-836, page 2A, enumeration district 107, image 844. He is listed as a physician. His wife is listed as Alice, age twenty-six, and born in New York, which might be a ploy to claim citizenship. They claim nine years of marriage, and there are six children listed, aged five months to thirteen years. Theirs is the only Lamb family listed in Butte at this time.

many of his patients   An ad for Dr. Lamb's services ran in the *Anaconda Standard*, September 20, 1909, under the headline "The Celebrated Chinese Herb Doctor." He guaranteed to cure diseases with his famous Chinese medicines, never before introduced into this country, and claimed he had cured thousands.

in a Christian service   *Occidental Board Bulletin*, May 1, 1901, 1.

teaching a Sunday school class   *Occidental Board Bulletin*, August 1, 1901, 9.

women could not attend   Lee, 4; "The Fifteenth Anniversary Program of the First Baptist Church, Butte, Montana, February 21–23, 1932"; and letter from James R. Lynch, Director of the Library, American Baptist Society, to George Everett, February 16, 1996, in Chinese file, Butte–Silver Bow Archives.

then a small girl   Martin, 43.

sweet and seemingly docile   The *Occidental Board Annual Report* of 1903 says "she has proved a beautiful character—polite and lovable in her manner," 60.

making Lon Ying wife number three   Quong Tuck Wing is listed as Tuck A. Duong or Quon Luck Wang in the Butte census of 1900. Choy Gay under the name of Lena Quon is listed as his wife, with Lon Ying as Lowyen Quon as a daughter. Butte Ward 6, Silver Bow, Montana, roll T-623-915, page 5A, enumeration district 119. Their address is the same as listed for Wing in numerous Butte city directories.

successfully challenged Quong Tuck Wing   *Occidental Board Bulletin*, August 1, 1902, 9.

successful Christian union   Correspondence to Ellen Crain, City Archives, Butte, from one of Lon Ying's granddaughters, Colleen Fong, Oakland, California, September 28, 1995.

developed enough sewing skill   *Occidental Board Annual Report* of 1903, 60, and 1907, 71.

population continued to drop   Everett, "The Butte Chinese," 9.

a forty-one-year-old veteran   "Du Toy," Butte Ward 6, Silver Bow, Montana, roll T623-915, page 10A, enumeration district 120; and Murphy, 58.

prostitute of the same name   "Du Toy," Helena, roll T9-742, page 277. This census lists her as being twenty-one, which may have been simply a marketing ploy of her owner.

"swells among the Chinese populations"   "No. 10 Chinatown," 341.

the editor ran the photograph   *Montana Standard*, September 2, 1936.

CHAPTER 6: RESPECTABLE PURPLE PATHS, 1900

Peter supported their family   Cornelius Hedges, *Progressive Men of the State of Montana* (Chicago: A. W. Bowen & Co., 1902), 705.

The property they rented   William D. Mangum, *The Clarks: An American Phenomenon* (New York: Silver Bow Press, 1941), 95–96.

reestablish himself as an oculist   The Butte city directory of 1891–1892 shows LaChapelle listed at a physician, but in 1893 he lists himself as "Oculist."

mining man Jim Murray   William R. Kershner, "'The Best Attractions at Popular Prices': Early Theatre in Butte," *Montana: The Magazine of Western History*, vol. 38, no. 2 (Spring 1988): 33.

Murray was not only   C. B. Glasscock, *War of the Copper Kings* (Helena: Montana Historical Society, 1962, originally published in 1935), 123–124.

Murray would later describe her   "Principals in the Wedding Whose Announcement Surprised Butte Yesterday," *Anaconda Standard*, July 13, 1904. "Histrionic" was a term used then relating to acting. Today the word is defined as "exaggerated emotional behavior calculated for effect."

Clark would later recall   "Wedding Took Place in Marseilles, France, More than Three Years Ago, but Announcement Is Made Only Now—Have Daughter Two Years Old," newspaper clipping with name that looks like it might be Moreford, New York, July 12, 1904, in William A. Clark file, Montana State Archives, Helena.

Clark, as president of the board, addressed the class   "Closing Exercises," *Silver State*, Deer Lodge, June 5, 1895, 2.

the most famous harpist   "Alphonse Hasselmans," *Information and Much More.* www.answers.com/topic/alphonse-hasselmans?cat=entertainment (accessed May 29, 2008).

he had arranged "Senator and Mrs. W. A. Clark and Their Infant Daughter Andree," *Butte Miner*, July 13, 1904, 1.

Spaniard named Joaquin Abascal James Miller Guinn, "Joaquin Abascal," *A History of California and an Extended History of Los Angeles and its Environs*, Volume 2 (Los Angeles: Historical Record Co., 1915), 286.

she introduced him Mangam, 97.

Clark's young son *Butte Weekly Miner*, March 12, 1896.

his quest had ended Michael Malone, *The Battle for Butte: Mining Politics on the Northern Frontier, 1864–1906* (Helena: Montana Historical Society Press, 1981), 128.

Williams had already debuted "Moving Picture Star," *Anaconda Standard*, July 2, 1911.

she had shaved four years Williams originally shaved a year or two off her age, and as her career progressed she claimed to be five years younger than she was. A write-up on her in her file from an unidentified book on actors at the Montana State Archives notes: "lost her beauty 'overnight,' leading to speculation she was much older than her admitted years: shocking indeed is a comparison between the radiant woman who starred for DeMille in 1918's *We Can't Have Everything* and the grim-lipped actress who, three years later, had the top supporting role in his *Forbidden Fruit . . .*"

Which is exactly what he did Letter to Mrs. Dan Pubols, Belmont, California, from Nora Lee of Butte, dated September 17, 1979, with Wesleyan graduation program in file of "Kathlyn Williams," Montana State Archives, Helena.

1902 city directory It is fascinating to track the rise of the LaChapelles in Butte city directories from the outskirts of the red-light district to the most exclusive district in town.

Four years after the fact Mangam, 97–100.

Clark's story was *Butte Miner*, July 13, 1904, 1.

a follow-up story *Anaconda Standard*, July 13, 1904, 7.

Yet he insisted Anna Mangam, 111.

actress Sarah Bernhardt *Anaconda Standard*, May 6, 1906.

Mary Haldron *Butte Miner*, August 27, 1910.

under whose management "Leslie Wheeler, Montana's Shocking 'Lit'ry Lady,'" *Montana: The Magazine of Western History*, vol. 27, no. 3 (Summer 1977): 22.

where Mary found herself Mary MacLane, *The Story of Mary MacLane by Herself* (Helena, MT: Riverbend Publishers, 2002; original edition by Herbert S. Stone and Company of Chicago, 1902), from new introduction by Dr. Julia Watson, xix. The family lived at 419 North Excelsior Street.

There were giant boarding homes Writers Project of Montana, *Copper Camp: The Lusty Story of Butte, Montana, the Richest Hill on Earth* (Helena, MT: Riverbend Publishing, 1973, first published by Montana State Department in 1943), 301.

mixed and mingled Malone, 61–64.

There are Irishmen Mary MacLane, 112–114.

And then only because Wheeler, 22–23.

She knows the heavy weight MacLane, 40–42.

For some time "Fannie Corbin," 1900 census, Butte, Ward 6, Silver Bow, Montana, roll T623-915, page 7 B, enumeration district 121; and Wheeler, 22–23. Corbin was born and raised in New York.

there was worse to follow There are various versions of this story, but this one comes from Margaret Thayer, daughter of Mary's sister, Dorothy, from an interview with the *Montana Standard*, August 14, 1994, A1.

Rejected, she was disinclined Wheeler cites an interview with Mrs. Kay Chester, daughter of Mary's sister Dorothy, 23.

I Am the Most Interesting Book A translation from French was first published by Cassell in New York. Also see MacLane's introduction by Watson, xi.

"Let us love dogs" "Marie Bashkirtseff," Answers.com. www.answers.com/topic /marie-bashkirtseff (accessed January 16, 2010).

"I, of womankind and of nineteen years" MacLane, 1, 14–15, 23, 126, 180, 319–320.

Lucy Monroe, a manuscript reader Novelguide.com. www.novelguide.com/a /discover/aww_03/aww_03_00843.html (accessed January 13, 2010).

H. L. Mencken MacLane, introduction by Watson, vii–viii.

A snippy *New York Times* reviewer Wheeler, 24–25.

Yet the public purchased MacLane, introduction by Watson, viii.

Insane craving for sensationalism May 1, 1902, 4.

But MacLane Wheeler provides an excellent summary of MacLane's reviews, 25–26.

"Patron Saint of American Poets," "Harriet Monroe, Poet, Dies in Peru," *New York Times*, September 27, 1936, N 15.

"You were so fascinating that day" Michael R. Brown, *Mary MacLane*, from material collected by his late wife, Elizabeth Pruitt, author *of Tender Darkness: A Mary MacLane Anthology* (Belmont, CA: Abernathy & Brow, 1993).www.mary maclane.com/mary/works/letters (accessed January 9, 2010).

was no insult Wheeler quotes the *Missoula Fruit-Grower*, July 25, 1902, 4.

"first, she is exceedingly pretty . . ." "The Real Mary MacLane" *The New York World*, August 17, 1902.

Two subsequent attempts "Mary MacLane's Colorful Writing Earned her World Fame," *Montana Standard*, August 14, 1994, A1.

She had squandered Barbara Miller, "'Hot as Live Embers: The Restless Soul of Butte's Mary MacLane," *Montana: The Magazine of Western History*, vol. 32, no. 4 (September 1982): 52.

He'd been at it so long W. Turrentine Jackson, "The Irish Fox and the British Lion: The Story of Tommy Cruse, the Drum Lummon, and the Montana Company, Limited (British)," *Montana: The Magazine of Western History*, vol. 9, no. 2 (Spring 1959): 29.

Margaret, who had recently attended college "A Hotel Corridor Group," clipping dated February 14, 1910, with no publication data except New York, from interview with Cruse in the Cruse family scrapbook, Tom Cruse file, Montana State Archives, Helena. Information on McQuaid comes from *Contributions to the History Society of Montana*, Volume 5 (Helena: Montana Historical Society, 1904), 274–275.

When she was only eight Arthur Brayly, Arthur Tarbell, and Joe Chapple, "Thomas Carter," *National Magazine*, vol. 25 (October 1911 to March 1912, Boston: Chapple Publishing, 1912): 368. Also see 1870 census, "Thomas Carter," Pana, Christian, Illinois, roll M593-194, page 91A, image 185, family history library film 545693.

ardent Catholics Cornelius Hedges, 1120.

Elizabeth Fisk "Fisk, Robert and Elizabeth, House Lewis and Clark County, Helena, Montana," www.nps.gov/history/nr/feature/wom/2009/elizabeth_fisk_house.htm

the best man Census data on best man T. L. Martin, thirty, who was Irish and later became a respected merchant. No data can be found on bridesmaid Netta Rosenbaum beyond the fact that she lived on the family farm in a part of town not thought to be classy.

The lavish reception *Helena Herald*, March 3, 1886.

briefly revived the temperance crusade Ellen Baumler, *Spirit Tailings: Ghost Tales from Virginia City, Butte and Helena* (Helena, Montana Historical Society Press, 2002), 104.

guest lists remained "unexclusive" Ellen Baumler, "The Cruse Tragedy," *Helena Independent Record*, November 23, 1995. The address was 328 Benton, still a good neighborhood.

Was he disappointed "A Sad Affliction," the *Helena Independent*, December 28, 1886; and Baumler, "The Cruse Tragedy" and *Spirit Tailings*, 104.

along with the cook "Mary A. Cruse," 1900 census, Helena, Ward 3, Lewis and Clark, Montana, roll T623-912, page 2B, enumeration district 172.

One of them Ann Conger, "Cruse: Tragedy in Life, Death," *Helena Independent Record*, August 15, 1971, 10.

He didn't approve The Cruse family scrapbook features half a dozen clippings from this excursion, but no dates, and only the publisher, *New York Times*, is noted.

Once Mary reached high school age "Mary M. Cruse Died Yesterday Morning," undated and unidentified clipping in "Thomas Cruse" file, Montana State Archives, Helena.

She became an expert equestrian "Col. Cruse's Child Weds," unnamed newspaper dated January 2, 1909, "Thomas Cruse" file, Montana State Archives, Helena.

Named Floral Queen "Floral Queen Is Announced," Cruse family scrapbook, undated.

Realizing it would be futile Conger, 10. Judge Loble, interviewed for this story, said Mary had set her heart on a good man who later proved himself.

But Mamie was looking "Mary M. Cruse Died Yesterday Morning."

According to one report "Col. Cruse's Child Weds."

Whether Cruse had the girl drugged Unidentified clipping with headline cut off except for the words "in Dragging Up Past life of Mary Carter," which according to datelines was probably dated June 24, 1925.

At the divorce hearing "Wife Rich, Shunned Work," *New York Times*, May 20, 1911.

ceremony was also illegal "Cotter–Cruse Wedding Illegal," undated clip with no publication information, in Cruse family scrapbook.

where she embarked Conger, 10.

"She would take" When the *Helena Daily Independent* reported that Cruse made the statement at a court during the hearing on Mary's estate, he demanded that they retract it, June 23, 1914. The paper stood by the court record.

The unexpected death of Anna LaChapelle's mother The final chapters of Anna Clark's life are well detailed by William Mangum. For information on Kathlyn Williams, see Kally Mavromatis's "Kathlyn Williams—Silent Star of April, 1998." www.csse.monash.edu.au/~pringle/silent/ssotm/Apr98/ (accessed August 30, 2006).

never made the list "Mrs. Anna Clark, Senator's Widow," *New York Times*, October 12, 1963, 18.

"[L]ove of any kind" Maybelle, "Mary MacLane Startles East with Another Book," *Butte Miner*, August 20, 1911, 15.

"It's not Death" Wheeler, 32–33.

A hero to many Conger, 15.

But even that wish was denied "Mrs. Cotter Kept in Confinement," *Helena Daily Independent*, June 20, 1914.

Mary Cruse Rae Unidentified clipping with headline cut off except for the words "in Dragging Up Past Life of Mary Carter."

"the favorite expression" "Plaintiff Rests in Cotter Case," *Helena Independent*, June 23, 1914.

the most expensive "Estate Inventory and Appraisment," Tom Cruse file, Montana State Archives, Helena.

Chapter 7: Reflection, 1900

just enough arsenic there Michael P. Malone and Richard B. Roeder, *Montana: A History of Two Centuries* (Seattle, London: University of Washington Press, 1976), 150.

wealthy social lions Helen Fitzgerald Sanders, *A History of Montana* (Chicago: Lewis Publishing Co., 1913), 1080–1081.

just turned thirty-seven Grace McGinnis, 1900 census, Butte Ward 5, Silver Bow, Montana, roll T623-914, page 2B, enumeration district 114.

the largest urban center Harry Fritz, *Montana Legacy: Essays on History, People and Place* (Helena: Montana Historical Society Press, 2002), 181.

$1 million a month Michael Malone, *The Battle for Butte: Mining and Politics on the Northern Frontier 1864–1906* (Helena: Montana Historical Society Press, 1981), 58; Writers Project of Montana, 303; and Fritz.

with an excellent view Ellen Baumler, "The Devil's Perch: Prostitute from Suite to Cellar in Butte, Montana," *Montana: The Magazine of Western History*, vol. 48, no. 3 (Summer 1998): 17–18; and *Tales of the Dumas: Parlor House, Butte Montana: The Mining City's Last Brothel, 1890–1982* (Butte, MT: Antiques Mall, 1995). The Dumas is at 45 East Mercury Street.

when the election was contested Writers Project of Montana, *Copper Camp: The Lusty Story of Butte, Montana, The Richest Hill on Earth* (New York: Hastings House, 1943; second edition Helena, MT: Riverbend Publishing, 1970), 301.

"I never bought a man" Writers Project of Montana, 41.

"Tsar of Butte's red-light district" Baumler, "The Devil's Perch," 9; and Mary Murphy, "Women on the Line: Prostitution in Butte, Montana, 1878–1917," master's thesis, University of North Carolina (Chapel Hill, 1983), 45–46.

thirty-nine-year-old veteran Mary Murphy, "Women on the Line," *Great Falls Tribune*, October 13, 1968, 62; and 1900 census, Butte Ward 5, Silver Bow, Montana, roll T623-914, page 3B, enumeration district 114.

"the most beautiful women in the world" Writers Project of Montana, 190.

most powerful man in the state Joseph Kinsey Howard, *Montana: High, Wide, and Handsome* (New Haven, CN: Yale University Press, 1943; third edition Lincoln and London: University of Nebraska Press, 1983), 56–57.

Gentlemen hoping to remain anonymous Two lipstick-smeared masks from the Dumas were shown on eBay on November 6, 1999. They were listed as Item 19483339 by mt.bigsky and priced at $100.

baring most of what they Interview with Rudy Giecek, owner of the Dumas, Butte, Montana, May 16, 1999.

CHAPTER 8: THE BEGINNING OF THE END, 1911

the fix was in on both sides   Paula Petrik, "Not a Love Story," *Montana: The Magazine of Western History*, vol. 41, no. 2 (Spring 1991): 46.

a relative newcomer from Mississippi   "John R. Bordeaux," 1880 census, Butte City, Deer Lodge, Montana, roll T9-742, family history film 1254742, page 107.3000, enumeration district 10, image 0220; and the 1891 and 1896 city directories for Butte showing him listed as a broker and "capitalist" at the classy address of 305 W. Broadway.

Then Campbell said   Petrik's feature "Not a Love Story" details the case from start to finish. Also see *Bordeaux v. Bordeaux* (1902), transcript 2-3, 585-65, Montana Historical Society, Helena.

dangerous to the lungs and internal organs   Joyce Litz, *The Montana Frontier: One Woman's West* (Albuquerque: University of New Mexico Press, 2004), 144. The author noted that Dr. Phillippe Marechale of Paris made American headlines when he tried to introduce a bill into the French Parliament placing corset manufacturers under state control. He declared that many young women who wore corsets died of pulmonary diseases or suffered from organic derangement through their entire life.

flooding into urban areas   William Moran, *The Belles of New England: The Women of the Textile Mills and the Families Whose Wealth They Wove* (New York: St. Martin's Press, 2002), is an excellent accounting of this phenomenon.

so engaged by 1900   Karen Abbott, *Sin in the Second City: Madams, Ministers, Playboys, and the Battle for America's Soul* (New York: Random House, 2007), 118. She cites Joanna Meyorowitz, *Women Adrift: Independent Wage Earners in Chicago, 1880–1930* (Chicago: University of Chicago Press, 1991), among others.

Women were members   Wim Wenders, "About Butte," *Montana: The Magazine of Western History*, vol. 56, no. 4 (Winter 2006): 62; and "The Butte–Anaconda National Historic Landmark," same issue, 68.

declaring himself a "miner-promoter"   "W. J. Kennedy," 1920 census, Butte Ward 6A, Silver Bow, Montana, roll T626-976, page 4A, enumeration district 226, image 702.

Yet the only successful arrest   "Pete Hanson Is Dead," *Anaconda Standard*, January 11, 1899, 10.

"She has been a woman of rare beauty"   January date obscured on clipping found in "Butte" general file of Montana State Archives, Helena.

"The so-called red light district"   *Butte Miner*, April 6, 1901, 7.

several walkways at the back   The Sanborn Insurance map for 1900 details this warren of walkways without naming the alleys. According to the census of that year, included were Model Terrace, New Terrace, Copper King Alley, Venus, and Old Fashioned Alley.

one-stop shopping mart for vice Ellen Baumler, "Devil's Perch: Prostitution from Suite to Cellar in Butte, Montana," *Montana: The Magazine of Western History*, vol. 48, no. 3 (Summer 1998): 7.

he mistakenly believed One of Ketchel's descendents, who prefers to remain unnamed, recalls that her great-uncle, Stanley's youngest brother, Arthur, said Stanley left home because of his "roving, adventurous nature." Note that sportswriters often added an extra "l" to Stanley's last name. James Carlos Blake, who fictionalized Ketchel's biography as a novel but stuck very close to the facts, suggested his exit was the result of a family fight. *The Killings of Stanley Ketchel* (New York: William Morrow, 2005), 9–14.

Ketchel then signed up Peter Walsh, "Stanley Ketchell: 1886–1910," Men of Steel, 1993, no publication data. Article sent in an e-mail from Jackie Corr, a famous Butte sportswriter, to Brian Shovers and Angelia Murray, Montana State Archives, Helena, June 6, 2002.

Boxing was huge in Montana "Stanley Ketchell," Boxrec Boxing Encyclopedia. http://boxrec.com/media/index.php/Stanley_Ketchell (accessed January 26, 2010).

big spender and a hard drinker Bob Gilluly, "Kid from Butte Knew How to Fight," *Great Falls Tribune*, June 9, 2002.

made a name for himself Frank Bell, *Gladiators of the Glittering Gulches* (Helena, MT: Western Horizon Books, 1985), 97.

leaving spectators spattered with blood Jackie Corr, "The Toughest Guy on the Planet," *'Round' Town Review*, Butte, May 2002.

where officials stopped the fight Bell, 97.

opponents who towered over "Ketchell in Straightened Circumstances, Left Butte to Become Famous as Middleweight Boxing Champ," a clipping without publishing data, "Stanley Ketchell" file, Butte–Silver Bow Public Archives. The piece was written after Ketchel was shot October 14, 1910.

utterly ruthless in action "Stanley Ketchell," Boxrec Boxing Encyclopedia.

Ketchel was a gentle and unusually thoughtful Nat Fleisher, "VF Stanley Ketchell," *Rig Magazine*, 1946, Montana State Archives, Helena; and Hype Igoe, "Ketchell Didn't Expect to Make 30," *Seattle Post-Intelligencer*, October 25, 1925.

kept a diary Ketchel descendent.

just twenty-four hours Berton Braley, *Pegasus Pulls a Hack: Memoirs of a Modern Minstrel* (New York: Minton, Blach & Co., 1934), 63–64.

high-rises had replaced John N. Dehaas Jr., *Historic Uptown Butte* (Billings, MT: John N. Dehass Jr., 1977), 7–9, 61.

"death grips with the subtle poisons" Warren Davenport, "editorial," *Butte X-Ray*, January 1, 1908. The bordello was at 7 and 9 East Mercury Street.

to open a bank Warren Davenport, *Butte and Montana Beneath the X-Ray: Being a Collection of Editorials from the Files of the Butte X-Ray During the Years 1907–08* (Butte and London: X-Ray Publishing Company, 1908), 39–44.

a strip of oilcloth Elliott West, "Scarlet West: The Oldest Profession in the Trans-Mississippi West," *Montana: The Magazine of Western History*, vol. 31, no. 2 (Spring 1981): 26.

"It was a tough hole" Writers Project of Montana, *Copper Camp: The Lusty Story of Butte, Montana, the Richest Hill on Earth* (Helena, MT: Riverbend Publishing, 1973, first published by Montana State Department in 1943), 188. Writers quote Wesley Davis, *Sketches of Butte*.

between two and five dollars Baumler, "Devil's Perch," 8; and Michael Rutter, *Upstairs Girls: Prostitution in the American West* (Helena, MT: Far Country Press, 2005), 23.

city fathers required Writers Project of Montana.

she quit to support herself "Mattie Mimmo [Mattie Mimms]," 1910 census, Butte Ward 5, Silver Bow, Montana, roll T624-836, page 7A, enumeration district 103, image 766.

Her death, just before her fortieth "Once a Favorite, She Dies Alone," *Butte Miner*, August 28, 1911.

she found herself segregated Butte city directory 1898; "Lizzie Hall," 1890 census, Butte Ward 5, Silver Bow, Montana, roll T623-914, page 3B; enumeration district 114.

and in the police courts Mary Murphy, *Women on the Line: Prostitution in Butte Montana 1878–1917*, master's thesis, University of North Carolina (Chapel Hill, 1983), 62.

"I's got a million dollars" Writers Project of Montana, 11.

Butte reported twenty-five hundred men Brian Shovers, "Housing on the Rocky Mountain Urban Frontier: Multifamily Building Forms in Butte, Montana, 1890–1916," *Drumlummon Views* (Spring 2009), 158. www.drumlummon.org/images/DV_vol3 -no1_PDFs/DV_vol3-no1_Shovers.pdf (accessed January 30, 2009).

Slower but surer Brian Shovers, "The Perils of Working in the Butte Underground: Industrial Fatalities in the Copper Mines, 1880–1920," *Montana: The Magazine of Western History*, vol. 37, no. 2 (Spring 1987): 26–39. The death total was tallied from 1907 to 1913, 28.

the mere threat of similar action Howard, 75.

the case dismissed Patrick F. Morris, *Anaconda Montana: Copper Smelting Boom Town on the Western Frontier* (Bethesda, MD: Swann Publishing, 1997), 201.

"Soirees were no longer staged" Baumler, "The Devil's Perch," 14.

"just about as dirty" Jerry Calvert, *The Gibraltar: Socialism and Labor in Butte, Montana, 1895–1920* (Helena: Montana Historical Society Press, 1988), 4–5.

officials unfailingly recognized "Butte, Montana," *AOL Hometown.*

last homestead act Timothy Egan, *The Worst Hard Time: The Untold Story of Those Who Survived the Great American Dust Bowl* (Boston and New York: Houghton Mifflin, 2006), 4.

causing a dramatic increase Paula Petrik, *No Step Backward: Women and Family on the Rocky Mountain Mining Frontier, Helena, Montana 1865–1900* (Helena: Montana Historical Society Press, 1987), 129.

majority still came from Ireland Calvert, 3.

she also met John Bottego "John B. Bottego," 1900 census, Butte Ward 8, Silver Bow, Montana, roll T623-915, page 9B, enumeration district 131.

abandoning California for Butte Robert S. Maloney, *Blessed are You . . . Because You Have Believed: Life of Mother Celestine Healy Bottego, Foundress of the Xaverian Missionaries of Mary* (Bologna, Italy: Editrice Missionaria Italiana, 2002), 3–5, 12.

became a personal friend Phone interview with Father Robert S. Maloney, Holliston, Massachusetts, January 27, 2010.

expanded streetcar service Brian Shovers, "Housing on the Rocky Mountain Urban Frontier: Multifamily Building Forms in Butte, Montana, 1890–1916," *Drumlummon Views* (Spring 2009), 153, 156–158, 173.

never-ending problems with renters Maloney, 11–13; and phone interview.

the best grammar school student Barbara LaBoe, "'Not Your Normal Nun,'" *Montana Standard*, July 21, 1999.

after carefully weighing Maloney, 16.

put his assets in his mother's name "Warren G. Davenport," folder SM016, Butte–Silver Bow Archives, letter collection.

"Vulgar manner, overfed" Davenport, *Butte and Montana Beneath the X-Ray*, 154.

twenty-five public and seven parochial Writers Project of Montana, 303.

estimated one thousand women Emmons, footnote 20.

let them post bail at the house *Butte Miner*, December 31, 1903.

seeking more civilized realms Clifford disappears from record after the census of 1910, which shows her working at the Victoria.

mailed in dirty clothes "From High Society to Hookers, Dye House Has Colorful Past," undated newspaper clipping in the author's possession. Feature is identified as part of a series written by the Historic American Engineer Records team that studied the mining city and provides a sketch of the business by Dave Hutchinson. Also interview with Sarah DeMuney, Butte, Montana, October 4, 2009, who was present when the building was restored.

"The red light district consisted" Charles Chaplin, *My Autobiography* (New York: Simon and Schuster, 1964), 128.

other society women "Butte Society Women Work Quietly Among Slums and Dope Fiends," *Butte Evening News*, August 28, 1910; and phone interview with local historian Charles Fisk, Butte, Montana, October 19, 2009.

the mistaken belief that he could cure Writers Project of Montana, 280.

no noticeable long-term improvements The *Butte Miner* and *Inter-Mountain News*, May 5, 10, 1905; and Baumler, "Devil's Perch," 10.

the Mann Act Abbott, 107–110.

"still possesses her 24-hour saloon" Davenport, *Butte and Montana Beneath the X-Ray*, 278.

"I have never seen a town" "Mrs. Nation Calls Taft an Infidel," *Anaconda Standard*, January 25, 1910, 7.

"Leave this hell hole" Dave Walter, "How Butte Beat Carrie Nation's Temperance Crusade," *Montana: The Magazine of Western History*, vol. 59, no. 2 (May–June 1982): 9–12, offers one of the best summaries of her visit.

"It was an odd spectacle" *Butte Miner*, January 27, 1910.

smack into the righteous reformer May Malloy appears in the Butte city directory in residence at 105 East Galena in 1889. The only Malloy listed in a red-light district census is Norma Malloy at 14 East Galena in 1900. Her birth date is listed as 1867. She was born in Iowa, as were her parents. Dorothy Raymond, twenty-five, was listed as being in charge of the Irish World when the census was taken in April 1910. Ruth Clifford has moved on to the Victoria.

propelled her aged adversary "Carrie Goes into the Slums and Offers a Helping Hand," *Butte Miner*, January 27, 1910.

an open letter to the bartenders "Carry A. Nation Addresses Letter to Bartenders' Union of Butte," *Butte Miner*, January 31, 1910, 6. Nation's given name was Carrey but she used "Carry" for her slogan. Editors used several spellings.

final words and valediction Doris Weatherford, *American Women's History* (New York: Prentice Hall General Reference, 1994), 240; and Herbert Asbury, *Carry Nation* (New York: Alfred A. Knopf, 1929), 305–306.

Nevin closed the district Mary Murphy, 347–348.

Based on the monthly fines *Butte Miner*, January 31 and February 1, 1911.

only to be ignored *Butte Miner*, February 20, 1911.

never been better Ellen Baumler, "The End of the Line: Butte, Anaconda, and the Landscape of Prostitution," *Drumlummon Views* (Spring 2009), 290. www.drumlummon.org/images/DV_vol3-no1_PDFs/DV_vol3-no1_Baumler.pdf (accessed December 2, 2010).

CHAPTER 9: NEW OPTIONS, 1916

daughter of a well-heeled farmer "David Knowles," 1870 census, Northwood, Rockingham, New Hampshire, roll M593-848, family history library film 552347, page 353, image 68. Ella's mother, Louise, was still living, as was a sister, Etta, age fourteen. Knowles reported real estate valued at $3,000 and personal savings of $800, considerably more than his neighbors in the 1870 census. Interviews refer to the fact that Ella worked her way through school, leading us to wonder if her father did not want her to go. Ella was living at home with David and his second wife, Mary, in the 1880 census.

following the death "They Paved the Way: Ella Knowles Haskell," Women for Women, Exeter, NH, February 29, 1979. The publication is unclear but the story was fifteenth in a series of articles on New Hampshire women. It was taken from the biographical file on Ella Knowles Haskell, Montana State Archives, Helena.

failed to finish her training *Progressive Men of the State of Montana* (Chicago: A. W. Bowen & Co., 1902), 472.

because her father remarried According to the 1880 Northwood census, Ella's father had recently remarried.

understood that field far better Richard B. Roeder, "Crossing the Gender Line: Ella L. Knowles, Montana's First Woman Lawyer," *Montana: The Magazine of Western History*, vol. 32, no. 3 (Summer 1982): 64–65.

kept the two quarters Ella Knowles Haskell, "My First Fee," *Anaconda Standard*, February 3, 1907.

an unusual number of women Roeder, 69.

first female ever nominated John Morrison and Catherine Wright Morrison, *Mavericks: The Lives and Battles of Montana Politicians* (Helena: Montana Historical Society Press, 1997), 445.

ought to protect Roeder, 70–72; and T. A. Larson, "Montana Women and the Battle for the Ballot," *Montana: The Magazine of Western History*, vol. 23, no. 1 (Winter 1983): 37.

first woman to plead a case "They Paved the Way."

from the U.S. secretary of interior *Progressive Men of the State of Montana*, 473.

restricted women's full development James J. Lopach and Jean A. Luckowski, *Jeannette Rankin: A Political Woman* (Boulder: University of Colorado Press, 2005), 50. The authors cite a letter from Rankin to a friend, Katherine Black; and Carroll Smith-Rosenberg, *Disorderly Conduct: Visions of Gender in Victorian America* (New York: Alfred A. Knopf, 1958), 254.

half-naked Indians Norma Smith, *Jeannette Rankin: America's Conscience* (Helena: Montana Historical Society Press, 2002), 31.

Olive took up teaching Kevin S. Giles, *Flight of the Dove: The Story of Jeannette Rankin* (Beaverton, OR: Touchstone Press, 1980), 20–21.

Olive wed him   Smith, 32.

ranch where they summered   Giles, 22–24.

varied viewpoints fostered debate   Lopach and Luckowski, 18.

"If you can take care of Jeannette"   Smith, 34.

the responsibility of raising five   Lopach and Luckowski, 19–29.

every Rankin child who could walk   Smith, 34–37.

still had plenty of work   Giles, 26.

might be hard on her health   Smith, 44–45.

actually riding astride   Donna M. Lucey, *Photographing Montana, 1894–1928: The Life and Work of Mrs. Evelyn Cameron* (Missoula, MT: Mountain Press, 2001), 204.

chaired the county Board of Health   Paula Petrik, *No Step Backward: Women and Family on the Rocky Mountain Mining Frontier, Helena, Montana 1865–1900* (Helena: Montana Historical Society Press, 1987), 21.

not the way she wanted to go   Smith, 43.

sentenced to forty years   A wonderful account of Bertie's adventure can be found in *More Montana Campfire Tales* by Dave Walker (Helena, MT: Far Country Press, 2002), 37–51.

failed to teach Jeannette to think   Smith, 43.

got a job teaching second grade   Lopach and Luckowski, 209. The quote comes from Ronald Schaffer's "Jeannette Rankin, Progressive Isolationist," doctoral thesis, Princeton University (Princeton, NJ, 1959), 6, which referenced Rankin's journals of 1902. Biographer Norma Smith noted in her "Essay on Sources," 224, that papers on "Jeannette's early life before going into politics" are no longer available.

parties, concerts, and dances   Photos of this period on display at the Jefferson Valley Museum, Inc., include many group shots of formally dressed young people engaged in these activities.

wife of one year   Interview with Roy E. Millegan, curator and founding member of the Jefferson Valley Museum, Inc., Whitehall, October 10, 2009; and "Nellie Packard," 1910 census, Whitehall, Jefferson, Montana, roll T624-832, page 9A, enumeration district 42, image 1245.

at its top speed   "Dr. Lawrence R. Packard" and "Fan' Packard," *Jefferson Valley News*, 1940 Progress edition for Whitehall, republished in 1990.

walked out on the interview   Lopach and Luckowski, 2. In an interview with this writer in Missoula, October 7, 2009, the authors said they had interviewed biographer Norma Smith, who had provoked Rankin's ire by asking what the Whitehall embarrassment had been, and that the writer, an experienced newspaper reporter, assumed it was of "of a sexual nature."

less-than-subtle public criticism   Giles, 24.

Some insist Jeannette No one in either court interviewed by this writer would put their name and opinion on record, nor would they discuss the subject when she queried them on it a second time.

befriended his second wife Millegan interview.

Rocky Mountain spotted (tick) fever Smith, 46.

added her father's family responsibilities Giles, 31; and Schaffer, 9.

most elaborate and diverse Giles, 33.

Apache chief Geronimo "Theodore Roosevelt Inaugural Address," March 4, 1905, *Great Books Online.* www.bartleby.com/124/pres42.html (accessed February 2, 2010).

as did her mother Smith, 47.

enrolled in a correspondence course Schaffer, 7, 12.

she escaped to visit an uncle Smith, 48.

New York School of Philanthropy Giles, 35–37.

"such well-trained college girls" Smith, 51–52.

thirteen died at the facility Giles, 35–36.

working as a seamstress Smith, 53–55. While other biographers have glossed over this period in Rankin's life, Norma Smith's in depth interview and research on Jeannette's stay in Washington State gives good insight into what motivated Jeannette later on.

posters promoting equal suffrage Giles, 41–42.

Washington women won their franchise Smith, 58–61.

New York Woman Suffrage Party Lopach and Luckowski, 83–85.

Oregon, Kansas, and Arizona "Voting Rights in America," Women of the West Museum. http://theautry.org/explore/exhibits/suffrage/suff_time.html (accessed February 14, 2010).

James Lissner of Helena Giles, 44–47.

"Men want women in the home" *Helena Independent,* February 2, 1911.

field secretary for the NAWSA Giles, 47–51.

A Butte newspaperwoman Smith, 83, 96; and Lopach and Luckowski, 92–93. The reporter was Mary O'Neill, who became Rankin's close friend.

put equal rights before the voters Smith, 81–82. The Senate vote was 26 to 2, while it was 74 to 2 in the House.

women in nine states *Anaconda Standard,* July 9, 1913, 7.

Mary Land "Mary Land," 1910 census, Missoula Ward 4, Missoula, Montana, roll T624-834, page 9A, enumeration district 71, image 1138. She was born in Sweden.

ignition required a hand crank Smith, 70–71.

half a million spectators Giles, 51–52.

who ignored police brutality "Woodrow Wilson, 1913–1921." www.whitehouse
.gov/about/presidents/woodrowwilson (accessed February 14, 2010); and Lopach
and Luckowski, 141–143, do an excellent job in documenting Wilson's insensitivity
to the police brutality and jailing of members of the Women's Party organized by
Alice Paul to picket him when he refused to consider equal rights.

the time was right Larson, 33–35.

Homemakers and men Petrik, 130–131; and Lopach and Luckowski, 95.

"Women in our organization" Smith, 82.

reacted with similar cool Giles, 64.

comfortable in buttonholing Giles, 55–57.

wage a successful congressional campaign Smith, 96–97.

planning a libel suit Lopach and Luckowski, 91.

any mention of her youthful indiscretion "Whitehall School District: Chrono-
logical Firsts," *Jefferson Valley News*, 1940 Progress edition for Whitehall, republished in 1990, 13.

"a rare combination of femininity and force" Lopach and Luckowski, 81–82.

fielding plenty of marriage proposals Giles, 61.

outlining the qualifications *New York Times*, November 18, 1916.

bested by a woman Lopach and Luckowski, 104, cite the *San Francisco Bulletin*,
May 5, 1917, and personal correspondence.

beholden to no man Lopach and Luckowski, 6.

Epilogue: The Wages of Sin

prohibiting houses of ill fame "Circular Letter Sent Out by Ford," *Butte Miner*,
January 7, 1917.

one doubted that he was serious "District Will Be Open Until Tuesday," *Butte
Miner*, January 1, 1917.

immediately filed ouster proceedings *Miles City Independent*, January 12, 1917.

five of the town's policemen Robert A. Harvie and Larry V. Bishop, "Police
Reform in Montana, 1890–1918," *Montana: The Magazine of Western History*, vol.
33, no. 2 (Spring 1983): 55.

charges against the women "Fail to Convict Landladies of the District," *Butte
Miner*, January 25, 1917.

She escaped conviction "Have Record Day in Police Court," *Butte Miner*, January 23, 1917.

"The public sure would laugh" "No Chance for a Woman to Be Good," *Butte
Miner*, January 18, 1917.

asking favors from no one "Scarlet Women Shun Offers of Help," *Butte Miner*, January 30, 1917.

in the name of venereal disease Ellen Baumler, "The End of the Line: Butte, Anaconda, and the Landscape of Prostitution," *Drumlummon Views* (Spring 2009), 291. www.drumlummon.org/images/DV_vol3-no1_PDFs/DV_vol3-no1_Baumler .pdf. Passage of the Chamberlain-Kahn Act in 1918 allowed the government to close such operations to prevent the spread of venereal disease.

"You can choose for yourself" "Closed District Would Bring Ruin," *Butte Miner*, January 3, 1917.

"the darkest black woman in Butte" Mary Murphy, "Women on the Line: Prostitution in Butte Montana 1878–1917," master's thesis, University of North Carolina (Chapel Hill, 1983), 62.

enjoying her services in Bannack "Lizzie Hall," Butte Ward 5, Silver Bow, Montana, roll T623-914, page 3B, enumeration district 114.

no figures to bear this out Butler's whole book (Urbana and Chicago: University of Illinois Press, 1987) is negative on the profession, yet she concedes that this class left few records or personal accounts. What she doesn't concede is that while suicides and drug busts made the news, prostitutes who did well were not prone to say so because the profession was usually illegal and, where it was legal, taxed.

"a far more interesting question" "Not the Same Old Story: Proulx, Prostitution, and the American West," HistoryTalk response posted by Paula Petrik, author of *No Step Backward*, June 26, 2005, in reaction to Annie Proulx, "How the West Was Spun," where she quoted Butler. http://historytalk.typepad.com/basic/2005/06 /proulx_prostitu.html (accessed August 8, 2009).

with a sympathetic introduction "Ben Lindsey," Answers.com. www.answers .com/topic/ben-lindsey (accessed February 22, 2010). Lindsey pioneered the creation of the American juvenile system.

Clinton Tyler Brainard "Court Convicts Head of Harpers," *New York Times*, January 24, 1920, 1.

women who sold themselves Anonymous, *Madeleine: An Autobiography* (New York: Persea Books, 1986), v–xi. Marcia Carlisle gives an excellent summation of what rankled moralists about the book in her introduction to this new edition.

reversed his conviction "Brainard Innocent, Upper Court Holds," *New York Times*, July 10, 1920.

"I should demand from life" McMaster's paper "The Girls Could Have the Prairies to Themselves: A Prostitute's View of the Canadian West" was delivered to the Congress of Humanities and Social Sciences in Toronto. Copy in possession of the author, quotation from page 9.

still well remembered E-mail communication with Bill Hillen, Coutts, Alberta, Canada, August 29, 2009.

apparently in the hopes Paula Petrik, *No Step Backward: Women and Family on the Rocky Mountain Mining Frontier, Helena, Montana 1865–1900* (Helena: Montana Historical Society Press, 1987), 36.

wed a younger woman "Charles E. Stanchfield," 1910 census, Burbank, Los Angeles, California, roll T624-79, page 8A, enumeration district 13, image 873.

under her original work name Polk's Missoula city directory, 1943.

the glowing write-up *A History of Montana* (Chicago: Lewis Publishing Co., 1913), 1080–1081.

later practiced in Lewistown *Harvard University Directory* (Cambridge: Harvard University Directory, 1913), 1847.

while Delia resided in splendor 1920 census, "Delia Nadeau," Butte, Silver Bow, Montana, series T625, roll 976, page 4; and "Joseph Nadeau," T624_ 976, page 85.

because of some scandal Off-the-record discussion with some staff members at Montana State Archives, Helena.

Nor was there any mention of the rest "Funeral of J. Nadeau Will Be Held Today," *Anaconda Standard*, April 4, 1925.

In 1908 in California "Ketchell, in Straightened Circumstances, Left Butte to Become Famous as a Middleweight Boxing Champ," newspaper clipping without publishing data, Stanley Ketchell file, Butte-Silver Bow Public Archives.

appreciated his energy "Stanley Ketchell," *Boxrec Boxing Encyclopedia*. http:// boxrec.com/media/index.php/Stanley_Ketchell (accessed January 26, 2010). For twenty-two years after his death a small notice appeared in the classified column.

Ziegfeld Follies star "Roundtown Review," Butte, Montana, July 1, 2002, an otherwise unidentified clipping in Ketchel's file at the Montana State Archives, Helena. The star's last name was Harting.

Nancy was discovered John Taliaferro, *Charles M. Russell: The Life and Legend of America's Cowboy* Artist (Boston, New York, Toronto, and London: Little, Brown and Company, 1996), 271.

misspelled but wonderful love letters Ginger K. Renner, "Charlie and the Ladies in his Life," *Montana: The Magazine of Western History*, vol. 34, no. 4 (Summer 1984): 54, cites letters of Charlie Russell to Nancy Russell, February 6–12, Britzman Collection, Colorado Springs Fine Art Museum.

Lady Minnie Lindsey "Mrs. Hoffman," 1888: Arrival: New York, United States, Microfilm serial M237, microfilm roll M237-525, line 22, list number 1234. The ship was the *City of Richmond*, arrival date September 10. Paget is not listed on the manifest but Minnie has the cabin next door.

the state's largest horse ranch Donna M. Lucey, *Photographing Montana, 1894–1928* (Missoula, MT: Mountain Press, 2001), 200.

and a one-year-old child "Mrs. Hoffman," Arrival: New York, United States, microfilm serial M 237, microfilm roll M237-538, line 34, list number 13260, *City of Rome*.

Sydney posed alone Mark H. Brown and W. R. Felton, *The Frontier Years: L. A. Huffman, Photographer of the Plains* (New York: Bramhball House, 1955), 150.

Big Horn Ranch Sam Morton, "Aiken and Big Horn; A History of Connection," *Aiken Polo Magazine*, 2008, 44–45. www.myvirtualpaper.com/doc/Aiken-Polo -Magazine/Aiken_Polo_Magazine_2008/2009031601/63.html (accessed August 24, 2009).

encamped in comfort Lucey, 199–200.

marrying a beautiful actress "Sydney Paget Fined $125," *New York Times*, March 23, 1906.

a major fire "After the Fire," *Yellowstone Journal*, August 8, 1886.

celebrated his tenth year Jean Freese, "Main Street Trail," *Centennial Roundup* (Miles City, MT: *Miles City Star*, 1987), 43; and "W. H. Bullard," *Illustrated and Historical Edition of the Yellowstone Journal, Supplement* (Miles City, MT: Yellowstone, September 27, 1900), 27.

they were still together "William H. Bullard," 1910 census, Justice Precinct 1, San Patricio, Texas, roll T624-1582, page 12 B, enumeration district 113, image 1179; and "William H. Bullard," 1920 census, Corpus Christi Ward 2, Nueces, Texas, roll T625-1838, page 1A, enumeration district 176, image 94.

recently survived a citizen's arrest Undated clipping from the *Yellowstone Journal* and an interview with Robin Gerber, Miles City Community College, October 12, 2009. Gerber, a trained historian, has done considerable research on Turner.

client sustained no apparent injury *Yellowstone Journal*, May 16, 1885.

woman's place was in the home "Crossing the Gender Line: Ella L. Knowles, Montana's First Woman Lawyer," *Montana: The Magazine of Western History*, vol. 32, no. 3 (Summer 1982): 68.

insisted on payment "The State vs. Hendricks," January 21, 1895, *Pacific Reporter*, vol. 39 (St. Paul, MN: West Publishing Co., 1895): 93–95.

openly declared its operation "Fannie French," 1900 census, Billings, Yellowstone, Montana, roll T623-915, page 32A, enumeration district 197.

a highly fictionalized account Calamity Jane, *Life and Adventures of Calamity Jane* (Billings, MT: self-published, 1896). www.gutenberg.org/etext/490 (accessed February 24, 2010).

friends buried her alongside Michael Griske, editor, *The Diaries of John Hunton: Made to Last, Written to Last, Sagas of the Western Frontier* (Westminster, MD: Heritage Books), 87–89, offers an interesting short view of Jane's life. The most detailed study to date comes from James D. McLaird, *Calamity Jane: The Woman and the Legend* (Norman: University of Oklahoma Press, 2005).

depended on the daughter Robert S. Maloney, *Blessed Are You . . . Because You Have Believed: Life of Mother Celestine Healy Bottego, Foundress of the Xaverian Missionaries of Mary* (Bologna, Italy: Editrice Missionaria Italiana, 2002), 14–15.

devoting the rest of her time Maloney, 44.

so well regarded *Progressive Men of Montana* (Chicago: A. W. Bowen & Co.,1902), 472–474.

when she died unexpectedly "Ella Knowles Haskell Passes Away," *Butte Miner*, January 28, 1911.

asked Congress for a declaration "Woodrow Wilson, *The White House*. www .whitehouse.gov/about/presidents/woodrowwilson (accessed February 14, 2010).

against the advice Norma Smith, *Jeannette Rankin: America's Conscience* (Helena: Montana Historical Society Press, 2002), 112.

igniting a series of strikes Brian Shovers, "The Perils of Working in the Butte Underground: Industrial Fatalities in the Copper Mines, 1880–1920," *Montana: The Magazine of Western History*, vol. 37, no. 2 (Spring 1987): 39.

roundly criticized Anaconda James J. Lopach and Jean A. Luckowski, *Jeannette Rankin: A Political Woman* (Boulder: University of Colorado Press, 2005), 155–160.

Anaconda saw to it Smith, 118–127.

living long enough to march Lopach and Luckowski, 204.

while they endowed Writers Project of Montana, *Copper Camp: The Lusty Story of Butte, Montana, the Richest Hill on Earth* (Helena, MT: Riverbend Publishing, 1973, first published by Montana State Department in 1943), 11.

it will take centuries Roberta Forsell Stauter, "EPA Releases Cleanup Plan for Butte Priority Soils Site," *Montana Standard*, December 20, 2004, 1.

the effects of the Dust Bowl Joseph Kinsey Howard, *Montana: High, Wide and Handsome* (Lincoln and London: University of Nebraska Press, 1983, originally published Yale University Press, 1943), 103.

had trouble supporting themselves Howard, 236–242; and Jeff Malcomson, "From the Society: Celebrating a Century of County Building in Montana," *Montana: The Magazine of Western History*, vol. 59, no. 3 (Autumn 2009): 67.

before moving operations Howard, 93.

She and her seven poodles John Kuglin, "Butte Madam Tells of Payoffs, Spurs Crusade Against Corruption," *Great Falls Tribune*, October 13, 1968.

female stereotypes in the American West "Western Women: Beginning to Come into Focus," *Montana: The Magazine of Western History*, vol. 32, no. 3 (Summer 1982): 2. At the time Armitage was director of the Women's Studies Program at Washington State University, Pullman.

big money selling babies Peter Chapin, "Gertie's Babies—Search for Birth Mothers Unearths Tale of Sold, Destroyed Lives," *Montana Standard*, March 15, 1992.

then returned to Montana Peter Chapin, "Gertrude Pitkanen—Butte's Notorious Abortionist." The writer's byline says he is the *Montana Standard* staff writer, but this feature was published in *Gertie's Babies*, by Mable Dean, Three Forks, Montana, February 28, 2010. www.gertiesbabies.com/gertrudepitkanen.html (accessed February 28, 2010). Also "Gertrude Pitkanen," 1930 census, Butte, Silver Bow, Montana, roll 1262, page 5A, enumeration district 40, image 716.0. According to the 1910 census, Gustavus was still single.

Gertrude took over   Clemens P. Work, author of *Darkest Before Dawn: Sedition and Free Speech in the American West*, via e-mail to this author, January 16, 2006.

her second husband was a detective   Barb Smith, "The Past Is a Mystery for Gertie's Babies," *Bozeman Daily Chronicle* article picked up by the Associated Press, August 29, 1994.

not the case with similar groups   Thomas Fields-Meyer and Vickie Bane in Butte, "Gertie's Babies," *People*, October 7, 1902, 93–94; and interview with Mable Dean, Three Forks, Montana, October 13, 2009.

especially difficult to trace   Chapin, "Gertrude Pitkanen."

INDEX